METROPOLITAN
MUSEUM
JOURNAL 52

METROPOLITAN MUSEUM
JOURNAL 52

VOLUME 52 / 2017

The Metropolitan Museum of Art
NEW YORK

This publication is made possible by a gift from Assunta Sommella Peluso, Ada Peluso, and Romano I. Peluso, in memory of Ignazio Peluso.

The *Metropolitan Museum Journal* is published annually by The Metropolitan Museum of Art.

Mark Polizzotti, Publisher and Editor in Chief
Gwen Roginsky, Associate Publisher and General Manager of Publications
Peter Antony, Chief Production Manager
Michael Sittenfeld, Senior Managing Editor
Edited by Elizabeth L. Block
Production by Lauren Knighton
Designed and typeset by Tina Henderson, based on original design by Lucinda Hitchcock
Image acquisitions by Josephine Rodriguez-Massop

Manuscripts submitted for the *Journal* and all correspondence concerning them should be sent to journalsubmissions@metmuseum.org. Guidelines for contributors are given on p. 6.

Published in association with the University of Chicago Press. Individual and institutional subscriptions are available worldwide. Please direct all subscription inquiries, back issue requests, and address changes to: University of Chicago Press, Journals Division, P.O. Box 37005, Chicago, IL 60637-0005, USA. Phone: (877) 705-1878 (U.S. and Canada) or (773) 753-3347 (international), fax: (877) 705-1879 (U.S. and Canada) or (773) 753-0811 (international), email: subscriptions@press.uchicago.edu, website: www.journals.uchicago.edu

ISBN 978-0-226-53684-2
(University of Chicago Press)
ISSN 0077-8958 (print)
ISSN 2169-3072 (online)

Library of Congress
Catalog Card Number 68-28799

Typefaces: Calibre, Lyon, and Harriet
Printed on Creator Silk, 150 gsm
Separations by Altaimage New York
Printed and bound by Puritan Capital,
Hollis, New Hampshire

Front and back cover illustration: Horace Pippin (American, 1888–1946). Detail of *The Lady of the Lake*, ca. 1936–39. See fig. 2, p. 97.

Illustration on p. 2: Paolo Veronese (Italian, 1528–1588). Detail of *Alessandro Vittoria*, ca. 1575. See fig. 1, p. 116.

Contents

MANUSCRIPT GUIDELINES
FOR THE METROPOLITAN MUSEUM JOURNAL

The *Metropolitan Museum Journal* is issued annually by The Metropolitan Museum of Art. Its purpose is to publish original research on works of art in the Museum's collection. Authors include members of the Museum staff and other art historians, conservators, scientists, and specialists.

The *Journal* publishes **Articles** and **Research Notes**. **Articles** contribute extensive and thoroughly argued scholarship. **Research Notes** typically present a concise, neatly bounded aspect of ongoing research, such as the presentation of a new acquisition or attribution, or a specific, resonant finding from technical analysis. All texts must take works of art in the collection as the point of departure. Contributions are not limited in length, but authors are encouraged to exercise discretion with the word count and the number of figure illustrations. Submissions should be emailed to: journalsubmissions@metmuseum.org.

Manuscripts are reviewed by the *Journal* Editorial Board, composed of members of the curatorial, conservation, and scientific departments.

To be considered for the following year's volume, an article must be submitted, complete including illustrations, by October 15.

Once an article or research note is accepted for publication, the author will have the opportunity to review it after it has been edited and again after it has been laid out in pages. The honorarium for image costs is $300, and each author receives a copy of the printed *Journal*. The *Journal* appears online at metmuseum.org/art/metpublications; journals.uchicago.edu/toc/met/current; and on JStor.

Manuscripts should be submitted as double-spaced Word files. In addition to the text, the manuscript must include endnotes, captions for illustrations, photograph credits, and a 200-word abstract.

For the style of captions and bibliographic references in endnotes, authors are referred to *The Metropolitan Museum of Art Guide to Editorial Style and Procedures*, which is available from the Museum's Publications and Editorial Department upon request, and to *The Chicago Manual of Style*. Please provide a list of all bibliographic citations that includes, for each title: full name(s) of author or authors; title and subtitle of book or article and periodical; place and date of publication; volume number, if any; and page, plate, and/or figure number(s). For citations in notes, please use only the last name(s) of the author or authors and the date of publication (e.g., Jones 1953, p. 65; Smith and Harding 2006, pp. 7–10, fig. 23).

When submitting manuscripts, authors should include a separate file with all illustrations. Please do not embed images within the main text document. If the manuscript is accepted, the author is expected to provide publication-quality images as well as copyright permissions to reproduce them in both the print and electronic editions of the *Journal*. The *Journal* requires either color digital images of at least 300 dpi at 8 x 10 in. in size, color transparencies (preferably 8 x 10 in. but 4 x 6 in. is also acceptable), or photographic prints (preferably 8 x 10 in. with white borders) of good quality and in good condition. TIFF files are preferable to Jpegs, and RGB color mode is preferable to CMYK.

In a separate Word file, please indicate the figure number, the picture's orientation, and any instructions for cropping. Reproductions of photographs or other illustrations in books should be accompanied by captions that include full bibliographic information.

The author of each article is responsible for obtaining all photographic materials and reproduction rights.

ABBREVIATIONS

MMA The Metropolitan Museum of Art
MMAB The Metropolitan Museum of Art Bulletin
MMJ Metropolitan Museum Journal

Height precedes width and then depth in dimensions cited.

METROPOLITAN MUSEUM
MUSEUM
JOURNAL 52

SEBASTIANO SOLDI

"Assyrian Clay Hands" in the Architecture of the Ancient Near East

The function of glazed clay hands in the architecture of Iron Age Mesopotamia (9th–8th century B.C.) and the Northern Levant has proven somewhat elusive even more than one hundred years after the first discovery of such objects in the Neo-Assyrian royal palaces of Nimrud, Khorsabad, Nineveh, and Ashur in northern Iraq and in the Aramaean kingdom of Zincirli (ancient Sam'al) in southern Turkey. Evidence in museum collections and from recent field excavations in northern Syria and southern Anatolia, however, allows an opportunity to reconstruct the placement of the hands in their original settlements and to suggest possible meanings of their shape (fig. 1). Through a brief review of their morphology, excavation contexts, and comparisons to other objects, this article aims to connect the so-called Assyrian clay hands with a long architectural tradition in Mesopotamia. In that tradition, temples and palace facades were

fig. 1 Glazed hand. Neo-Assyrian, Nimrud (ancient Kalhu), probably Northwest Palace, ca. 883–859 B.C. Terracotta, glaze, 8¼ × 3¾ × 2⅜ in. (21 × 9.5 × 6 cm). British Museum, London (BM 92095)

fig. 2 Reconstructed clay cone-mosaic columns decorating a staircase in the E-anna Precinct, Uruk. Late Uruk, ca. 3300–3000 B.C. Staatliche Museen zu Berlin, Vorderasiatisches Museum

decorated with various architectural elements that had multiple functions, combining symbolic and decorative purposes with structural needs.[1]

The utilization of multifunctional elements had been in place since the beginning of monumental architecture in southern Mesopotamia, where the imposing buildings in the E-anna sacred area of Uruk, dated to the end of the fourth millennium B.C., had peculiar facade decorations. The niches and projecting pilasters along the walls of major town buildings were decorated with multicolored stone and clay cones systematically inserted into the plaster. The flat bottoms of the cones were arranged in a geometric, mosaic motif on the surface of the building (fig. 2).[2] Beside the cones, other clay or stone figurative objects were displayed on the surface, fixed into the walls through a stem, in a format that

continued from the late Uruk period (ca. 3200–3000 B.C.) until the Early Dynastic period (ca. 2900–2350 B.C.). The practice is observed across a large geographic area and a long time span, as attested in the Eye Temple in Tell Brak, in northern Syria, where the cones and a composite gold and limestone frieze were excavated together with a series of stone rosettes once fixed to the walls of the sanctuary.[3] Furthermore, in the Ninhursag temple in Tell al 'Ubaid, near Ur, in southern Mesopotamia, spectacular copper-alloy with limestone and shell-inlay friezes were found along with stone and clay rosettes similar in shape and function to those at Tell Brak (fig. 3).[4]

In later periods the tendency to integrate decorative solutions within architecture became more articulated, culminating with the introduction of molded bricks during the Middle and Late Bronze Age in the second millennium B.C. In Tell Leilan and Tell al Rimah, respectively in northeastern Syria and northwestern Iraq, archaeologists have revealed imposing temple facades characterized by mud-brick half-columns in the shape of palm-tree trunks and spiral columns, obtained by juxtaposing molded bricks cut in the required forms to obtain the complex pattern.[5] In Uruk, during the reign of Kara-indash, king of the Kassite dynasty ruling over Babylon at the end of the fifteenth century B.C., a small shrine dedicated to the goddess Inanna was erected. The exterior walls of the small temples were decorated with repeated images of lifesize deities inserted in the niches and framed by circular elements.[6] A similar system of adornment with mythological figures represented in the molded bricks is attested in Susa during the Middle Elamite period (twelfth century B.C.), in the temple erected by King Shilhak-Inshushinak and dedicated to the great Iranian god Inshushinak, patron god of Susa and of the dynasty of the Shutrukides.[7] These instances testify to how architecture and figurative decoration in a variety of materials have a long reciprocal history in the Near East. Assyrian palaces and temples appear along the line of this tradition.[8]

Assyrian clay hands were first discovered in the mid-nineteenth century by British and French archaeologists among the remains of palaces and temples of major Assyrian cities in northern Iraq. As these were the first excavations carried out in the Near East, archaeological methods were at their very beginning, and excavators were mainly focused on major finds such as sculpted reliefs and gigantic statues of winged gatekeeper figures. Many of the latter would form the core of the first Mesopotamian galleries in European and American museums.[9] Nevertheless, many small finds were collected and sometimes recorded in field notes, so that a certain number of clay hands found in the debris of the royal buildings were catalogued and shipped to museums.

In 1991, Grant Frame, who analyzed most of the known examples, recorded 171 clay hands, a number he warned was partially incomplete because some items mentioned by early explorers in Iraq were not accessioned and were left at the site.[10] About thirty more hands must be added to the total after recent excavations, mainly from northern Syria and southern Turkey. Sites where clay hands have been identified so far are the historical Assyrian capitals of Nimrud, Khorsabad, Nineveh, Ashur, Kar-Tukulti-Ninurta, and a few other smaller settlements in the Mosul area.[11] Westward, a few hands have been found at two sites in the Khabur region of northeastern Syria, and, far from the Assyrian heartland, in Zincirli, capital of the ancient Aramaean kingdom of Sam'al, located in the Karasu river valley, in the Amanus region of the northeastern Mediterranean (fig. 4).[12]

The Metropolitan Museum of Art has in its collection two Assyrian clay hands, found in the Northwest Palace at the site of Nimrud (figs. 5, 6).[13] With the exception of the Zincirli pieces, which present some peculiarities typical of items from that site, all other clay hands are closely related in shape, surface treatment, and chronology. The objects are generally composed of an "arm" segment, rectangular in shape and left in an unfinished and unpolished state, and a "hand" part in the shape of a clenched or cupped fist; the fingers are individually marked, and the thumb is always represented as a fifth finger without distinction from the other four (figs. 7, 8). The hand usually has a section that is wider and higher than the arm:[14] this characteristic, together with the rough finishing of the arm part in contrast with the definition of the fingers in the hand, suggests that the arm would have been inserted into the mortar among the brickwork with the function of a tenon (fig. 9), leaving the fist as the only visible part of the object.[15] Some works have a clear indication of fingernails, which do not continue in the direction of the arm but seem to turn toward the wrist (figs. 1, 6, 8). Frame observes that "it remains uncertain whether these objects were intended to represent cupped hands, fists, or simply hands with fingers outstretched."[16] Finally, some hands exhibit a surface treatment, such as a blue or greenish glaze covering, in most cases (figs. 1, 11), or a bitumen coating. The treatment is associated only with the fingers and fist, leaving the rest of the object blank and rough.

About one-third of the preserved hands bear an inscription on the fingers or on one side of the hand (see figs. 5, 6, 8).[17] The inscriptions, except for a single case related to the reign of Shalmaneser III, are connected to Ashurnasirpal II, who reigned between 883 and 859 B.C. There are a few standardized types, repeating a common series of elements, such as the king's royal titles and genealogy denoted in different ways. A few objects bear indications that they belong to the palace

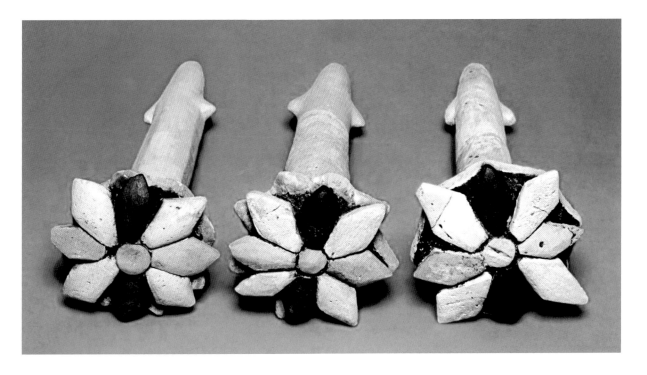

fig. 3 Rosettes. Sumerian (Early Dynastic III), ca. 2400–2250 B.C. Ninhursag temple, Tell al 'Ubaid. Terracotta, stone, and bitumen, each 7⅞ × 4⅞ in. (20 × 12.3 cm). University of Pennsylvania Museum of Archaeology and Anthropology, Philadelphia (B15795; B15796; B15888)

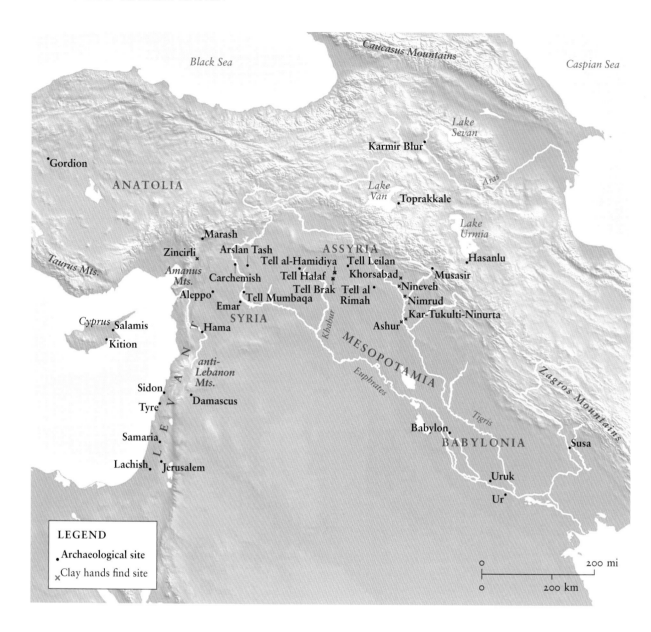

fig. 4 Map of the Ancient Near East and the Eastern Mediterranean in the second and first millennia B.C.

of the king or to the temple of Ishtar in Nimrud, signaling that the objects were designed for specific places. The two works in the Metropolitan Museum, both from Nimrud (ancient Kalhu), have similar inscriptions, in one case displayed on the three central fingers, and in the other, subdivided along all five fingers of the cupped fist:

MMA 54.117.30 (fig. 5):
Palace of Ashurnasirpal II, king of the world, king of Assyria, son of Tukulti-Ninurta II, king of the world, king of Assyria, son of Adad-Narari II, (who was) also king of the world (and) king of Assyria.[18]

MMA 57.27.30 (fig. 6):
Palace of Ashurnasirpal II, great king, mighty king, king of the world, king of Assyria,

son of Tukulti-Ninurta II, king of the world, king of Assyria, son of Adad-Narari II, (who was) also king of the world (and) king of Assyria. Property of the city of Kalhu.[19]

Without entering here into a specific analysis of these inscriptions and others in the catalogue of known clay hands, which has been so well carried out by other scholars, we turn now to observations addressing the possible origin and function of the clay hands, relying on the few iconographic sources and archaeological data. A few clay hands have been found in situ, but in most cases, the exact location of origin is not clear, leading scholars to speculate on how they were used. The most complete documentation is provided by the Old Palace excavation in Ashur, where the German expedition directed by Walter Andrae in 1903–14

fig. 5 Glazed and inscribed hand. Neo-Assyrian, Mesopotamia, Nimrud (ancient Kalhu), Northwest Palace, ca. 883–859 B.C. Terracotta, glaze, 3⅞ × 8¾ × 2⅜ in. (9.8 × 22.2 × 5.9 cm). The Metropolitan Museum of Art, Rogers Fund, 1954 (54.117.30)

fig. 6 Inscribed hand. Neo-Assyrian, Nimrud (ancient Kalhu), Northwest Palace, ca. 883–859 B.C. Terracotta, bitumen, 2¼ × 5⅝ × 3½ in. (5.75 × 14.2 × 9 cm). The Metropolitan Museum of Art, Rogers Fund, 1957 (57.27.30)

recorded a collapsed wall with a row of clay hands set at a regular distance from one another in a vertical orientation (fig. 10).[20] Conrad Preusser notes that mud-bricks in "Raum 2" of the Old Palace, where clay hands were found in situ, measured 47 × 47 × 7 centimeters, and bore the stamped inscription of King Ashurnasirpal II.[21] Recently, Friedhelm Pedde and Steven Lundström reviewed the documentation of the excavations of the Old Palace and proposed that the distance between the hands was 25 centimeters.[22] The thickness of the clay hands, which are on average between 4 centimeters in height in the arm part and 7 centimeters in the hand segment, is compatible with the height of the bricks (7 centimeters, according to Preusser).[23] The average dimensions of the hands and the bricks would thus allow the clay hands to be inserted as corbels in the horizontal rows of the brickwork. The vertical position in which the hands were found in the Old Palace is

explained by the frontal collapse of the wall and the ceiling.

In Nimrud and Khorsabad too, British and French archaeologists respectively discovered clay hands inserted into the wall plaster. George Smith recorded finding them in a vertical position, "planted upright in the wall, embedded in mortar between the bricks," noting at the same time that the wall itself was ruined and in very bad condition.[24] Although a reuse of such artifacts cannot be excluded, it is more likely that the hands were found in a vertical position only because of the building structure's collapse, as was the case in Ashur. In addition, French archaeologists at Khorsabad observed the hands protruding horizontally out of the walls.[25] Considering both the excavation contexts and the manner in which the clay hands are left rough and without surface treatment along the arm part, we can confidently state that their original position was

fig. 7 Multiple views of a fragment of a clay hand. Neo-Assyrian, Nimrud (ancient Kalhu), ca. 883–859 B.C. Terracotta, 4⅝ × 3⅞ × 2 in. (11.7 × 9.7 × 5.2 cm). British Museum, London (BM 1994,1105.8)

fig. 8 Multiple views of a fragment of a clay hand. Neo-Assyrian, Nimrud (ancient Kalhu), ca. 883–859 B.C. Terracotta, 5⅛ × 3⅜ × 2⅛ in. (13 × 8.5 × 5.3 cm). British Museum, London (BM 90976)

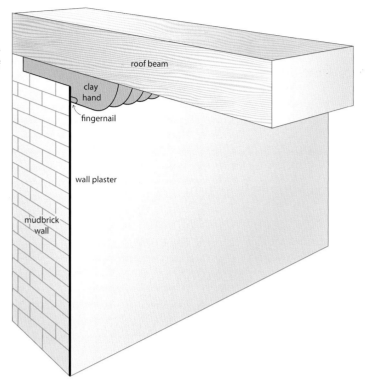

fig. 9 Diagram showing possible usage of clay hands underneath roof beams

horizontal, inserted in the brickwork and extending out of the walls. As noted above in the case of Ashur, dimensions of the mud bricks used during the Neo-Assyrian period are compatible with those of the hands and the arm section with the function of tenon. During the Iron Age, bricks tended to become thicker than in previous periods, with an average height between 7 and 12–13 centimeters.[26]

The clay hands were certainly used inside the rooms of palaces and temples, as attested by the Old Palace in Ashur and by field notes relating the objects to the vicinity of the throne room in Nimrud, but due to the dearth of archaeological records from the find sites we cannot state if the interior use was exclusive or if they were also used as exterior decoration.[27] The exact use of the objects is debated among scholars, who alternately favor a general apotropaic purpose, use as supports for roof beams, use as window ledges, or a purely decorative function.[28] The apotropaic possibility derives from uses of the hand as symbolic representation against the evil eye in many Mediterranean and Near Eastern cultures. The presence of the hands along the perimeter of sacred palaces and temples could have protected an area and purified it from evil spirits.[29] The blue glazed coating has been interpreted in this manner because of its historical connections with amulets and magical objects made of glass, faience, or Egyptian blue, but the explanation must be contested, because, as mentioned above, some hands do not have any surface treatment, or are covered by black bitumen.

Other scholars regard the hands along the wall as a means to support the roof, or roof beams, or as window-ledge fixtures.[30] Alternatively, the hands may have framed tapestries or other textiles on the walls, a hypothesis that cannot be proven because textiles from ancient Mesopotamia were rarely preserved.[31] Given the state of current research, it is best to consider the objects as decorative elements or as supports for light weights, rather than structural elements in the architecture, since the baked clay would easily break in the junction between arm and hand due to the static stress

fig. 10 Neo-Assyrian, Old Palace, Qalat Sherqat (ancient Ashur), reign of King Ashurnasirpal II (883–859 B.C.). Collapsed wall in "Raum 2" as found by the German expedition between 1903 and 1914. Clay hands were found in situ, inserted at a regular distance into the brickwork, originally in a horizontal orientation, but seen here vertically in the collapsed wall structure. Note the fallen clay hand to the left of the seated workman.

fig. 11 Hand sheathings. Neo-Assyrian, Nimrud (ancient Kalhu) and Kouyunjik (ancient Ninua/Nineveh), 9th–8th century B.C. Bronze, 4⅞ × 2½ × 3¾ in. (12.3 × 5.9 × 9.4 cm). British Museum, London (BM 55-12-5; BM 48-11-4; BM 313-4)

of the ceiling timbers' weight.[32] This observation leads to the analysis of a related class of materials: bronze casings in the shape of embossed hands.

When excavating the debris of entrance D to the throne room B of the palace of Ashurnasirpal II at Nimrud in 1846, Sir Austen Henry Layard observed the following:

> In clearing the earth from this entrance, and from behind the fallen lion, many ornaments in copper, two small ducks in baked clay, and tablets of alabaster inscribed on both sides were discovered. Amongst the copper mouldings were the head of a ram or a bull, several hands (the fingers closed and slightly bent), and a few flowers. The hands may have served as a casing to similar objects in baked clay, frequently found amongst the ruins, and having an inscription, containing the names, titles, and genealogy of the King, graved upon the fingers.[33]

Layard noted therefore a similarity between the bronze sheathing hands (fig. 11a–c) and the clay ones he found in abundance throughout the debris of the buildings in his excavations, although his suggestion that the bronze sheathings served as a cover for the clay hands has not been supported by evidence.[34] John Curtis recently published the only existing examples of bronze hands in his volume on Assyrian metalwork in the British Museum.[35] The bronze hands, four from Nimrud and two from Nineveh, are embossed and hammered from the inside, with fingers and fingernails carefully delineated. Their measurements are comparable with the clay hands, so that they can properly be considered as an overlay sheathing covering some objects with similar dimensions. As suggested by Curtis, who notes the presence of a nail to fix them to an underlying material, it is unlikely that they were used to cover the actual clay hands, which never bear a nail-hole. They might, however, have covered a wooden structure, such as the ends of roof beams protruding from the exterior walls, which could have been carved in the shape of the hand. Even though Layard recalls "several" bronze hands, their number does not compare with the clay hands, two hundred of which remain. Bronze was often melted and reused in antiquity and metals would have been among the objects most likely pillaged from the royal palaces after the fall of the Assyrian empire;[36] moreover, wood is rarely found in Mesopotamian archaeology because of conservation issues related to the moisture levels of the soil.

If the hypothesis of the bronze hands as overlaid sheathing repoussé is correct, we may suggest that the bronze hands may have covered the protruding end of wooden beams employed in Assyrian buildings to

fig. 12a Architectural model
with ridged elements. Meskene
(ancient Emar), Syria, Tour A,
14th–13th century B.C.
Terracotta, 46⅛ × 30¾ ×
30¾ in. (117 × 78 × 78 cm).
National Museum, Aleppo, Syria

fig. 12b Detail of architectural
model in fig. 12a showing
ridged protuberances encircling the window of Emar
Tour A

fig. 12c Detail of architectural
model in fig. 12a showing
ridged protuberances underneath the rooftop of Emar
Tour A

a

b

c

support the roof, whereas the clay hands were displayed with a purely decorative function as a sort of skeuomorphic replica of those bearing a static function.[37] Further objects support this proposal. The first group is composed of Late Bronze Age architectural models (fourteenth to thirteenth century B.C.) from the Syrian mid-Euphrates area representing towers, houses, and temples, with particular attention to those from Emar and Tell Mumbaqa. These *maquettes architecturales* have been collected in a vast corpus by Béatrice Muller, who discusses in detail the evolution and typologies of such works from the Eastern Mediterranean to Iran.[38] With regard to the architectural models from the mid-second millennium B.C. from Emar and Tell Mumbaqa, Muller suggests that a few elements, such as the ridged

protuberances encircling the window and underneath the rooftop (figs. 12a–c), might relate to the Assyrian clay hands.[39] Olivier Callot, who studied the use of wood in the architecture of Syria and the Levant, focuses on the ridged elements represented in the architectural models, identifying them as the roof-supporting beams protruding from the buildings' facades, a treatment that is still used in traditional mud-brick architecture in Syria and Iraq.[40] As Béatrice Muller and Jean-Claude Margueron point out, the architectural models were not necessarily intended to be exact representations of ancient buildings.[41] Nevertheless they display distinct features that help us to reconstruct details of the original, lost buildings, especially when the information matches that from excavations. One such feature is the

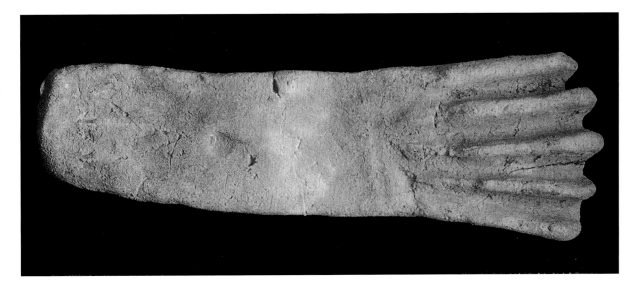

fig. 13 Clay hand. Tell al-Hamidiya (ancient Ta'idu), Syria, 15th century B.C. Terracotta, 21 × 6¾ × 3⅛ in. (53.5 × 17 × 8 cm). Museum, Deir ez-Zor, Syria (TH 41/42-38)

ridges that appear at junctures between wall and roof or wall and window on some architectural models. We can therefore begin to establish a parallel between the bronze casings that Layard excavated in Nimrud and Nineveh, probably meant to cover a wooden core, and these ridged elements.

One substantial problem posed by comparing the Assyrian hands with the architectural models lies in the chronological and geographic gap between the sets of objects. The bronze and clay hands are attested in Assyria between the ninth and eighth century B.C., whereas the architectural models are found in the Syrian area of the middle Euphrates between the fifteenth and thirteenth centuries B.C. Unfortunately, there is a lack of archaeological evidence in that area in the middle of the second millennium B.C., but recently published excavations in eastern Syria provide new information. In Tell al-Hamidiya, in the Khabur region, the Swiss archaeological expedition identified between 1988 and 2001 some twenty-eight examples of clay hands, unglazed and unpainted, in a secondary-use context in the palace attributed to the Mittanian period, which should be dated to the fifteenth century B.C. (fig. 13).[42] Although of slightly different shape—the definition of the single fingers is flatter and rougher than those in the Assyrian models—the Hamidiya hands must now be considered the most ancient artifacts of this class of materials.

A date in the thirteenth century B.C. had already been tentatively proposed for some hands found in Kar-Tukulti-Ninurta, one of the first Assyrian capitals in northwestern Iraq, but the uncertain stratigraphic position of the objects led archaeologists to reconsider the attribution to the later Neo-Assyrian period.[43] Another single clay hand is recorded from the plowed surface in

Tell Brak, where an imposing Mittanian and Middle-Assyrian occupation is also attested, but the British archaeologists working at the site hypothesized that this single object must have belonged to a disappeared Neo-Assyrian level (about the ninth to eighth century B.C.), rather than attributing it to the Mittanian or Middle-Assyrian buildings.[44]

David and Joan Oates and Helen McDonald considered the recent findings from nearby Tell al-Hamidiya, but they excluded a chronological relationship between the two, since the Brak example appears more similar to types from the Neo-Assyrian period than to the flat and long-armed pieces from Hamidiya. Importantly, however, archaeologists report that in Brak no occupation levels or materials belonging to the Neo-Assyrian period are attested within the site itself. As we have seen, the presence of Assyrian clay hands is always related, except in a few cases from an Ashur grave, to official buildings such as palaces and temples, which in this case would not have left a trace on the ground, not even with other eroded materials and pottery shards below the slope of the tell. Also, the height of the small hand fragment from Brak is reported to be nine centimeters, a measurement comparable with the findings at Hamidiya. These factors lead us to retain the possibility that the clay hand from Brak might have belonged to one of the official buildings dated to the Mittanian or Middle-Assyrian periods on the top of the tell and could be roughly contemporaneous with the items at Hamidiya. If this hypothesis is correct, we could state the following: hand-shaped devices were first in use in eastern Syria, then in Assyria, as early as the fifteenth to thirteenth century B.C., as attested by the iconography of clay architectural models and by recent finds in archaeological excavations.

fig. 14 Glazed pair of cupped hands (external and internal views). Syro-Hittite, Zincirli (ancient Sam'al), Turkey, 8th century B.C. Terracotta, glaze, 7½ × 5¾ × 4 in. (19 × 14.5 × 10 cm). Vorderasiatisches Museum, Berlin (S 2302)

fig. 15 Altar or funerary stele. Syro-Hittite, Karamanmaraş (ancient Gurgum), Turkey, late 8th–early 7th century B.C. Basalt, 29⅞ × 22¼ × 12⅜ in. (76 × 56.5 × 31.5 cm). Archaeological Museum, Antakya, Turkey (17915)

Another group of clay hands must be brought into the discussion: the only site in the Northern Levant where glazed hands have been found is Zincirli, in the Karasu river valley in the Amanus mountains.[45] Here the German expedition directed by Felix von Luschan at the end of the nineteenth century and recently the joint expedition of the Universities of Chicago and Tübingen directed by David Schloen have revealed several glazed hands in the ruins of the palaces of the ancient capital of the Aramaean kingdom of Sam'al (about the ninth to eighth century B.C.), which was conquered by the Assyrians in the eighth century B.C. The Zincirli hands, labeled "Handkonsolen" by the German archaeologists, present one main difference from those from the Assyrian region: they are represented as pairs of joined hands, with eight fingers and the two thumbs clearly represented in the correct position and not as an indistinct fifth finger (fig. 14), as in the Assyrian examples. No fingernails are represented, but a cupped hole, sometimes interpreted as an indentation, is present in the middle of the hands on the upper side, in some cases connecting with a hole passing through thumb and forefinger.[46] New fragments of Zincirli hands have been excavated by the Chicago-Tübingen expedition and are currently under study by the present author. It is difficult to place the Zincirli hands in relation to those from Assyria, or to understand their possible function, given that few indications of their stratigraphic provenance were recorded.[47] For the moment we can state that hands with a generic architectural function and a thick glaze coating were used in the far western province on the border between Syria and Anatolia, probably introduced by the new Assyrian rulers and locally readapted in shape and function as a regional variation.[48]

The same area of Zincirli presents another striking piece of evidence for the clay hands in their original setting: a funerary stele, or more probably an altar, from the city of Marash (ancient Gurgum), dated to the late eighth–early seventh century B.C., with a frontal depiction of a woman wearing a finely decorated dress and seated on a bed (fig. 15).[49] The stele is represented as an architectural frame, and underneath the stepped crenellations,[50] which have also been found in glazed ware in Zincirli,[51] are four protruding hands just below the ceiling, with all four fingers and thumb clearly defined.[52] The work provides a clear representation of the hands within their original architectural framework, recalling the visual suggestion provided by the Late Bronze Age Syrian architectural models.

We may never completely understand the significance for the people of the ancient Near East of such hands in different shapes and materials created from Assyria to western Syria in a span of time between the second half of the second millennium B.C. and the beginning of the first millennium B.C. Probably all the abovementioned hypotheses are partially true, beginning with a structural function coexisting with a symbolic and religious meaning. The hand always played an important role in Mesopotamian representations, as seen in the hand gestures on numerous Assyrian reliefs.[53] The fact that the hands bear the name of King Ashurnasirpal II, and mention his palace or one of the temples in Nimrud, could be a reference, at least in Assyria, to the role of the king as builder of palaces and temples, a topos that characterizes Mesopotamian kings from the earliest Dynastic periods onward. In this case the hand would be a symbol for the embodiment of the *roi bâtisseur* within the palace that he erected with his own hands, putting in place or transporting the mud bricks for construction, as represented in art contemporary with and even much earlier than the clay and bronze hands. For example, during the Neo-Assyrian period

King Ashurbanipal and his brother Shamash-shum-ukin, formerly king of Babylon before Ashurbanipal unified the crown of Assyria and Babylon, left three steles of their restoration works in the Esagila temple in Babylon, representing themselves carrying a basket of earth upon their heads (figs. 16, 17).[54]

Another possible explanation for the use of hands protruding out of the walls could be connected to the act of supporting the roof, the hand being a sort of *pars pro toto* for a figure of an Atlas or Telamon upholding the highest part of the building. Representations of mythological figures supporting the heavenly vault or the winged sun disk are common in the ancient Near East, especially on stone reliefs from Syro-Hittite citadels and on Assyrian and Babylonian seals. In these cases the anthropomorphic deities support the sky by holding it with their hands (fig. 18).[55]

This article has reviewed most of the archaeological and visual documentation related to the Assyrian glazed hands and has identified their employment as far back as the Late Bronze Age in northern Syria and Mesopotamia. Although the visual sources helpful to

fig. 17 Stele of Ashurbanipal, king of Assyria, represented as builder. Neo-Assyrian, Esagila Temple (Babylon), 668–655 B.C. Marble, H. 14 ½ in. (36.8 cm), W. 8 ¾ in. (22.2 cm). British Museum, London (ME 90864)

fig. 18 Cylinder seal belonging to the priest of Adad, Nabu-shar-usur, with a figure of Atlas holding a winged sun disk. Neo-Assyrian, ca. late 9th century–8th century B.C. Chalcedony, 1 ⅜ × ⅝ in. (3.6 × 1.5 cm). British Museum, London (BM 89082)

reconstruct their use are sparse, the monument from Marash, though outside of the Assyrian heartland, provides striking evidence that they were placed in an architectural setting consistent with that suggested by the excavated hands still embedded in the fallen wall of Room 2 in the Old Palace at Ashur. Furthermore, the Late Bronze Age Syrian architectural models offer a means by which to interpret the function of the hands in the second millennium B.C., as they can now be paired with archaeological remains of clay hands in a building presumably dated to the Mittanian period. The wide usage of these objects in the Assyrian palaces therefore seems to continue a long tradition in the architecture of the Near East, probably beginning in the last centuries of the second millennium B.C. in the region between the Syrian middle Euphrates and northern Mesopotamia. The origin of the hand-shaped objects in this area and their subsequent spread throughout Assyria in the early first millennium B.C.,

and most likely extending to the western provinces of the Northern Levant, could explain the variations in shape and surface treatment between the extant works, revealing once more the persistence of cultural interconnections between these regions already in place during the Late Bronze Age.

ACKNOWLEDGMENTS
I am grateful to the Department of Ancient Near Eastern Art for hosting me as a Jane and Morgan Whitney fellow. Sarah Graff and Michael Seymour offered especially valuable advice and fruitful discussions with regard to my research on glazed ceramics of the Iron Age.

SEBASTIANO SOLDI
Registrar, National Archaeological Museum, Florence, and Research Associate, University of Tübingen

NOTES

1 Edgar Peltenburg used the label "Assyrian clay fists" in his article of 1968. Grant Frame redefined them as "Assyrian clay hands" in his article of 1991, the most complete study on these objects. The pieces also became popular in the archaeological literature with the name "Hands of Ishtar," a definition that is best avoided, as correctly advised by Roger Moorey (1985, p. 180), since no clear reference in cuneiform texts or other visual sources relates the objects to the Mesopotamian goddess of love and war.

2 See the detailed study of the motifs and disposition of the cones in Brandes 1968.

3 Mallowan 1947, pp. 93–95, pls. 3–5.

4 Collins 2003a; Collins 2003b.

5 Weiss 1985; Oates 1967.

6 Evans 2008, pp. 200–201, fig. 66.

7 Harper 1992; Caubet 2003.

8 Anastasio 2011, pp. 35–65.

9 On the first excavations in the Near East, see Matthiae 1986 and Matthews 2003, pp. 1–19.

10 Frame 1991, p. 335n1.

11 See Peltenburg 1968 and Frame 1991.

12 Luschan and Andrae 1943; Peltenburg 1968.

13 MMA 54.117.30 and 57.27.30, excavated by the British School of Archaeology in Iraq in 1952.

14 In specific cases the hand and arm have identical widths, as in some examples of clay hands from Ashur (Preusser 1955, pl. 17e–h) or all the specimens from Khorsabad in the Oriental Institute Museum of the University of Chicago (Guralnick 2008).

15 See the hypothesis of employment in Frame 1991, p. 358, fig. 4.

16 Ibid., p. 338.

17 Ibid.

18 See the transliteration and translation in ibid., p. 348 (Inscription F).

19 See the transliteration and translation in ibid., p. 350 (Inscription H).

20 Preusser 1955, p. 21, pl. 14:B.

21 Ibid., p. 19.

22 Pedde and Lundström 2008, p. 45; see the two images in ibid., figs. 54, 55 (the first one was not published in Preusser 1955), where missing clay hands can be detected within the wall mud bricks.

23 Frame 1991, pp. 336–38.

24 Smith 1875, pp. 76 and 429.

25 Place 1867–70, vol. 2, p. 86.

26 See the detailed study by Martin Sauvage (1998, especially pp. 147–50) devoted to the brick and its employment through different periods of the ancient Near East.

27 Frame 1991, p. 356; Moorey (1985, p. 180) notes that the glaze or the bituminous covering on some of the examples was not treated in this manner to avoid damages caused by water in an outdoor environment, as the glaze would not be enough to resist the effect of flowing water.

28 Frame 1991, pp. 355–59.

29 Van Buren 1945, pp. 58–59.

30 The explanation of the use as a window ledge is proposed by Edgar Peltenburg (1968, p. 62) on the basis of a parallel with a basalt architectural decoration with lion talons from the citadel of Hama (ancient capital of the Aramaean kingdom of Hamath and Luash, in western Syria, ninth–eighth century B.C.).

31 Pedde 2011, p. 43.

32 Moorey 1985, p. 180.

33 Layard 1849, vol. 1, pp. 115–16.

34 In a portrait of Sir Austen Henry Layard by Ludwig Johann Passini (Austrian, 1832–1903), now in the National Portrait Gallery in London (NPG 1797), he is represented at his desk writing notes, with an Assyrian clay hand lying on the table in front of him.

35 Curtis 2013, pp. 61–62.

36 Frame 1991, p. 339.

37 The main objection to this hypothesis is that the dimension of the bronze sheathing hand is smaller than the eventual average diameter of a wooden timber supporting the roof, but we cannot exclude that the terminal part could be carved and adjusted to fit within the casing of the bronze hand.

38 Muller 2002.

39 Muller 2001, p. 337; Muller 2002, pp. 97–98; this hypothesis would harmonize well with Peltenburg's suggestion to interpret the hands as window ledges; Peltenburg 1968, p. 62.

40 See Callot 2001, especially p. 283, discussion with Peltenburg, who proposes a relationship between the wooden timber beams and the Assyrian clay hands.

41 Muller 2001; Margueron 1976; Margueron 2001.

42 Wäfler 1993, pp. 195, 464 no. 327; Wäfler 2003.

43 Eickhoff 1985; Dittmann et al. 1988, p. 121. See discussion in Hausleiter 1999, p. 277.

44 Oates, Oates, and McDonald 1997, pp. 153–54, fig. 178.

45 Luschan and Andrae 1943, pp. 60–61, 155, pl. 31:d–e; Pucci 2008, pp. 72–73.

46 See especially Luschan and Andrae 1943, p. 61, fig. 72, pl. 31:d–e; Peltenburg 1968, pp. 58–59, fig. 1c.

47 According to Felix von Luschan and Walter Andrae, the Zincirli hands were found in a pit south of the Hilani III, with other similar glazed objects (hands and rings); see the discussion of the possible stratigraphic attribution for the pit and related material in Pucci 2008, pp. 72–73.

48 An interesting but doubtful case of hands carved in stone from the Syro-Hittite area comes from Karkemish: Leonard Woolley (1921, p. ix, pl. A.16,e) describes two fragments of stone hands with Luwian inscriptions from the Lower Palace as fragments of a bowl. We cannot exclude that such hands were part of a larger statue that was lost or were part of a lost architectonic decoration similar to the Zincirli cupped hands with indentation.

49 Schachner and Schachner 1996; Bonatz 2000, p. 22 (C59), pl. XX.

50 For the hypothesis of the stele's use as an altar, see the comparison with another altar from the citadel of Marash in Garbini 1959 with the striking similarity in the stepped crenellation (Schachner and Schachner 1996, pp. 211–12).

51 Luschan and Andrae 1943, pp. 61, 155, pl. 31:a–c.

52 Schachner and Schachner 1996, p. 212, figs. 1, 9; see also the detailed color images posted by Tayfun Bilgin on the website Hittite Monuments, accessed January 9, 2016, www.hittitemonuments.com.

53 See the comprehensive analyses of Assyrian hand gestures in Gruber 1980, Goldman 1990, and Cifarelli 1998.

54 Tallis 2014.

55 One apparent incongruence to this hypothesis is that the clay hands with represented fingernails have the fingernails leaning on the side of the wall and not to the roof, looking as if a hand would come out from the roof above, and not supporting the roof itself (see Frame 1991, pp. 357, 358, fig. 4). It must be stressed, however, that if the clay hands did belong to an Atlas supporting the roof, fingernails would be represented as they are in a cupped open hand, as in images of Atlantes in stone slabs and seals (see fig. 18), and thus with fingernails leaning on the side of the wall.

REFERENCES

Anastasio, Stefano
2011 *Costruire tra i due fiumi: Introduzione all'edilizia in Mesopotamia tra Neolitico ed Età del Ferro.* Florence: Museo e Istituto Fiorentino di Preistoria "Paolo Graziosi."

Aruz, Joan, ed., with Ronald Wallenfels
2003 *Art of the First Cities: The Third Millennium B.C. from the Mediterranean to the Indus.* Exh. cat. New York: MMA.

Bonatz, Dominik
2000 *Das syro-hethitische Grabdenkmal: Untersuchungen zur Entstehung einer neuen Bildgattung in der Eisenzeit im nordsyrisch-südostanatolischen Raum.* Mainz: Philipp von Zabern.

Brandes, Mark A.
1968 *Untersuchungen zur Komposition der Stiftmosaiken an der Pfeilerhalle der Schicht IVa in Uruk-Warka.* Baghdader Mitteilungen, Beiheft 1. Berlin: Mann.

Callot, Olivier
2001 "De l'architecture à la maquette: Usage et représentation du bois en Syrie au Bronze récent." In *"Maquettes architecturales" de l'Antiquité: Regards croisés (Proche-Orient, Égypte, Chypre, bassin égéen et Grèce, du Néolithique à l'époque hellénistique); Actes du colloque de Strasbourg, 3–5 décembre 1998,* edited by Béatrice Muller, pp. 273–83. Strasbourg: Université Strasbourg; Paris: De Boccard.

Caubet, Annie
2003 "Le temple d'Inshushinak de Suse et l'architecture monumentale en 'faïence.'" In *Culture through Objects: Ancient Near Eastern Studies in Honour of P. R. S. Moorey,* edited by Timothy Potts, Michael Roaf, and Diana Stein, pp. 325–32. Oxford: Griffith Institute.

Cifarelli, Megan
1998 "Gesture and Alterity in the Art of Ashurnasirpal II of Assyria." *Art Bulletin* 80, no. 2, pp. 210–28.

Collins, Paul
2003a "Al Ubaid." In Aruz and Wallenfels 2003, p. 84.
2003b "Wall Nails Inlaid with Rosettes." In Aruz and Wallenfels 2003, pp. 86–87, no. 45a–c.

Curtis, John
2013 *An Examination of Late Assyrian Metalwork: With Special Reference to Nimrud.* Oxford: Oxbow Books.

Dittmann, Reinhard, Tilman Eickhoff, Rainer Schmitt, Roland Stengele, and Sabine Thürwächter
1988 "Untersuchungen in Kâr-Tukultī-Ninurta (Tulūl al-'Aqar) 1986." *Mitteilungen der Deutschen Orient-Gesellschaft zu Berlin* 120, pp. 97–138.

Eickhoff, Tilman
1985 *Kâr Tukulti Ninurta: Eine mittelassyrische Kult- und Residenzstadt.* Abhandlungen der Deutschen Orient-Gesellschaft 21. Berlin: Gebr. Mann.

Evans, Jean M.
2008 "Kassite Babylonia." In *Beyond Babylon: Art, Trade, and Diplomacy in the Second Millennium B.C.,* edited by Joan Aruz, Kim Benzel, Jean M. Evans, pp. 200–202. Exh. cat. New York: MMA.

Frame, Grant
1991 "Assyrian Clay Hands." *Baghdader Mitteilungen* 22, pp. 335–81.

Garbini, Giovanni
1959 "A New Altar from Marash." *Orientalia,* n.s., 28, pp. 206–8.

Goldman, Bernard
1990 "Some Assyrian Gestures." In "Aspects of Iranian Culture in Honor of Richard Nelson Frye," *Bulletin of the Asia Institute,* n.s. 4, part 1 (pub. 1992), pp. 41–49.

Gruber, Mayer I.
1980 *Aspects of Nonverbal Communication in the Ancient Near East.* 2 vols. Studia Pohl 12. Rome: Biblical Institute Press.

Guralnick, Eleanor
2008 "Assyrian Clay Hands from Khorsabad." *Journal of Near Eastern Studies* 67, no. 4, pp. 241–46.

Harper, Prudence O.
1992 "Brick Relief with Bull-Man, Palm Tree, and Frontal Figure." In *The Royal City of Susa: Ancient Near Eastern Treasures in the Louvre,* edited by Prudence O. Harper, Joan Aruz, and Françoise Tallon, pp. 141–44, no. 88. Exh. cat. New York: MMA.

Hausleiter, Arnulf
1999 "Neuassyrische Kunstperiode. VI. Keramik." *Reallexikon der Assyriologie und voderasiatischen Archäologie* 9, no. 3/4, pp. 274–77.

Layard, Austen Henry
1849 *Nineveh and Its Remains . . . .* 2 vols. London: John Murray.

Luschan, Felix von, and Walter Andrae
1943 *Ausgrabungen in Sendschirli.* Vol. 5, *Die Kleinfunde von Sendschirli.* Mitteilungen aus den orientalischen Sammlungen 15. Berlin: Walter de Gruyter.

Mallowan, Max E. L.
1947 "Excavations at Brak and Chagar Bazar." *Iraq* 9, pp. 1–259.

Margueron, Jean-Claude
1976 "'Maquettes' architecturales de Meskene-Emar." *Syria* 53, no. 3–4, pp. 193–232.
2001 "Maquette et transparence architecturale." In *"Maquettes architecturales" de l'Antiquité: Regards croisés (Proche-Orient, Égypte, Chypre, bassin égéen et Grèce, du Néolithique à l'époque hellénistique); Actes du colloque de Strasbourg, 3–5 décembre 1998,* edited by Béatrice Muller, pp. 227–56. Strasbourg: Université Strasbourg; Paris: De Boccard.

Matthews, Roger
2003 *The Archaeology of Mesopotamia: Theories and Approaches.* London: Routledge.

Matthiae, Paolo
1986 *Scoperte di archeologia orientale.* Rome and Bari: Laterza.

Moorey, P. R. S.
1985 *Materials and Manufacture in Ancient Mesopotamia: The Evidence of Archaeology and Art; Metals and Metalwork, Glazed Materials and Glass.* British Archaeological Reports International Series 237. Oxford: British Archaeological Reports.

Muller, Béatrice
2001 "L'homme qui fabriquait les maquettes au Proch Orient . . . ." In *"Maquettes architecturales" de l'Antiquité: Regards croisés (Proche-Orient, Égypte, Chypre, bassin égéen et Grèce, du Néolithique à l'époque hellénistique); Actes du colloque de Strasbourg, 3–5 décembre 1998,* edited by Béatrice Muller, pp. 331–56. Strasbourg: Université Strasbourg; Paris: De Boccard.
2002 *Les "maquettes architecturales" du Proche-Orient ancien: Mésopotamie, Syrie, Palestine du IIIe au milieu du Ier millénaire av. J.-C.* 2 vols. Bibliothèque Archéologique et Historique 160. Beirut: Institut Français d'Archéologie du Proche-Orient.

Oates, David
1967 "The Excavations at Tell al Rimah, 1966." *Iraq* 29 (Autumn), pp. 70–96.

Oates, David, Joan Oates, and Helen McDonald
1997 *Excavations at Tell Brak.* Vol. 1, *The Mitanni and Old Babylonian Periods.* Cambridge: McDonald Institute for Archaeological Research, University of Cambridge; London: British School of Archaeology in Iraq.

Pedde, Friedhelm

2011 "Der Alte Palast in Assur: Ausgrabungen und Neubearbeitung." In *Assur–Gott, Stadt und Land: 5. Internationales Colloquium der Deutschen Orient-Gesellschaft 18.–21. Februar 2004 in Berlin*, edited by Johannes Renger, pp. 33–62. Colloquien der Deutschen Orient-Gesellschaft 5. Wiesbaden: Harrassowitz.

Pedde, Friedhelm, and Steven Lundström

2008 *Der Alte Palast in Assur: Architektur und Baugeschichte; Faltpläne*. Wissenschaftliche Veröffentlichung der Deutschen Orient-Gesellschaft 120. Wiesbaden: Harrassowitz.

Peltenburg, Edgar J.

1968 "Assyrian Clay Fists." *Oriens Antiquus* 7, pp. 57–62.

Place, Victor

1867–70 *Ninive et l'Assyrie*. 3 vols. Paris: Imprimierie Impériale.

Preusser, Conrad

1955 *Die Paläste in Assur*. Wissenschaftliche Veröffentlichung der Deutschen Orient-Gesellschaft 66. Berlin: Gebr. Mann.

Pucci, Marina

2008 *Functional Analysis of Space in Syro-Hittite Architecture*. British Archaeological Reports International Series 1738. Oxford: Archaeopress.

Sauvage, Martin

1998 *La brique et sa mise en oeuvre en Mésopotamie: Des origines à l'époque achéménide*. Paris: Ministère des Affaires Etrangères.

Schachner, Şenay, and Andreas Schachner

1996 "Eine späthethitische Grabstele aus Maraş im Museum von Antakya." *Anatolica* 22, pp. 203–26.

Smith, George

1875 *Assyrian Discoveries: An Account of Explorations and Discoveries on the Site of Nineveh, during 1873 and 1874*. London: Sampson Low, Marston, Low and Searle.

Tallis, Nigel

2014 "Stele of Ashurbanipal." In *Assyria to Iberia at the Dawn of the Classical Age*, edited by Joan Aruz, Sarah B. Graff, and Yelena Rakic, pp. 342–43, no. 206. Exh. cat. New York: MMA.

Van Buren, Elizabeth Douglas

1945 *Symbols of the Gods in Mesopotamian Art*. Rome: Pontificium Institutum Biblicum.

Wäfler, Markus

1993 "Tell al-Ḥamidiya" and catalogue entries. In *L'Eufrate e il tempo: Le civiltà del medio Eufrate e della Gezira siriana*, edited by Olivier Rouault and Maria Grazia Masetti-Rouault, pp. 193–98, 464. Exh. cat., Sala dell'Arengo and Palazzo del Podestà, Rimini. Milan: Electa.

2003 *Tall al-Hamīdīya*. Vol. 4, *Vorbericht 1988–2001*. Orbis Biblicus et Orientalis, Series Archaeologica 23. Fribourg: Academic Press; Göttingen: Vandenhoeck & Ruprecht.

Weiss, Harvey

1985 "Rediscovering: Tell Leilan on the Habur Plains of Syria." *Biblical Archaeologist* 48 (March), pp. 5–34.

Woolley, C. Leonard

1921 *Carchemish: Report on the Excavations at Jerablus on Behalf of the British Museum*. Part 2, *The Town Defences*. London: Trustees of the British Museum; Oxford: University Press.

LUCA BOMBARDIERI

A Possible Cypriot Origin for an Assyrian Stone Mixing Bowl in the Cesnola Collection

The comprehensive publication of the Cesnola Collection of Cypriot stone sculpture in The Metropolitan Museum of Art from 2014 sheds new light on iconographic and ideological aspects of major stone statuary, as well as a variety of other stone objects.[1] Of particular interest is a shallow basalt bowl that had previously remained unpublished (fig. 1). Part of a small group of ten hard-stone vessels purchased by the Museum in 1874–76 from the Cesnola Collection, the basalt bowl appears to be a typical Assyrian mixing bowl.[2]

The production of different types of stone mixing bowls began in northern Mesopotamia in the Early Iron Age and increased considerably, developing distinctive features, throughout the Neo-Assyrian period and the Post-Assyrian/Neo-Babylonian period (eighth to sixth century B.C.). The most widespread types were primarily shallow bowls made of basalt with a simple base, or a

fig. 1 Mixing bowl. Cyprus. Iron Age, ca. 8th–6th century B.C. Basalt, H. 2 in. (5 cm); Diam. 8 in. (20.3 cm). The Metropolitan Museum of Art, The Cesnola Collection, Purchased by subscription, 1874–76 (74.51.5054)

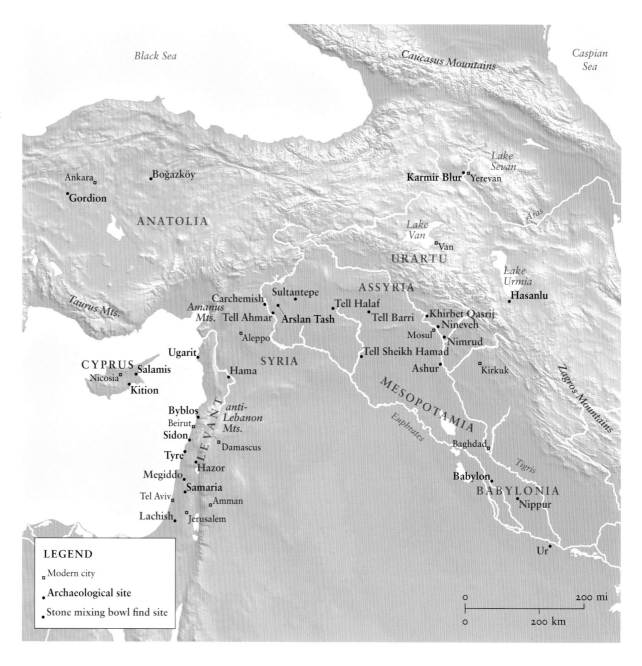

fig. 2 Map of the Ancient Near East and the Eastern Mediterranean in the first millennium B.C., with find sites of Assyrian stone mixing bowls (8th–6th century B.C.) mentioned in this article, and select second millennium B.C. sites

ring base, or a disk base, which usually have a distinctive form of double rim, or discontinuous rim with bar handle. Pedestal bowls and tripods can also have the same form of rim.[3] Analogous shapes and comparable decoration patterns are documented in contemporary ceramic production.[4]

The lower rim of the Metropolitan Museum's bowl serves as both a handle and a suitable place for securing a lid. The bowl could be held by placing the finger below the rim to take the weight, while the thumb could be hooked upward through the discontinuous rib and toward the interior of the bowl. Many bowls of this type, deriving from Assyrian palaces, bear inscriptions with royal titles and names of the Neo-Assyrian kings, and

occasionally with hieroglyphs that assign them to royal property. Production of the bowls originated from central Assyria and is attested across a vast area comprising southern Mesopotamia, inner Syria, and the Palestinian Levant, extending as far as the central Anatolian plateau and—hypothetically—Cyprus (fig. 2).

At the main city of Ashur, a significant number of mixing bowls come from the sacred area of the Temple of Ishtar, from the levels that can be dated to the reign of Shalmaneser III and Sin-šar-iškun (fig. 3).[5] On the whole, this production was well attested at Ashur at least from the beginning of the eighth century B.C. and throughout the entire Neo-Assyrian and the Post-Assyrian/Neo-Babylonian periods, within a

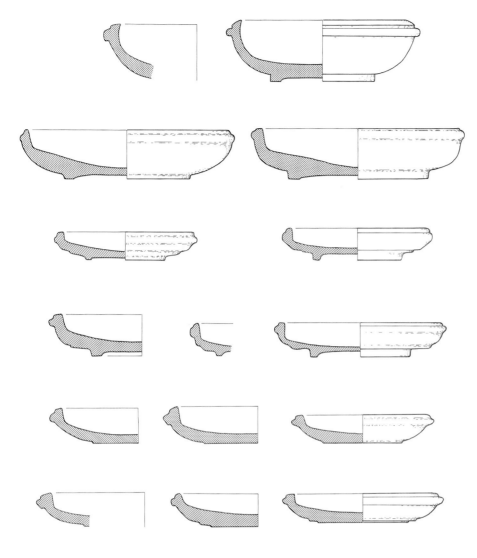

fig. 3 Drawing of stone mixing bowls from Ashur, 8th–7th century B.C.

fig. 4 Stone mixing bowl. Tell Halaf

chronological range similar to that documented in Nimrud and Nineveh.[6] In these central capital cities, several stone mixing bowls bear inscriptions of the kings Sennacherib, Esarhaddon, and Ashurbanipal. At least two stone mixing bowls were also found at Persepolis in the fourth century B.C., and we may assume that both came from Assyria during the seventh century B.C. and were used there for a long time.[7]

In the immediate periphery of the Assyrian empire, the production is well documented at Carchemish and Tell Halaf as well as in the provincial northern Mesopotamian towns of Tell Ahmar, Tell Barri, and Tell Sheikh Hamad, where Assyrian (and then Neo-Babylonian) governors' palaces were located (fig. 4).[8] Outside of northern Mesopotamia, the production of mixing bowls has been sporadically traced from southern Mesopotamia (Ur and Nippur) to central Anatolia (Phrygian Boğazköy), in the period between 650 B.C. and the conquest of Croesus in 547 B.C.[9] The production of mixing bowls has been much more widely documented in western Syria (from the royal quarters at Hama), the Levant (from Lachish in a seventh-century B.C. level; and from Megiddo and Hazor, dated before the destruction of 732 B.C.), and in Cyprus.[10]

Based on a definition by L. A. Moritz suggesting that similar containers, named *mortaria*, were used for various purposes related to the preparation of food, especially for small quantities of ingredients, the containers in question may be considered functional mixing bowls.[11] *Mortaria*—which did not function as mortars, despite the name—and the Assyrian mixing bowls were probably employed for rubbing and mixing, rather than pounding, small quantities of easily crushed substances.[12] The mixing bowls were made for royalty and high officials and are strictly connected with royal banquet ceremonies in Neo-Assyrian palaces. Analogous forms of the bowls would have served the same purpose at meals taken by peripheral and Assyrianized elites.

The Assyrian menu for royal banquets was celebrated far outside Assyria and contributed to the wide appeal of Assyrian culture, its impact lasting long after the fall of the empire, attested by the topos of Assyrian decadence in Greek literature.[13] The role of food as a means to disseminate royal culture is well exemplified by the Banquet Stele of Ashurnasirpal II. The famous text emphatically lists the food served at the inauguration of the royal palace at Nimrud in 869 B.C., probably the most exquisite and enormous Assyrian feast, to which sixty-nine thousand guests from diverse provinces and surrounding regions were invited.[14] The text reveals the wide variety of ingredients and dishes served by the cooks of the Assyrian royal kitchens, especially the assorted meat-based courses seasoned with aromatic condiments. The stele lists the following common spices of royal cuisine: cardamom, watercress, spicy salts, onion, garlic, cumin, thyme, and fennel, along with herbs and unidentified ingredients such as *karkartu*, *ḫabbaqūqu*, and *saḫunu*.[15]

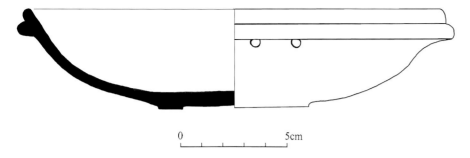

Meat and spices figured prominently in elite food, but were absent in the daily diets of commoners, which were based on cereals (bread and beer), vegetables, and dairy products.[16] Sheep, goats, calves and steers, fishes, ducks, doves, and other winged animals were cooked in ovens, roasted over the fire (*šube/šume*), or on spit roasts (*gabbubu*). Special joints of meat were salted (*midlu*) long before being cooked or boiled in large bronze cauldrons.[17] The boiling of meat appears to be represented in a relief scene from the Southwest Palace of Sennacherib at Nineveh, in which a large bronze open vessel is transported on a wood raft together with a beheaded steer ready to be cooked.[18]

Mixing bowls were customarily placed on the table during meals, and it seems possible that bowls such as the one in the Metropolitan Museum may have been utilized to grind aromatic ingredients like salt and herbs. The two items, used in small quantities, sometimes required light crushing at the table, and would be kept covered to preserve the fragrance during the banquet.[19]

The stone mixing bowls bear a clear Assyrian character, and convey new information about how that culture prepared and consumed food. The widespread diffusion of exclusive objects demonstrates how Assyrian elements were adopted and assimilated by peripheral and foreign elites, in particular, the Cypriot ruling classes. The complexity of cultural relations between Cyprus and Assyria and the role of the island in the Neo-Assyrian and Post-Assyrian economic and ideological system are still being debated.[20] The traditional view of an Assyrian domination in Cyprus in the eighth to seventh century B.C., as initially argued by Einar Gjerstad in the 1940s, has been reconsidered by most scholars, who reject the former emphasis on the disruptions brought about by military incursions from outside the island.[21] It seems beneficial to approach this controversial issue not by exclusively focusing on possible evidence of direct cultural interactions between Cyprus and Assyria, but by evaluating more complex phenomena of assimilation and adoption of

fig. 5 Drawing of ceramic bowl. Sacred area at Kition Kathari (Area II, Temple 1; 2221). Gray and black polished ware

fig. 6 Stele of Sargon II. Kition, Larnaca. Neo-Assyrian, after 707 B.C. Gabbro/basalt, H. 82¼ in. (209 cm), W. 27 in. (68.5 cm). Staatliche Museen zu Berlin, Vorderasiatisches Museum, Purchase 1845 (VA 968)

cultural elements from a wider Eastern Mediterranean perspective. It is important to consider that the contacts between Cyprus and Assyria were mostly mediated through the influence of the Phoenicians, particularly through Kition.[22] A ceramic Phoenician import from the sacred area at Kition Kathari (Area II, Temple 1) provides a relevant point of discussion (fig. 5).[23] The

fig. 7 Octagonal pyramidal seal. Cyprus. Neo-Babylonian, 6th century B.C. Blue chalcedony, seal face ¾ × ½ in. (1.9 × 1.3 cm), H. 1⅛ in. (2.8 cm), string hole 1/16 in. (.2 cm). The Metropolitan Museum of Art, The Cesnola Collection, Purchased by subscription, 1874–76 (74.51.4422)

shallow bowl in gray and black polished ware has an everted rim with a horizontal depression at its midpoint, forming two rolls—features that are also characteristic of the Metropolitan Museum's Assyrian stone mixing bowl. The co-presence of this type of bowl in both ceramic and basalt in Phoenicia and Assyria has been proven previously.[24] Furthermore, it has been argued that in Cyprus the repertoire of gray and black polished ware imitates stone prototypes, especially basalt vessels, and the depositing of these vessels in funerary and sacred areas can be attributed to their use for food and liquid offerings.[25] Contacts between Assyria and Cyprus, mediated by Phoenicians, could have provided the common underlying network for the introduction of such objects to the island.

Whereas Assyrianizing works of art were presumably imported to the island or imitated by local artists during the Archaic period (as is most evident with seals, ivory inlays, and stone sculpture), the only truly Assyrian object found in Cyprus is a royal Neo-Assyrian stele (fig. 6).[26] This well-known victory stele, which is attributed to Sargon II (721–705 B.C.), was found in 1845 at Kition, and is now in the Vorderasiatisches Museum in Berlin.[27] The iconography of the king on the stele connotes Assyrian manufacture and a strictly royal ritual context; the position of the arms and cudgel clearly points to a kingship ceremony witnessed by the gods, represented in front of the king. The cuneiform inscription along the sides of the stele records that seven kings of Cyprus took fright upon

hearing of the deeds of Sargon, and sent a series of appeasing gifts.[28]

Examples of imported Assyrianizing objects in Cyprus are the stamp seals in the Pierides Museum in Larnaca and in the Cesnola Collection of the Metropolitan Museum, cut in both elaborate and common styles that can be associated with Neo-Assyrian and Neo-Babylonian glyptic (fig. 7).[29] Perhaps the clearest evidence of demand for Assyrianizing prestige objects by Cypriot elites is represented by the decorated ivory inlays imported to the island during the Archaic period. For example, the majority of ivory panels from the Royal Cemetery at Salamis belongs to the "ornate" style, of which the main centers of production were likely located in Phoenicia, and shows an Assyrianizing character, with iconographic elements widely shared in contemporary Mesopotamia and the Levant.[30] The mixed provenance of the ivory panels resulted in the hybrid style that is most characteristic of a wide Eastern Mediterranean shared cultural milieu.

In addition to imported objects, the imitation of Assyrian motifs in Cypriot figurative art is evident, especially in the stone sculpture of male votaries. The significance and prestige ascribed to these representations of dignitaries and officials during the Archaic period are conveyed by their colossal size, as attested by the limestone head of a bearded man in the Cesnola Collection in the Metropolitan Museum (fig. 8).[31] While the identity of the figure, his rank in religious ceremonies, and probable military role remain uncertain, the elaborate dress with conical helmet indicates high social status. The dress code adopted by such members of the Cypriot elite again strongly suggests an Assyrian-style model evenly diffused since the end of the eighth century B.C. from the Levantine coast to Cilicia and Cyprus.[32]

Although the Assyrianizing elements in Cypriot art appear evident, the presence of Assyrian objects imported to the island remains sporadic and questionable. Unfortunately, the provenances of the stamp seals from both the Pierides Museum and the Metropolitan Museum are unclear. Both Pierides and Cesnola were actively involved in the antiquities market, and we must allow for the possibility that the objects could have been brought to the island in modern times.[33] One of six Neo-Babylonian–style stamp seals from Cyprus that are datable to the seventh to sixth century B.C. has a firm attribution, however. The seal bears a Cypro-Syllabic inscription and epigraphic analysis confirmed that it was certainly imported to the island and re-engraved during the Cypro-Archaic I period.[34]

fig. 8 Limestone head of a bearded man. Cyprus, sacred area of Golgoi *Ayios Photios*. Archaic, early 6th century B.C. Limestone, 35 × 14 × 23 in. (88.9 × 35.6 × 58.4 cm). The Metropolitan Museum of Art, The Cesnola Collection, Purchased by subscription, 1874–76 (74.51.2857)

Caution must be taken when attempting to draw a conclusive hypothesis about the unprovenanced and unique Assyrian stone mixing bowl in the Metropolitan Museum. If we accept that the provenance from Cyprus is genuine, the bowl may provide further significant evidence of an elite, Assyrian-style object at the island during the period from the eighth century to the first half of the sixth century B.C. Without question, however, the function, dating, and geographic associations of the Metropolitan Museum's stone mixing bowl support the notion that Cyprus took part in a wide Eastern Mediterranean cultural network. This active participation may have resulted in the progressive assimilation of ideological and cultural elements from Assyria, the most influential political and cultural entity in the Eastern Mediterranean at the time. The Cypriot elite appear to have fashioned their image of power through the adoption of Assyrian-style status objects and behaviors, such as codified dining practices.

ACKNOWLEDGMENTS

I am grateful to Annie Caubet, Antoine Hermary, Markus Hilgert, and Adriano Orsingher for their support, helpful comments, and suggestions.

LUCA BOMBARDIERI
Researcher, Department of Humanities,
Università di Torino

NOTES

1 Hermary and Mertens 2014.

2 Ibid., p. 411, no. 618; MMA 74.51.5054; H. 2 in. (5 cm); Diam. 8 in. (20.3 cm).

3 Searight, Reade, and Finkel 2008, p. 51.

4 Fiorina, Bombardieri, and Chiocchetti 2005; Kreppner 2006.

5 Miglus 1996, pls. 58–60.

6 Searight, Reade, and Finkel 2008, pp. 51–53; Bombardieri 2010, pp. 122–28, 212–18.

7 Schmidt 1957, pls. 60.4, 61.3; Searight, Reade, and Finkel 2008, pp. 52–53.

8 For Carchemish, see Searight, Reade, and Finkel 2008, nos. 397, 415. For Tell Halaf, see Hrouda 1962, pp. 66–67, and Searight, Reade, and Finkel 2008, no. 414. For the other northern Mesopotamian towns, see Bunnens 1990, pp. 18–22; Trokay 2000; Kreppner 2006; and Bombardieri 2010, pp. 122–28, 212–18.

9 For southern Mesopotamia (Ur and Nippur), see Woolley 1965, pl. 35, and Zettler 1993, p. 137. For central Anatolia (Phrygian Boğazköy), see Bossert 2000, pl. 93.103, 104.

10 For western Syria, see Riis and Buhl 1990. For Megiddo and Hazor, see Lamon and Shipton 1939, pl. 113.2,4,14; Loud 1948, pl. 263.21; Tufnell 1953, pl. 65.8; and Yadin et al. 1958, p. 51.

11 Moritz 1958, pp. 22–23.

12 Bombardieri 2010, p. 119.

13 As exemplified in Diodorus Siculus, *Bibliotheca Historica* 2.23.2.

14 Grayson 1991, p. 292, text A.0.101.30, line 114.

15 Bottéro 2004, pp. 69, 101–3; Gaspa 2012, pp. 182–83.

16 Gaspa 2012, p. 183.

17 Ibid., p. 180.

18 Barnett, Bleibtreu, and Turner 1998, pl. 147a.

19 Searight, Reade, and Finkel 2008, p. 62.

20 Reyes 1994; Iacovou 2001; Cannavò 2007.

21 Gjerstad 1948, pp. 449–52. See also Tatton-Brown 1989, p. 73.

22 Cannavò 2007; Hadjisavvas 2007; Cannavò 2015.

23 Bikai 1981, p. 27, no. 70, pls. XXII.11, XXVI.9. The main assemblages of gray and black polished ware come from Kition and its territory during the Cypro-Geometric III to Cypro-Archaic I periods; see Bikai 2003 (Kition Kathari); Fourrier 2015 (Kition Bamboula); Papageorghiou 1990 (Aradippou, tomb 1); Flourentzos 2008, p. 102, fig. 101 (from a rescue-excavated tomb in the area of the Larnaca International Airport).

24 Kreppner 2006; Bombardieri 2010, p. 128.

25 Georgiou and Karageorghis 2013; Orsingher n.d., forthcoming.

26 Karageorghis 1974; Reyes 2001; Nenna 2006; Caubet 2014.

27 Börker-Klähn 1982, pp. 202–3; Morandi 1988, pp. 113–17, 147, table B1; Reyes 1994, pp. 50–51; Karageorghis 2002, pp. 153–54; Radner 2010, pp. 433–35; Merrillees 2016.

28 Radner 2010, pp. 440–41.

29 Reyes 1994, p. 61.

30 Herrmann 1986, pp. 35–36. One of the characteristic elements of the "ornate style" is the sacred tree. The motif is depicted on one of the openwork panels forming the scrollwork back of a chair from Tomb 79 (Karageorghis 1974, pls. A, B, LXI–LXIII) and finds immediate parallels with the well-known ivories from Room SW 37, Fort Shalmaneser at Nimrud (Herrmann 1986, pls. 288, 289, 325, 326; Pappalardo 2006). The lion motif is also common to the style, seen in the S-shaped ivory table leg with a lion motif (Karageorghis 1974, pl. F). Comparisons from SW 37 are the larger lion paws on ivory furniture legs (Herrmann 1986, p. 379; Pappalardo 2006, pl. L) and the panels depicting opposing human-headed sphinxes and kneeling figures, in Egyptian dress, framed by notched palm branches and separated by a stylized tree, coming from the rows of the ivory panels originating from a bed (Karageorghis 1974, pls. LXVII, LXVIII). The same motif occurs on openwork furniture plaques from Nimrud and Samaria (Herrmann 1986, pls. 288, 160; Mallowan 1966, fig. 479; Crowfoot and Crowfoot 1938, pl. II.2). See also Cecchini, Mazzoni, and Scigliuzzo 2009.

31 Hermary and Mertens 2014, p. 28.

32 Hermary 1989, pp. 22–23.

33 Reyes 1991; Reyes 2001.

34 Masson 1983, p. 344, n.353; Morpurgo Davies 1988, p. 106; Tuplin 1996, p. 48; Egetmeyer 2010, p. 31.

REFERENCES

Barnett, Richard D., Erika Bleibtreu, and Geoffrey Turner
  1998 *Sculptures from the Southwest Palace of Sennacherib at Nineveh.* 2 vols. London: British Museum Press.
Bikai, Patricia M.
  1981 "The Phoenician Imports." In *Excavations at Kition IV: The Non-Cypriote Pottery,* edited by Vassos Karageorghis, pp. 23–35. Nicosia: Department of Antiquities, Cyprus.
  2003 "Statistical Observations on the Phoenician Pottery of Kition." In *Excavations at Kition VI: The Phoenician and Later Levels, Part II,* by Vassos Karageorghis, pp. 258–64. Nicosia: Department of Antiquities, Cyprus.
Bombardieri, Luca
  2010 *Pietre da macina, macine per mulini: Definizione e sviluppo delle tecniche per la macinazione nell'area del Vicino Oriente e del Mediterraneo orientale antico.* Oxford: Archaeopress.
  2015 *Orgoglio e pregiudizi: L'archeologia cipriota di Luigi Palma di Cesnola alla luce dei documenti e delle corrispondenze con l'Italia.* Rome: Artemide.
Börker-Klähn, Jutta
  1982 *Altvorderasiatische Bildstelen und vergleichbare Felsreliefs.* Mainz am Rhein: Philipp von Zabern.
Bossert, Eva-Maria
  2000 *Die Keramik phrygischer Zeit von Boğazköy: Funde aus den Grabungskampagnen 1906, 1907, 1911, 1912, 1931–1939 und 1952–1960.* Boğazköy-Ḫattuša 18. Berlin: Mann.
Bottéro, Jean
  2004 *The Oldest Cuisine in the World: Cooking in Mesopotamia.* Translated from French by Teresa Lavender Fagan. Chicago: University of Chicago Press.
Bunnens, Guy, ed.
  1990 *Tell Ahmar 1988 Season.* Publications of the Melbourne University Expedition to Tell Ahmar, Abr-Nahrain Suppl. 2. Leuven: Orientaliste.
Cannavò, Anna
  2007 "The Role of Cyprus in the Neo-Assyrian Economic System: Analysis of the Textual Evidence." *Rivista di studi fenici* 35, no. 2, pp. 179–90.
  2015 "Cyprus and the Near East in the Neo-Assyrian Period." *Kyprios Character: History, Archaeology & Numismatics of Ancient Cyprus,* June 7, http://kyprioscharacter.eie.gr/en/t/AL.
Caubet, Annie
  2014 "Alabastron." In *Assyria to Iberia at the Dawn of the Classical Age,* edited by Joan Aruz, Sarah B. Graff, and Yelena Rakic, pp. 168–69, no. 60. Exh. cat. New York: MMA.
Cecchini, Serena Maria, Stefania Mazzoni, and Elena Scigliuzzo, eds.
  2009 *Syrian and Phoenician Ivories of the Early First Millennium BCE: Chronology, Regional Styles and Iconographic Repertories, Patterns of Inter-regional Distribution.* Ricerche di archeologia del Vicino Oriente 3. Pisa: Edizioni ETS.
Crowfoot, J. W., and Grace M. Crowfoot
  1938 *Early Ivories from Samaria.* Samaria-Sebaste: Reports of the Work of the Joint Expedition in 1931–1933 and of the British Expedition in 1935, no. 2. London: Palestine Exploration Fund.
Egetmeyer, Markus
  2010 *Le dialecte grec ancien de Chypre.* 2 vols. Berlin and New York: Walter de Gruyter.
Fiorina, Paolo, Luca Bombardieri, and Lucia Chiocchetti
  2005 "Kalhu-Kahat: Elementi di continuità attraverso il periodo neoassiro finale e l'età neobabilonese caldea in Mesopotamia settentrionale." *Mesopotamia* 40, pp. 81–102.

Flourentzos, Pavlos
  2008 *Annual Report of the Department of Antiquities for the Year 2006.* Lefkosia: Department of Antiquities, Cyprus.
Fourrier, Sabine
  2015 "La céramique chypriote et levantine d'époque géométrique et archaïque." In *Kition-Bamboula,* vol. 6, *Le sanctuaire sous la colline,* by Annie Caubet, Sabine Fourrier, and Marguerite Yon, pp. 111–72. Lyon: Maison de l'Orient et de la Méditerranée.
Gaspa, Salvatore
  2012 "La cucina del dio e del re nell'alimentazione dell'impero assiro." In *Mangiare divinamente: Pratiche e simbologie alimentari nell'Antico Oriente,* edited by Lucio Milano, pp. 177–231. Florence: LoGisma.
Georgiou, Giorgos, and Vassos Karageorghis
  2013 *A Cypro-Archaic Tomb at Xylotymbou and Three Cypro-Classical Tombs at Phlasou: From Exuberance to Recession.* Studies in Mediterranean Archaeology 140. Uppsala: Aströms Förlag.
Gjerstad, Einar
  1948 *The Cypro-Geometric, Cypro-Archaic, and Cypro-Classical Periods.* The Swedish Cyprus Expedition 4, part 2. Stockholm: Swedish Cyprus Expedition.
Grayson, A. Kirk
  1991 *Assyrian Rulers of the Early First Millennium BC, I (1114–859 BC).* Toronto, Buffalo, and London: University of Toronto Press.
Hadjisavvas, Sophocles
  2007 "The Phoenician Penetration in Cyprus as Documented in the Necropolis of Kition." *Cahiers du Centre d'Etudes Chypriotes* 37, pp. 185–95.
Hermary, Antoine
  1989 *Catalogue des antiquités de Chypre: Sculptures.* Musée du Louvre. Département des Antiquités Orientales. Paris: Editions de la Réunion des Musées Nationaux.
Hermary, Antoine, and Joan R. Mertens
  2014 *The Cesnola Collection of Cypriot Art: Stone Sculpture.* New York: MMA.
Herrmann, Georgina
  1986 *Ivories from Room SW 37, Fort Shalmaneser.* 2 vols. London: British School of Archaeology in Iraq.
Hrouda, Barthel
  1962 *Tell Halaf.* Vol. 4, *Die Kleinfunde aus historischer Zeit.* Berlin: De Gruyter.
Iacovou, Maria
  2001 "Cyprus from Alashiya to Iatnana: The Protohistoric Interim." In *IΘAKH [Ithakē]: Festschrift für Jörg Schäfer zum 75. Geburtstag am 25. April 2001,* edited by Stephanie Böhm and Klaus-Valtin von Eickstedt, pp. 85–92. Würzburg: Ergon.
Karageorghis, Vassos
  1974 *Salamis.* Vol. 5, *Excavations in the Necropolis of Salamis III.* 3 parts. Nicosia: Department of Antiquities, Cyprus.
  2002 *Early Cyprus: Crossroads of the Mediterranean.* Los Angeles: J. Paul Getty Museum.
Kreppner, Florian Janoscha
  2006 *Die Keramik des "Roten Hauses" von Tall Šēḫ Ḥamad/Dūr-Katlimmu: Eine Betrachtung der Keramik Nordmesopotamiens aus der zweiten Hälfte des 7. und aus dem 6. Jahrhundert v. Chr.* 2 vols. Berichte der Ausgrabung Tall Schech Hamad/Dūr-Katlimmu 7. Wiesbaden: Harrassowitz.

Lamon, Robert S., and Geoffrey M. Shipton
  1939 *Megiddo*. Vol. 1, *Seasons of 1925–1934, Strata I–V*. University of Chicago Oriental Institute Publication 42. Chicago: University of Chicago Press.

Loud, Gordon
  1948 *Megiddo*. Vol. 2, *Seasons of 1935–39*. 2 vols. University of Chicago Oriental Institute Publication 62. Chicago: University of Chicago Press.

Mallowan, M. E. L.
  1966 *Nimrud and Its Remains*. Vols. 1, 2. London: British School of Archaeology in Iraq; Collins.

Masson, Olivier
  1983 *Les inscriptions chypriotes syllabiques: Recueil critique et commenté*. Reprint of 1961 ed., with additions. Etudes chypriotes 1. Paris: E. de Boccard.

Merrillees, Robert S.
  2016 "Studies on the Provenances of the Stele of Sargon II from Larnaca (Kition) and the So-called Dhali (Idalion) Silver Bowls in the Louvre." *Cahiers du Centre d'Etudes Chypriotes* 46, pp. 349–86.

Miglus, Peter A.
  1996 *Das Wohngebiet von Assur: Stratigraphie und Architektur*. 2 vols. Berlin: Mann.

Morandi, Daniele
  1988 "Stele e statue reali assire: Localizzazione, diffusione e implicazioni ideologiche." *Mesopotamia* 23, pp. 105–55.

Moritz, L. A.
  1958 *Grain-Mills and Flour in Classical Antiquity*. Oxford: Clarendon Press.

Morpurgo Davies, Anna
  1988 "Problems in Cyprian Phonology and Writings." In *The History of Greek Language in Cyprus: Proceedings of an International Symposium Sponsored by the Pierides Foundation, Larnaca, Cyprus, 8–13 September, 1986*, edited by Jacqueline Karageorghis and Olivier Masson, pp. 99–126. Nicosia: Pierides Foundation.

Nenna, Marie-Dominique
  2006 "Les verres d'époque archaïque, classique et hellénistique du sanctuaire d'Aphrodite à Amathonte." In *Amathonte*, vol. 6, *Le sanctuaire d'Aphrodite des origines au début de l'époque impériale*, by Sabine Fourrier and Antoine Hermary, pp. 142–49. Athens: Ecole Française d'Athènes.

Orsingher, Adriano
  n.d. "A Stopover along the Journey of Elissa: Kition between Tyre and Carthage." In *The Many Face(t)s of Cyprus: 14th Meeting of Postgraduate Cypriot Archaeology*. Forthcoming publication of paper delivered November 15, 2014.

Papageorghiou, Athanasios
  1990 "Chronique des fouilles et découvertes archéologiques à Chypre en 1989." *Bulletin de correspondance hellénique* 114, pp. 941–85.

Pappalardo, Eleonora
  2006 "Avori dagli scavi italiani a Forte Salmanassar (Nimrud): Figure umane, elementi vegetali, leoni." *Mesopotamia* 41, pp. 57–156.

Radner, Karen
  2010 "The Stele of Sargon II of Assyria at Kition: A Focus for an Emerging Cypriot Identity?" In *Interkulturalität in der Alten Welt: Vorderasien, Hellas, Ägypten und die vielfältigen Ebenen des Kontakts*, edited by Robert Rollinger, Birgit Gufler, Martin Lang, and Irene Madreiter, pp. 429–50. Wiesbaden: Harrassowitz.

Reyes, Andres T.
  1991 "The Stamp Seals in the Pierides Collection, Larnaca." *Report of the Department of Antiquities, Cyprus*, pp. 117–28.
  1994 *Archaic Cyprus: A Study of the Textual and Archaeological Evidence*. Oxford: Clarendon.
  2001 *The Stamp-Seals of Ancient Cyprus*. Monograph 52. Oxford: Oxford University, School of Archaeology, Institute of Archaeology.

Riis, P. J., and Marie-Louise Buhl
  1990 *Hama, fouilles et recherches de la Fondation Carlsberg, 1931–1938*. Vol. 2, no. 2, *Les objets de la période dite Syro-Hittite (Âge du Fer)*. Copenhagen: Fondation Carlsberg.

Schmidt, Erich F.
  1957 *Persepolis*. Vol. 2, *Contents of the Treasury and Other Discoveries*. Chicago: University of Chicago Press.

Searight, Ann, Julian Reade, and Irving Finkel
  2008 *Assyrian Stone Vessels and Related Material in the British Museum*. Oxford: Oxbow Books.

Tatton-Brown, Veronica A., ed.
  1989 *Cyprus and the East Mediterranean in the Iron Age: Proceedings of the Seventh British Museum Classical Colloquium, April 1988*. London: British Museum Publications.

Trokay, Madeleine
  2000 "Le matériel de broyage en basalte du Tell Ahmar (Area C, fouilles de 1989–1996)." In *Proceedings of the First International Congress on the Archaeology of the Ancient Near East, Rome, May 18th–23rd, 1998*, edited by Paolo Matthiae, Alessandra Enea, Luca Peyronel, and Frances Pinnock, vol. 2, pp. 1665–[77]. Rome: Dipartimento di Scienze Storiche, Archeologiche e Antropologiche dell'Antichità.

Tufnell, Olga
  1953 *Lachish III (Tell ed Duweir): The Iron Age*. 2 vols. London: Oxford University Press.

Tuplin, Christopher
  1996 *Achaemenid Studies*. Stuttgart: Franz Steiner.

Woolley, Leonard
  1965 *The Kassite Period and the Period of the Assyrian Kings*. Ur Excavations 8. London: British Museum; Philadelphia: University Museum.

Yadin, Yigael, Yohanan Aharoni, Ruth Amiran, Trude Dothan, Emanuel Dunayevsky, and Jean Perrot, eds.
  1958 *Hazor*. Vol. 1, *An Account of the Second Season of Excavations, 1955*. Jerusalem: Magnes Press, Hebrew University.
  1960 *Hazor*. Vol. 2, *An Account of the Second Season of Excavations, 1956*. Jerusalem: Magnes Press, Hebrew University.

Zettler, Richard L.
  1993 *Nippur III: Kassite Buildings in Area WC-1*. Chicago: University of Chicago Press.

**ANDREA BAYER AND
MICHAEL GALLAGHER
WITH SILVIA A. CENTENO,
JOHN DELANEY, AND EVAN READ**

Andrea del Sarto's *Borgherini Holy Family* and *Charity*: Two Intertwined Late Works

> For Giovanni Borgherini Andrea painted another picture almost exactly like the one of Charity mentioned above, containing a Madonna, a little S. John offering to Christ a globe that represents the world, and a very beautiful head of S. Joseph.[1]
> —Giorgio Vasari, *Lives of the Painters, Sculptors and Architects*

TWO PAINTINGS AND THEIR HISTORICAL BACKGROUND

Since Giorgio Vasari first published his *Vita* of Andrea del Sarto (1486–1530) in 1550, it has been clear that late in his career the artist painted two works that contemporaries saw as closely related, *The Holy Family with the Young Saint John the Baptist* and *Charity* (figs. 1, 2). The former, painted for the Florentine Giovanni Borgherini (1496–1559) and commonly referred to as the *Borgherini Holy Family*, later descended through the Rinuccini and Corsini families in Florence. Charles Fairfax Murray purchased it in 1905, and the panel was sold to The Metropolitan Museum of Art in 1922.[2] It is among the artist's most admired, studied, and copied compositions

fig. 1 Andrea del Sarto (Italian, 1486–1530). *The Holy Family with the Young Saint John the Baptist*, also known as the *Borgherini Holy Family*, 1528 or 1529. Oil on wood, 53½ × 39⅝ in. (135.9 × 100.6 cm). The Metropolitan Museum of Art, Maria DeWitt Jesup Fund, 1922 (22.75)

fig. 2 Andrea del Sarto. *Charity*, 1528 or 1529. Oil on wood, 47 × 36½ in. (119.5 × 92.5 cm). National Gallery of Art, Washington, D.C., Samuel H. Kress Collection (1957.14.5)

and universally hailed as one of the most significant works of his last years. Vasari tells us that *Charity* was meant for Francis I of France, for whose court Sarto had worked a decade earlier, but it did not reach him.[3] Instead, after Sarto's death in 1530, his widow sold it to the painter Domenico Conti, who in turn sold it to Niccolò Antinori; the painting is now in the collection of the National Gallery of Art, Washington, D.C. Conservation of the Metropolitan Museum's *Holy Family* in 2013 provided an opportunity to look more closely at these two works and think again about their relationship. As this article will explore, Sarto's two late masterpieces are interwoven at every level, from their conception and making to their meaning, patronage, and place in Florentine history. The strong resemblance between the two, seen when the compositions are side by side, is made even more palpable by the repetition of the orb at the center. Depicted prominently in *The Holy Family*, the object emerges as a ghostly form in *Charity* (fig. 3). How did the compositions come to be this way?

Sarto painted the *Borgherini Holy Family* and *Charity* between 1528 and 1530—that is, when Florence had declared itself a republic (for the last time) and expelled the Medici family, taking on as adversaries both the Medici pope Clement VII and the Hapsburg emperor Charles V. That tense historical moment is integral to the meaning of both paintings. The rather romantically termed Last Florentine Republic of 1527–30 was a fleeting moment of self-rule in the city—the preface to one new law called it the "present free and popular government"—between a relatively brief period of domination by the Medici family and the family's return following a disastrous siege of the city in 1529–30.[4] The wealthy patron of *The Holy Family*, Giovanni Borgherini, was at the very center of the republican ferment of those years.[5] His connection with Venice, where he had spent part of his childhood and which was ruled historically as a republic, may have been the basis of his fascination with the ideas of republican rule. In 1525, Borgherini invited the Florentine humanist scholar Donato Giannotti to travel with him to the Veneto, a trip that led up to Giannotti's celebrated dialogue *Della repubblica de' veneziani* (On the Venetian Republic), written that year and the next. Borgherini appears as an interlocutor in the text, receiving instruction on the Venetian constitution and guiding the discussions toward a political theory that would urge Florentines to follow the Venetian model. Giannotti returned to Florence soon after the Medici were expelled in May 1527 and Niccolò Capponi, the opposition leader, was elected gonfalonier.[6] By September, the new government had assigned Giannotti to an important post and asked him to consider the republic's constitution.[7]

Borgherini's ties to the new republican government could hardly have been closer. He was married to Selvaggia Capponi, Niccolò Capponi's daughter, and experienced with her family all the early euphoria and then bitter moments of the following years. For Capponi and his cohort, some of the necessary justification of republican rule—rule not dominated by a single family—had been amply expressed by the Dominican preacher Girolamo Savonarola in Florence in the 1490s. This confluence—of Borgherini, Capponi, and Savonarola—helps explain the iconography of the devotional painting that Sarto painted for the Florentine patriot.

Savonarola had aimed to convince the Florentines that they needed no one but Christ as their king. In one of his last sermons, the defiant reformer had declaimed: "Come on, Florence, what do you want, what leader, what king can give himself to you. . . . God wants to make you happy and give you . . . a king to govern you. . . . Take Christ for your king and live under his law."[8] During the terrible outbreak of plague in 1527, Capponi reminded the members of the Great Council, the city's expanded governing body, of Savonarola's preaching, and early the following year he proposed that Christ be elected king of Florence; the voting in favor was well-nigh unanimous. The Council decided to place an inscription naming the city's new sovereign over the portals of the Palazzo della Signoria; during the republic's brief life, the resolution was celebrated in an annual procession, held on February 9, with all officers of state parading from the Duomo to the church of the Santissima Annunziata.[9] As the threat to the city deepened, with the Medici pope Clement VII demanding ever greater submission, the Great Council reaffirmed in June 1529 the resolution that Christ alone was Lord and King of Florence.[10] This revival of Savonarola's teachings had unfortunate aspects—the call for the expulsion of Jews from Florence, for example—but the fervor it inspired provided backbone at a time when the emperor's advancing troops, in league with Clement VII, were squeezing the increasingly isolated Florentines.[11]

It is easy to understand how *The Holy Family* would have had particular resonance for Giovanni Borgherini, for the artist carefully wove Savonarolan themes into the structure of the painting. The Virgin tenderly cradles a vigorous, indeed sculptural, Christ Child, who strides across the center of the painting to embrace an orb and cross, the *Globus cruciger*, representing Christ's dominion and often found as part of royal regalia. Its tones of blue contribute to its appearance as representing "the world."[12] The more mature Saint John the Baptist, patron saint of Florence, holds the orb top and bottom. No image could proclaim more vividly the republican belief that Florence belonged under the aegis of its sacred protectors alone. The play of the hand gestures—the Virgin supporting Christ and holding his *cangiante* (changeable in color) cloth across his middle, the three hands straddling the globe—are at the core of the picture's rhythm and draw attention to the affective interplay among these figures, the carriers of the painting's message.

Sarto painted *Charity* believing that it would enter the collection of the French king, Francis I. As will become clear below, the artist reconceived for this new work a panel already well under way with a design matching that of the *Borgherini Holy Family*. We can best understand his decision to change course and embark on a new subject by reviewing the role of the French king in Florentine affairs during these years. Florence's success in throwing off the domination of the Medici family coincided with Pope Clement VII's own political difficulties and his powerlessness to reassert control over his native city. His pontificate had reached a low point in 1527, when troops allied with Emperor Charles V sacked Rome. It was generally assumed that the enmity between pope and emperor would endure thereafter for a long time, but in April 1529 Sir Gregory Casale, an English agent in Rome, wrote the following to Cardinal Wolsey in London: "I have persuaded myself, and have been assured . . . a thousand times, that the Pope would never join the Emperor. Now I should not be surprised if he did, for the persecution of

fig. 4 Andrea del Sarto. *Charity*, 1518. Oil on canvas, transferred from wood, 72⅞ × 54 in. (185 × 137 cm). Signed and dated on sheet depicted at lower left: *ANDREUS. SARTUS. FLORENTINUS. ME PINXIT MDXVIII.* Musée du Louvre, Département des Peintures, Paris (712)

his [Clement's] friends and relatives will be a great incentive for him to do so. The French ought to prevail on the Florentines to restrain themselves."[13] By this, Casale meant that a future alignment of the papacy and the Hapsburg empire seemed inevitable, and that the French, known as longtime allies of the Florentines, would do well to force the rebellious city to reach a compromise with the pope. Casale's words proved prophetic a few months later, when Charles V entered into

a solemn alliance with Clement. The treaty included a fatal ninth clause in which the emperor pledged to restore Clement's kinsmen to their native city.[14]

Events moved swiftly after the declaration of this alliance. Imperial troops under the command of the professional soldier Philibert de Chalon, Prince of Orange, marched through Tuscany ready to set siege to the city. The Florentine government debated whether to submit or defend themselves, finally deciding that they would see "Florence in ashes rather than under the Medici."[15] The die was cast, and by October 29, 1529, Philibert's artillery was attacking the Florentine positions at San Miniato.

Artists and artworks were involved in the siege of Florence in a myriad of ways, but perhaps the most significant was the grand project conceived by the Florentine Battista della Palla (1489–1532). He intended to procure significant works of art for Francis I as part of a larger scheme to reinforce the alliance of the French king with the Florentine Republic and inspire him to lend assistance at this critical juncture.[16] Della Palla began his career within Medici circles, but in the early 1520s his allegiances shifted; he began to harbor strong republican sympathies, which he discussed in letters sent from the safety of a residency at the French court. He was adamant that no concession be made to the pope, saying, "He who goes down one step of the ladder must go down all."[17] He believed that he could induce Francis I to support the Florentines, cultivating the king's good will by adding materially to his highly prized collection. A letter from della Palla, then in Florence, to Filippo Strozzi in Lyon in early 1529 set out his objectives: "to provide them [the French] with large quantities of excellent antiquities of whatsoever sort, of marbles and bronzes and medals and paintings by masters worthy of His Majesty, in which things he has delighted all his life, and is now more immersed than ever."[18]

Vasari recounts that della Palla asked Andrea del Sarto to produce for the king two paintings, one depicting the Sacrifice of Isaac, and the other, Charity. We do not know precisely how these subjects were chosen.[19] Charity probably had particular significance for both artist and patron: when, a decade earlier, Sarto worked at the French court, he had painted for Francis I a grand panel of the subject, a work that showed him fully able to compete with the great Italian artists already known to the court (fig. 4). In addition, themes of Christian Virtue were of deep iconographic interest to the Valois court. Among the many references to Charity documented there from these years is a poem of 1515 in which each letter of the king's name was associated with a particular Virtue—C corresponding to Charity: "Of good will is the fifth letter of the noble name of François, powerful king: it shows him flourishing through Charity, who leads and loves him."[20] Sarto would have known the theme was appropriate for the patron and also for this particular moment, given the exhortatory purpose of the commission. He had every reason to wish to produce inspiring works for Francis, having departed abruptly from the court a decade earlier (an act for which Vasari condemned him), leaving with some monies that were not returned or accounted for.[21] Sarto had attempted to revive the relationship in the early 1520s, without success; here appeared another opportunity to reignite interest in his work beyond the Alps.

UNDERSTANDING SARTO'S ARTISTIC PRACTICE THROUGH TECHNICAL EXAMINATION AND THE ANALYSIS OF DRAWINGS

Technical examination confirms that the painting on the panel of *Charity* began as a slightly smaller version of *The Holy Family*; therefore, the planning for the devotional image must have moved forward first. Comparison of the evidence provided by an array of imaging techniques (infrared reflectography [IRR], X-radiography, multi-spectral imaging, and macro-X-ray fluorescence [MA-XRF] imaging) at the Metropolitan Museum and the National Gallery of Art reveals that the entire Holy Family group was drawn and partially painted on what is now the Charity panel before Sarto morphed the figures to depict an entirely different subject.[22]

Owing to the natural, increased transparency of oil paint as it ages, some of the original compositional elements that Sarto painted over are now partially visible to the naked eye, in particular the abovementioned orb supported by the young Saint John the Baptist and the Christ Child in the Borgherini picture. The figure of the Virgin needed little elaboration to be transformed into the allegorical figure of Charity: the neckline of her garment was simply revised to reveal her breast. By changing the position of Saint John the Baptist's arm and reducing the drapery around his body to a narrow, decorative swag, Sarto converted the figure into an accompanying, almost naked, boy. In contrast, the heroic, frontally facing Christ Child was completely rethought. His body was reduced in size and turned more toward Charity, and his head was turned to direct his gaze toward the boy on the left of the composition. The head of Saint Joseph was replaced entirely with that of a smiling child, who, like Joseph, looks out in order to directly engage the onlooker.

The information provided in the infrared reflectogram of *Charity* is occasionally difficult to decipher, owing to some of the radical changes in composition and consequent proliferation of overlapping forms (fig. 5). However, it seems that much of the preparatory underdrawing concealed beneath the paint layers is freehand: unrefined but bold and confident in its application and evident purpose to anchor forms and resolve contours.

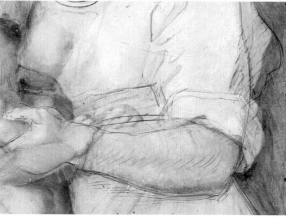

fig. 5 Infrared reflectogram of *Charity* (fig. 2) showing abundance of overlapping forms indicative of compositional changes

fig. 6 Detail of infrared reflectogram in fig. 5 revealing bold, freehand underdrawing

The emphatic reinforcement of certain lines and features and the cursory hatching delineating a fold falling into shadow or the play of light on a limb—elements frequently seen in Sarto's small-scale drawings on paper—are here writ large (fig. 6).[23]

The underdrawing in the *Borgherini Holy Family* is much easier to read but of a fundamentally different character (figs. 7, 8). The rather angular, abbreviated lines—especially evident in the Virgin's drapery—indicate the use of cartoons, full-scale compositional drawings that were transferred to the painting support by placing carbon-black-coated paper underneath the

cartoons and tracing the lines of the design with a stylus. Use of this technique was widespread in Florentine Renaissance art but is characteristic of Sarto and his workshop, as demonstrated in the recent exhibition "Andrea del Sarto: The Renaissance Workshop in Action."[24] Exploiting an essentially mechanical process, the artist created a highly efficient method for generating new works or revising existing compositions. Details and variations were frequently added or edited freehand, a process of revision that continued into the painting stage, occasionally resulting in compositions that were far different from those transferred from the cartoons.[25]

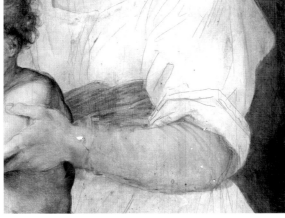

fig. 7 Infrared reflectogram of the *Borgherini Holy Family* (fig. 1)

fig. 8 Detail of infrared reflectogram in fig. 7 revealing angular, abbreviated underdrawing traced on the ground layer by means of a cartoon

fig. 9 Detail of fig. 5 (infrared reflectogram of *Charity*, fig. 2) showing freehand repositioning of the underlying Christ Child's proper left leg

fig. 10 Detail of fig. 7 showing repositioning of the Christ Child's proper left leg similar to that in fig. 9

fig. 11 MA-XRF image of lead distribution in the *Borgherini Holy Family* (fig. 1) showing original drapery of the same length as that revealed in fig. 12

fig. 12 MA-XRF image of lead distribution in *Charity* (fig. 2). The red overlay shows the original lower edge of the Christ Child's drapery.

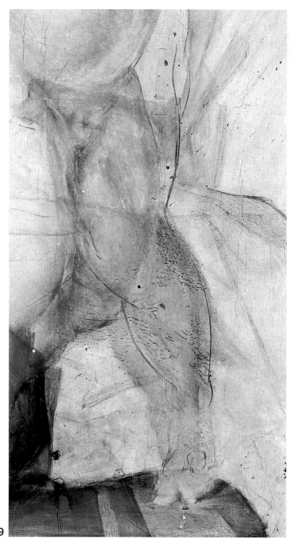

9

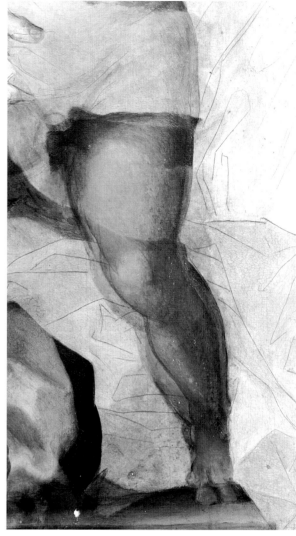

10

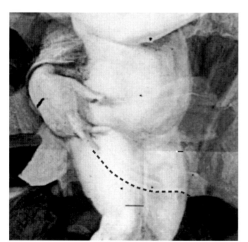

12

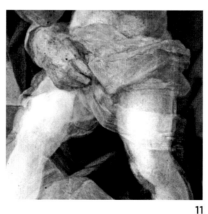

11

In the case of *Charity* and the *Borgherini Holy Family*, the relationship between the compositions and their evolution is intriguing, because it is evident that the two panels must have been produced simultaneously, despite the fact that the *Borgherini Holy Family* is eleven percent larger. The evidence lies in the presence on the Borgherini panel of identical pentimenti found in both the underdrawing and initial laying-in of the Holy Family composition beneath *Charity*.[26] The same revision to the position of the Christ Child's outstretched legs can be seen in the underdrawing in both paintings (figs. 9, 10). Similarly, the drapery around the infant's middle initially fell to just above the right knee but later was raised much higher—a significant change that was made at the painting stage in both pictures (figs. 11, 12). And a sacklike cushion corresponding to a preparatory drawing now in the Gallerie degli Uffizi, Florence (6445F verso), to which we will return below, was also laid-in on each panel and subsequently covered with an expanse of drapery (supplemented in *The Holy Family* with the Baptist's reed cross and in *Charity* with a book) (figs. 13, 14).

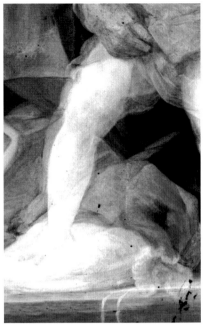

It would seem that many features of the composition that underlies *Charity* were only partially or thinly painted prior to Sarto's rethinking of the subject. These paint layers probably correspond to the wash-like applications of diluted color that can be seen in several of the artist's unfinished works, such as *The Sacrifice of Isaac* in the Cleveland Museum of Art (fig. 15).[27] The incomplete and preparatory nature of certain passages perhaps accounts for the intermittency of the information provided by the X-ray and XRF maps of the pentimenti. Still, XRF confirms that the background drapery in the *Borgherini Holy Family* was begun beneath the rock formation in *Charity* (revealing as well the initial placement of Joseph's head) (figs. 16, 17).

How the freehand drawing of the main figures on the *Charity* panel was enlarged for the cartoon remains a matter of speculation. The close correlation between the *Charity* and *Holy Family* compositions and their highly consistent proportional relationship would indicate a method of mechanical scaling. Incised, arcing lines present on several of Sarto's paintings, including *Charity*, support the idea that a proportional compass or similar device may have been deployed.[28] Interestingly, although a significant number of incised lines in *Charity* merit attention, the same cannot be said of the *Borgherini Holy Family*, where the few surface incisions could possibly be attributed to scrapes that occurred during the preparation of the gesso ground. The disparity perhaps suggests that *Charity* bears the marks of measuring and notation that permitted the creation of the scaled-up cartoons.[29]

Of the handful of drawings for these paintings that have come down to us, most relate to the initial

composition of *The Holy Family*, although they continued to be relevant to the elaboration of *Charity*. Our investigation of the panels and the evidence revealed by technical imaging have clarified the function of these preparatory drawings and provide further evidence of Sarto's relentless refinement of the principal figures, their gestures, movements, and relationships. On one side of a sheet in the Louvre, the artist has analyzed in red chalk the Virgin's left arm and hand as she holds Christ's arm; various inflections of her right hand as it will touch his waist (just implied); and the Baptist's fingertips atop the orb (fig. 18). The verso of this drawing is a study for the hanging curtain, with color notes.[30] Four drawings in the Uffizi relate to the paintings.[31] On the recto of one of these (Uffizi 6444F), done in red chalk on rose-tinted paper, the artist delicately drew the Virgin's head and the set of her shoulders, focusing on the fall of light across her neck and the subtle angle of her body. She wears a plain but thick headband resembling the final solution seen in *Charity*.

fig. 16 MA-XRF image of copper distribution in *Charity* (fig. 2) revealing initial inclusion of background curtain

fig. 17 Detail of the *Borgherini Holy Family* (fig. 1) showing background curtain

fig. 18 Andrea del Sarto. Study for the *Borgherini Holy Family*, ca. 1528–29. Red chalk, 6⅛ × 9½ in. (15.7 × 24 cm). Musée du Louvre, Cabinet des Dessins, Paris (1714A)

fig. 19 Andrea del Sarto. Study for the *Borgherini Holy Family*, ca. 1528–29. Red chalk, 6 × 9 in. (15.3 × 22.9 cm). Gallerie degli Uffizi, Gabinetto dei Disegni e delle Stampe (6445F recto)

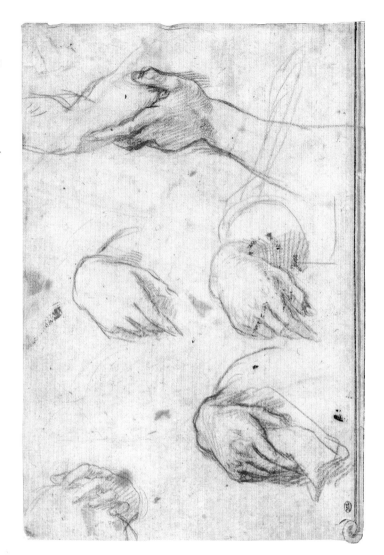

The recto of Uffizi 6445 presents another sketch of the Virgin's arm, drapery bunched at the elbow, but most of the sheet is given over to a study of the shadowy face of Saint Joseph, seen in reverse of the painted head (fig. 19). John Shearman believed the head in the drawing was likely a self-portrait, drawn *allo specchio* (in the mirror), which helps to account for the subsequent reversal.[32] It can be argued that the saint appears considerably older than the artist, who died soon thereafter at the age of forty-four, but the sharply defined features are close to those of other known self-portraits, and it may be that the artist was representing the great strain of the historical moment in the hollowed eyes and furrowed brow. Interestingly, a study of this same head but with somewhat softened features and drawn in black and red chalk has recently surfaced; its specific relation to *The Holy Family* cannot yet be determined.[33]

Technical imaging shows that this conception of Joseph was not Sarto's first for the figure. The traced underdrawing lines and initial laying-in describe a head turned more to the left, gazing across to John the Baptist (figs. 20, 21).[34] The underlying head bears a strong resemblance to a black-chalk head study (fig. 22) for the figure of Joseph in *The Holy Family with Saint John the Baptist* of about 1527, in the State Hermitage Museum (fig. 23). This painting also includes a close model for the Baptist depicted in the *Borgherini Holy Family*. In addition, the Christ Child in the Hermitage painting appears to be derived from an earlier red-chalk compositional study, *The Madonna and Child with Saint John*, in the Uffizi (fig. 24). By shifting the diagonal axis of the Christ Child's figure in this drawing to the vertical, a strong affinity emerges with the foreground child in *Charity* (figs. 25, 26).

There are other examples of the characteristic fluid and expedient methods of adaptation and reuse by the artist and his workshop. Two beautiful head studies, one of a child, the other of a woman, were probably prototypes for the heads of John the Baptist and the Virgin in the *Borgherini Holy Family*; each was reused in multiple compositions, including *Charity*.[35] Small but

20

fig. 20 Tracing of underdrawing beneath the head of Saint Joseph in the *Borgherini Holy Family* (fig. 1)

fig. 21 MA-XRF image of lead distribution, revealing initial iteration of the head in the *Borgherini Holy Family* (fig. 1).

fig. 22 Andrea del Sarto. Detail of *Head of a Man Looking Up*, ca. 1527. Black chalk, with later red chalk additions, 9¾ × 7 in. (24.7 × 17.7 cm). Ashmolean Museum of Art and Archaeology, University of Oxford (WA1944.141)

21

22

fig. 23 Andrea del Sarto. *The Holy Family with Saint John the Baptist*, ca. 1527. Oil on wood, 50⅞ × 39⅜ in. (129 × 100 cm). State Hermitage Museum, Saint Petersburg (GE-6680)

significant departures from the drawings were made in the paintings: for example, the painted John the Baptist is considerably older than the figure represented in the drawing. Sarto's willingness to rethink compositional elements well into the painting process is shown by the partial cancellation of the characteristic sacklike cushion sketched in a drawing in the Uffizi and in preparatory layers on both panels, as was illustrated earlier.

FINAL OBSERVATIONS

Sarto undertook the complex back-and-forth between these two panels so that the one already under way could be transformed from a Holy Family into a Charity. It is intriguing and somewhat frustrating not to know why the artist did not simply finish the Holy Family on the smaller panel and transfer the relevant aspects to the larger panel to create a Charity. The answer could lie in Sarto's

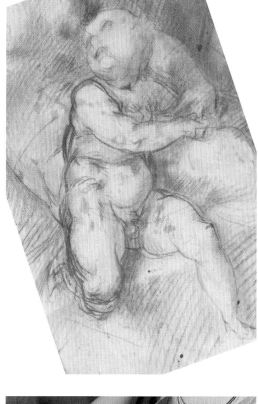

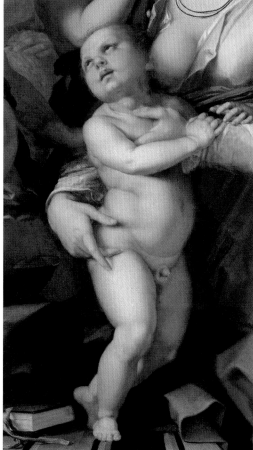

fig. 24 Andrea del Sarto. Studies for the *Borghese Madonna*, ca. 1516. Red chalk, 12⅜ × 9⅛ in. (31.4 × 23.2 cm). Gallerie degli Uffizi, Gabinetto dei Disegni e delle Stampe (304F recto)

fig. 25 Detail of fig. 24, with the axis of the Christ Child's figure shifted to a vertical position, revealing affinity with infant in fig. 26

fig. 26 Detail of *Charity* (fig. 2)

creative preoccupations and the dialogue generated by working on the paintings simultaneously. However, the reason may be more mundane, linked to details of the commission—even to something as basic as cost. Perhaps reworking portions of the Holy Family that was under way on the smaller panel was simply cheaper.

What is certain is that he successfully adapted the composition of the partially completed Holy Family to fit the description of Caritas, called Love by Saint Paul, who considered it the greatest of the three theological virtues—the others being Faith and Hope (1 Corinthians 13). Artists generally represented Caritas as a woman with three children, one for each of the three Virtues, with a nursing child a symbol of Charity herself and of the nourishment provided by charitable love. Charity is usually attired in red, as Cesare Ripa later affirmed in his *Iconologia* (1611), and on occasion is shown with an aureole, as here.[36] Although Sarto must have had his earlier composition for Francis I in mind when undertaking this work, he made changes that showed off the newer elements of his style: increasingly monumental, broad forms with a strong, sculptural three-dimensionality and a powerfully vibrant palette. He also chose to depart from certain norms in the iconography of the group. A flame—the *ignis caritatis*—is characteristic of the imagery and is usually depicted held by Charity or in a nearby vessel. Instead, Sarto represents the flame as a conflagration burning in the upper right of the composition, at the far end of a claustrophobia-inducing range of towering rocks that cramp the figures in a shallow space in the foreground. Could it be that Sarto meant to suggest the walls of the besieged city, or the conflagration that threatened it? Certainly, he has gone out of his way to distinguish the background from the open, sunny landscape of his earlier version for the king. In these new circumstances, the more threatening imagery might have had some power as an appeal to Francis. Admittedly speculative, this reading, with its emphasis on historic events then taking place, allows us to understand how the two panels can have been so intertwined in the artist's mind. Both were in specific service to the Florentine Republic, with traditional iconographies varied to address the state's vital needs.

Many of the art objects della Palla gathered together for the French king reached their destination, but not all. News of the grand project went quiet in December 1529. Sarto's paintings were never sent, as Florence was conquered the following summer, allowing in soldiers and disease and leading to the artist's death. Vasari's words paint a grim picture: "The siege being finished, Andrea was waiting for matters to mend although with little hope that his French project would succeed, since Giovan Battista della Palla had been taken prisoner, when Florence became filled with soldiers. . . . Among those soldiers were some lansquenets sick with the plague who . . . shortly afterwards left it infected." Sarto's death following a brief illness "was a very great loss to the city and to art."[37] Della Palla had indeed been taken prisoner; he was incarcerated by the Medici in the Fortress of Pisa, where he died, poisoned, in 1532.[38]

Nor did Giovanni Borgherini, owner of *The Holy Family*, escape the turmoil of these events. As a member of the republican government, he had been sent out of the city in August 1529 as part of a delegation and then chose to retreat to Venice, not returning to Florence. Following the fall of the city, and once the Medici had reasserted their authority, Borgherini immediately wrote them pledging his support. He was not punished but never held official position again.[39] These dates suggest that Sarto's work for him is probably to be dated between early 1528 (when Savonarolan themes began to dominate) and the summer of 1529.

Vasari ended his *Vita* of Sarto with a melancholy statement about the artist's truncated career, noting that his loss was great because "he went on always improving from one work to another."[40] In this instance, we have found him indeed moving from one work to another, with energetic purpose. These two paintings, at first glance relatively simple in subject matter and composition, have built into them a complex creative process that gives them a unique place in the history of Florentine art of the period.

ACKNOWLEDGMENTS

Andrea Bayer and Michael Gallagher thank the following individuals: Carmen Bambach, curator, Department of Drawings and Prints, The Metropolitan Museum of Art; Julian Brooks, Alessandro Cecchi, Rodolfo Maffeis, and Eva Reifert; and colleagues at the National Gallery of Art, Washington, D.C., especially Joanna Dunn and Gretchen Hirschauer.

ANDREA BAYER
Jayne Wrightsman Curator, Department of European Paintings, The Metropolitan Museum of Art

MICHAEL GALLAGHER
Sherman Fairchild Conservator in Charge, Department of Paintings Conservation, The Metropolitan Museum of Art

SILVIA A. CENTENO
Research Scientist, Department of Scientific Research, The Metropolitan Museum of Art

JOHN DELANEY
Senior Imaging Scientist, Department of Scientific Research, National Gallery of Art, Washington, D.C.

EVAN READ
Associate Manager of Technical Documentation, Department of Paintings Conservation, The Metropolitan Museum of Art

1 Vasari 1996, vol. 1, p. 851. For the original Italian, see Vasari (1568) 1976, vol. 4, p. 391: "Fece un altro quadro Andrea quasi simile a quello della Carità già detta, a Giovanni Borgherini, dentrovi una Nostra Donna, un San Giovanni putto che porge a Cristo una palla figurata per il mondo, e una testa di Giuseppo molto bella."

2 For the provenance of the *Borgherini Holy Family*, see www.metmuseum.org/art/collection/search/437609; for *Charity*, see Shapley 1968, vol. 2, pp. 128–29.

3 Vasari 1996, vol. 1, p. 850; Vasari (1568) 1976, vol. 4, pp. 389–90.

4 Roth 1925; Stephens 1983, p. 216; Cecchi 2017.

5 Gilbert 1977, whose text is fundamental for the political meaning explored here.

6 Ibid., p. 284; Starn 1968, pp. 18–19: also in May 1527, Niccolò Capponi requested a report from Giannotti on the Venetian constitution; see Stephens 1983, p. 209.

7 Starn 1968, pp. 20–21; Roth 1925, pp. 92–93.

8 "Orsù, Firenze, che vorresti tu, che capo, che re ti si può dare.... Iddio ti vuol contentare e darti . . . uno re che ti governi. E questo è Cristo . . . El Signore ti vuole reggere Lui, se tu vorrai . . . piglia Cristo per tuo re e sta sotto la sua legge"; G. Savonarola, *Prediche italiane ai Fiorentini, I (Novembre e dicembre del 1494)*, excerpted in O'Gorman 1965, p. 503n14, with translation on p. 503. The Savonarolan context of the painting was first explored by James O'Gorman (1965).

9 Roth 1925, pp. 76–77, 197; Stephens 1983, pp. 215, 219.

10 Roth 1925, p. 141.

11 On the treatment of the Jews, see Stephens 1983, pp. 214–25; one skeptical contemporary observer, Baccio Carnescchi, who wrote an account of the Republic, said that it was possible to hold a city down through force or religion, and Florence had opted for religion; see ibid., p. 219.

12 Vasari 1996, vol. 1, p. 851.

13 Gregory Casale to Wolsey, April 21, 1529, in Brewer 1875, p. 2417, doc. 5478, www.british-history.ac.uk/letters-papers-hen8/vol4/pp2414-2427.

14 Roth 1925, pp. 139, 153n44.

15 Ibid., pp. 174, 219n80. Feelings against the Medici ran so high that the governing Council of the Eight received a violent denunciation of Cosimo de' Medici's epitaph as "Pater Patriae" on his tomb in the church of San Lorenzo; see Stephens 1983, p. 234.

16 For the fullest analysis of della Palla's scheme, see Elam 1993; on the broader topic, Cecchi 2017.

17 "Consulte e pratiche 71," September 7, 1529, Archivio di Stato, Florence, as translated in Elam 1993, p. 43.

18 Della Palla to Strozzi, January 21, 1529, Carte Strozziane, sec. V, 1209, fasc. I, no. 24, Archivio di Stato, Florence, as translated in Elam 1993, pp. 47, 88.

19 Vasari 1996, vol. 1, p. 850; Vasari (1568) 1976, vol. 4, pp. 389–90. On the Sacrifice of Isaac, see Brooks 2015 and Steele 2015.

20 Cox-Rearick 1996, pp. 187, 449, no. 142, and, for the original French, no. 143: "De bon vouloir tiens la letter cinquiesme / Du noble nom de François, roy puissant, / Lequel se doibt démonstrer florissant / Par Charité qui le conduit et ayme." For an analysis and overview of the literature on the painting and the theme, see ibid., pp. 185–88, no. V-14.

21 Vasari 1996, vol. 1, pp. 837–38; Vasari (1568) 1976, vol. 4, pp. 367–69. For Sarto's time at the French court, see Delieuvin 2009.

22 At the Metropolitan Museum, infrared reflectography was undertaken using an Indigo Systems Merlin near-infrared camera (InGaAs sensor range: 900–1700 nanometers) with a StingRay Optics macro lens optimized for this range, in conjunction with a National Instruments IMAQ PCI-1422 frame grabber card and IRvista 2.51 software. Macro-X-ray fluorescence (MA-XRF) imaging was carried out using a Bruker M6 Jetstream instrument. The painting was scanned at 90 msec/pixel, with a 400 micron spot size, an 850 micron step size; the X-ray source operated at 50 kV and 500 mA. The spectra were processed using the Bruker® software. At the National Gallery of Art, infrared reflectography was undertaken in the 1500 to 1800 nm spectral band using a novel, near-infrared camera system consisting of an interference filter (1500-1800 nm bandpass), a custom macro near-infrared lens (F/2.3 EFL 50 mm, Stingray Optics, NH), and an Indium Antimonide IR focal plane array (SBF-193, Santa Barbara Focal Plane, CA). The individual images were collected using a computerized easel (SmartDrive, Cambridge UK), and then mosaicked and registered to a reference color image using custom software (Conover, Delaney, and Loew 2015). The MA-XRF imaging was done using a system designed in-house. The X-ray source is a rhodium tube operating at 50 kV and 750 mA (XOS) with polycapillary focusing optics set for a 1 mm spot size. A Vortex-90EX detector (Hitachi High-Technologies Science America, Inc.) operates at a peaking time of 0.1 ms and 13.7 eV sampling. The painting was scanned at 100 msec/pixel using a computer-controlled easel. The element maps were calculated using an in-house semi-empirical fitting procedure. Because the surface of the panel painting deviates from planarity by 2.5 cm, both imaging modalities were collected in vertical zones and mosaicked together.

23 Faietti 2015.

24 J. Paul Getty Museum, Los Angeles, and Frick Collection, New York, 2015–16. See Brooks, Allen, and Salomon 2015.

25 For other examples, see Keith 2001; Buzzegoli and Kunzelman 2006; and Szafran and Chui 2015.

26 When a digital tracing of the *Holy Family*—reduced by eleven percent—is laid over an image of *Charity*, the outlines of the Virgin and Charity match almost exactly, but the tracing needs to be moved to correspond with other figures and details. It therefore appears that several enlarged cartoons were developed from the composition that lies below *Charity*. The digital tracing and image overlays were executed by Evan Read.

27 Neugebauer et al. 2009, pp. 154–60; Steele 2015, p. 199; Szafran and Chui 2015, pp. 16–17.

28 Szafran and Chui 2015, pp. 14–16; Steele 2015, pp. 198–99.

29 Technical aspects of these processes are explored in the forthcoming article on Andrea del Sarto's *Sacrifice of Isaac* by Marcia Steele, senior conservator of paintings, Cleveland Museum of Art, in *Kermes: La revista del restauro*.

30 Musée du Louvre, Cabinet des Dessins, Paris, 1714A; Shearman 1965, vol. 2, pp. 377–78; Cordellier 1986, pp. 87–88.

31 Gallerie degli Uffizi, Gabinetto dei Disegni e delle Stampe, nos. 6444F recto and verso; 6445 recto and verso; 631E recto and verso; 653E recto and verso; ibid., pp. 344–45, 350, 354, 355.

32 Ibid., vol. 1, p. 127.

33 Gestas & Carrère, Pau, Cabinet de Bayser, "Andrea del Sarto (1486-1530), Vente d'un dessin inédit," December 17, 2016. The verso of the drawing includes sketches for an unrelated eye and, possibly, lip. The same figure appears in two other paintings by Sarto, the *Panciatichi Assumption*, 1522–25 (Galleria Palatina, Florence, inv. 1912, no. 191) and the *Passerini Assumption*, 1526–28 (Galleria Palatina, Florence, inv. 1890, no. 225). While the importance of this portrait (or self-portrait) to the artist is clear, its reappearance at different moments in the 1520s, and in

both drawing and painting, cannot be fully explained. Only in the *Holy Family* has the direction of the head been flipped.

34 Examination with MA-XRF imaging indicates that Sarto partially painted this figure in.

35 The drawing of the child's head is Uffizi 631E recto; the drawing of the woman's head is Uffizi 653E, as above. On the reuse of 631E, see Brooks, Allen, and Salomon 2015, pp. 137–39, no. 40.

36 Ripa 1611, p. 71. The unusual shape of the aureole is not unlike those found in Benedetto Buglioni's sculptures of the Theological Virtues of Hope and Faith of about 1510–20 (private collection); see Cambareri 2016, p. 166, nos. 86, 87, ill. p. 123.

37 Vasari 1996, vol. 1, p. 852. For the original Italian, see Vasari (1568) 1976, vol. 4, p. 393: "Finito l'assedio, se ne stava Andrea aspettando che le cose si allargassino, se bene con poco speranza che il disegno di Francia gli dovesse riuscire, essendo stato preso Giovambatista della Palla, quando Fiorenza si riempié dei soldati . . . fra i quali soldati essendo alcuni Lanzi appestati . . . e poco appresso la lasciarono infetta. . . . Fu la morte d'Andrea di grandissimo danno alla sua città et all'arte."

38 Elam 1993, p. 71.

39 Starn 1968, p. 106n1.

40 Vasari 1996, vol. 1, p. 852. For the original Italian, see Vasari (1568) 1976, vol. 4, pp. 393–94: "andò sempre di cosa in cosa migliorando di sorte."

REFERENCES

Brewer, J. S., ed.
1875 *Letters and Papers, Foreign and Domestic, Henry VIII.* Vol. 4, *1524–1530*. London: Her Majesty's Stationery Office. *British History Online*, www.british-history.ac.uk/letters-papers-hen8/vol4.

Brooks, Julian
2015 "The Sacrifice of Isaac." In Brooks, Allen, and Salomon 2015, pp. 185–97.

Brooks, Julian, Denise Allen, and Xavier F. Salomon
2015 *Andrea del Sarto: The Renaissance Workshop in Action.* Exh. cat., J. Paul Getty Museum, Los Angeles; Frick Collection, New York. Los Angeles: J. Paul Getty Museum.

Buzzegoli, Ezio, and Diane Kunzelman
2006 "Re-use of Cartoons on Paintings by Andrea del Sarto and Pontormo: A Study with High Resolution Digital Scanned IRR." In *La peinture ancienne et ses procedes: Copies, repliques, pastiches*, edited by Hélène Verougstraete and Jacqueline Couvert, pp. 67–78. Le dessin sous-jacent et la technologie dans la peinture, Colloque 15. Leuven: Peeters.

Cambareri, Marietta
2016 *Della Robbia: Sculpting with Color in Renaissance Florence.* Exh. cat., Museum of Fine Arts, Boston; National Gallery of Art, Washington, D.C. Boston: Museum of Fine Arts Publications.

Cecchi, Alessandro
2017 "Storia e arte dell'ultima Repubblica fiorentina." In *Michelangelo e l'assedio di Firenze, 1529–1530*, edited by Alessandro Cecchi, pp. 25–35. Exh. cat., Casa Buonarotti, Florence. Florence: Edizioni Polistampa.

Conover, Damon M., John K. Delaney, and Murray H. Loew
2015 "Automatic Registration and Mosaicking of Technical Images of Old Master Paintings." *Applied Physics A* 119, no. 4, pp. 1567–75.

Cordellier, Dominique
1986 *Hommage à Andrea del Sarto.* Exh. cat., Musée du Louvre, Paris. Paris: Editions de la Réunion des Musées Nationaux.

Cox-Rearick, Janet
1996 *The Collection of Francis I: Royal Treasures.* New York: Harry N. Abrams.

Delieuvin, Vincent
2009 "Andrea del Sartos Gemälde für den französischen Hof." In Syre, Schmidt, and Stege 2009, pp. 53–77.

Elam, Caroline
1993 "Art in the Service of Liberty: Battista della Palla, Art Agent for Francis I." *I Tatti Studies: Essays in the Renaissance* 5, pp. 33–109.

Faietti, Marzia
2015 "The Red-Chalk Drawings of Andrea del Sarto: Linear Form and Luminous Naturalism." In Brooks, Allen, and Salomon 2015, pp. 28–33.

Gilbert, Felix
1977 "Andrea del Sartos 'Heilige Familie Borgherini' und Florentinische Politik." In *Festschrift für Otto von Simson zum 65. Geburtstag*, edited by Lucius Grisebach and Konrad Renger, pp. 284–88. Frankfurt am Main: Propyläen Verlag.

Keith, Larry
2001 "Andrea del Sarto's 'The Virgin and Child with Saint Elizabeth and Saint John the Baptist': Technique and Critical Reputation." *National Gallery Technical Bulletin* 22, pp. 42–53.

Neugebauer, Wibke, Patrick Dietemann, Heike Stege, and Jan
Schmidt, with Ursula Baumer, Irene Fiedler, and Cornelia Tilenschi
  2009 "'Die Gewänder sind zum Staunen schön, . . . seine
  Farben . . . außerordentlich und wirklich göttlich': Zur Maltechnik
  und den Materialien der *Heiligen Familie* in der Alten
  Pinakothek." In Syre, Schmidt, and Stege 2009, pp. 133–67.
O'Gorman, James F.
  1965 "An Interpretation of Andrea del Sarto's *Borgherini Holy
  Family*." *Art Bulletin* 47, no. 4, pp. 502–4.
Ripa, Cesare
  1611 *Iconologia; overo, Descrittione d' Imagini delle virtu . . . .*
  Padua: Pietro Paolo Tozzi.
Roth, Cecil
  1925 *The Last Florentine Republic.* London: Methuen & Co.
Shapley, Fern Rusk
  1968 *Paintings from the Samuel H. Kress Collection.* Vol. 2,
  Italian Schools, XV–XVI Century. London: Phaidon Press.
Shearman, John
  1965 *Andrea del Sarto.* 2 vols. Oxford: Clarendon Press.
Starn, Randolph
  1968 *Donato Giannotti and His* Epistolae: *Biblioteca
  Universitaria Alessandrina, Rome, MS 107.* Geneva:
  Librairie Droz.
Steele, Marcia
  2015 "*The Sacrifice of Isaac*, Cleveland Museum of Art:
  Observations on the Infrared Image and the Painting." In Brooks,
  Allen, and Salomon 2015, appendix, pp. 198–99.
  n.d. "Andrea del Sarto Sacrifice of Isaac, Technical Research
  and Comparative Study" [working title]. In "Attorno ad Andrea
  del Sarto/Around Andrea del Sarto," *Kermes: La revista del
  restauro.* Forthcoming, Spring 2017.
Stephens, J. N.
  1983 *The Fall of the Florentine Republic, 1512–1530.* Oxford:
  Clarendon Press.
Syre, Cornelia, Jan Schmidt, and Heike Stege, eds.
  2009 *Göttlich gemalt. Andrea del Sarto: Die Heilige Familie in
  Paris und München.* Exh. cat., Alte Pinakothek, Bayerische
  Staatsgemäldesammlungen, Munich. Munich: Hirmer.
Szafran, Yvonne, and Sue Ann Chui
  2015 "A Perfectionist Revealed: The Resourceful Methods of
  Andrea del Sarto." In Brooks, Allen, and Salomon 2015,
  pp. 13–19.
Vasari, Giorgio
  1976 *Le vite de' più eccellenti pittori scultori e architettori nelle
  redazioni del 1550 e 1568.* Edited by Rosanna Bettarini and
  Paola Barocchi. Vol. 4. Florence: Studio per Edizioni Scelte.
  1996 *Lives of the Painters, Sculptors and Architects* [1568].
  Translated by Gaston du C. de Vere. 2 vols. New York and
  Toronto: Alfred A. Knopf. First published 1912–14 in 10 vols.

**KATHARINE BAETJER
WITH MARJORIE SHELLEY,
CHARLOTTE HALE, AND CYNTHIA MOYER**

Benjamin Franklin, Ambassador to France: Portraits by Joseph Siffred Duplessis

fig. 1 Joseph Siffred Duplessis (French, 1725–1802). *Benjamin Franklin* (VIR Portrait or Fur Collar Portrait), 1778. Oil on canvas, oval, 28½ × 23 in. (72.4 × 58.4 cm). Signed, dated, and inscribed (right center): *J.S. Duplessis / pinx. Parisis / 1778.* The Metropolitan Museum of Art, The Friedsam Collection, Bequest of Michael Friedsam, 1931 (32.100.132)

The best-known portrait of Benjamin Franklin (1706–1790) was painted by a French artist, Joseph Siffred Duplessis (1725–1802). For the better part of a century The Metropolitan Museum of Art has owned and exhibited the primary version of the so-called VIR Portrait, painted in 1778 in oil on canvas (fig. 1). It is the only one that is signed and dated, and it retains the elaborate carved and gilded frame in which it was exhibited at the 1779 Paris Salon. The cartouche on the frame is inscribed in Latin *VIR*, or "man," and surely the usage arose from the fact that this singularly famous and accomplished individual needed no further identification. The primary objective of the present study has been to discover what relation might exist between the Museum's iconic painting and an important pastel of the same sitter by the same artist in the New York Public Library (fig. 2). Very little known because, owing to its sensitivity to light,

fig. 2 Joseph Siffred Duplessis. *Benjamin Franklin* (Gray Coat Portrait), ca. 1777–78. Pastel on parchment, 28¾ × 23½ in. (73 × 59.7 cm). The New York Public Library, Astor, Lenox and Tilden Foundations

fig. 3 Jean-Baptiste Greuze
(French, 1725–1805). *Benjamin
Franklin*, 1777. Pastel on paper,
oval, 31½ × 25⅛ in. (80 ×
63.8 cm). Diplomatic Reception
Rooms, United States
Department of State,
Washington, D.C., 1976 (73.6)

days before Christmas 1776. No later than March 1777 he had settled in Passy, between Paris and Versailles; he would live there until 1785. Franklin's reputation was well established in Paris, where he had long been lauded for his many literary and scientific achievements. As a prolific writer and inventor, and in his new role as a patriot, politician, and statesman, he was welcomed to France by everyone from the porter in the street to the most enlightened members of society. He was the subject of many portraits, the most important of which were painted between 1777 and 1780, when he was at the height of his fame.

In America, after many difficult months of combat, on October 17, 1777, the British under General John Burgoyne suffered a major defeat at Saratoga, New York, at the hands of the American general Horatio Gates. Franklin's negotiations with the French Crown then began to secure important results. Having promoted the treaty aligning his country with France and against Britain, he soon became the first American minister accredited to a foreign government. The American war was a hugely popular cause at court and in the capital, where the old diplomat's simplicity of dress and manner were admired. While his self-presentation—untidy, thin, receding, and unpowdered hair; a thick waist; plain clothes—was natural to him, certainly his "Quaker style" (he was not a Quaker) was carefully maintained for effect. The extent of public interest in Franklin is astonishing. Among those who portrayed him early in his stay were Jean Jacques Caffiéri and Jean Antoine Houdon, whose terracotta portrait busts were shown at the Salons of 1777 and 1779 respectively;[2] Jean-Baptiste Nini, the first of whose terracotta plaques went into production in 1777;[3] Augustin de Saint-Aubin, whose portrait drawing of Franklin in a fur hat was engraved by Charles Nicolas Cochin II for publication in 1778; and Jean Honoré Fragonard, two of whose allegorical drawings were engraved, by Marguerite Gérard and by the Abbé de Saint-Non, for publication in 1778.[4] Nevertheless, Franklin did not like to pose, and, with the exception of Caffiéri, few artists had the advantage of direct contact with the elderly American statesman. Among painters, he accorded sittings only to Jean-Baptiste Greuze, Anne Rosalie Bocquet Filleul, and Joseph Siffred Duplessis.

According to the contemporary writer and critic Louis Petit de Bachaumont, Greuze received a request to paint Franklin on March 8, 1777, from the well-known attorney Jean-Baptiste Jacques Elie de Beaumont.[5] A pastel, which the artist retained, was completed by June 10 (fig. 3), and Beaumont's oil (private collection) seems to have been ready for delivery by July 25.

it is rarely exhibited. We hoped also to revisit the question of the dating of the pastel, and to establish how precisely a painted replica belonging to the Metropolitan Museum (and perhaps other replicas) conforms to the design of the primary version. Our findings, including new information about the frame, were presented in a 2016 dossier exhibition and are reviewed here in the wider context of Franklin portraits from the late 1770s and of the sitter's critically important role in European and American politics of that time.

Benjamin Franklin promoted the first major treaty of alliance between the fledgling United States of America and the government of Louis XVI, which was signed at Versailles on February 6, 1778.[1] Born in 1706, Franklin was then seventy-two years old and had visited France as a private citizen on two occasions in the 1760s. On his third visit, he went in an official capacity as the most important of three commissioners sent by the American Continental Congress. After a difficult voyage, he landed unannounced at a remote location in Brittany and, traveling by coach, reached Paris several

fig. 4 Anne Rosalie Bocquet Filleul (French, 1752–1794). *Benjamin Franklin,* ca. 1777–78. Oil on canvas, 35 ⅞ × 28 ½ in. (91.1 × 72.4 cm). Philadelphia Museum of Art, Gift of the Honorable Walter H. Annenberg and Leonore Annenberg and the Annenberg Foundation, 2007 (2007-13-2)

Another oil by Greuze that may have been a direct commission is recorded in 1780 with a well-known private collector, the Abbé de Véri (now American Philosophical Society, Philadelphia). Franklin's wily character and apparent lack of pretension should have appealed to the unconventional Greuze, but his portraits of the American are austere and distant. Franklin draws away from the observer, his face and torso elongated. Atypically, the sitter wears a satin waistcoat and a satin sable-trimmed coat. The artist did not show at the Salons, but on September 6, 1777, he displayed a painting of Franklin to visitors to his studio. Greuze's portraits were not engraved.

Anne Rosalie Bocquet Filleul (1752–1794), a minor figure among women artists of the period, had direct access to Franklin because she was a neighbor.[6] Doubtless she painted him at home, pointing to a map of Philadelphia and with his spectacles on the table beside him (fig. 4). The project must have been initiated by her father, Blaise Bocquet, a fan painter and dealer who published a reproductive engraving after Filleul's Franklin by Louis Jacques Cathelin, an example of which was exhibited at the 1779 Salon. Madame Filleul, relatively inexperienced, may have seen one of Greuze's portraits, since the way she depicted Franklin's clothes and his elongated form are similar. Her painting, of someone she knew reasonably well, is in fact livelier and more engaging than his, although Cathelin's engraving lacks equivalent distinction. We would have had a very different picture of the patriot had any of these images captured public attention.

Duplessis is not well known in general and hardly at all outside France.[7] He was born in 1725 at Carpentras and, like many other young artists from the south, received his further training in Rome, as a pupil of Pierre Subleyras. Duplessis left the South of France in 1751, arrived in Paris thereafter, and finally exhibited with the painters' guild, the Académie de Saint-Luc, in 1764. As a candidate member of the most important arts organization, the Académie Royale de Peinture et de Sculpture, he first showed portraits at the 1769 Salon but was not admitted as a full member of the Académie until 1774, when he was nearing fifty. Louis XVI sat to Duplessis for a state portrait (lost; a replica is in the Musée Carnavalet, Paris), which was exhibited as number 119 in 1777, and he became the king's official painter. Two years later, he showed his portrait of Franklin in a red coat with a fur collar. The portrait and its astonishing frame, decorated with the sitter's attributes and symbols of his homeland, won praise after the opening of the Salon on August 25, 1779. Among the artist's other exhibits that year were portraits of the king's brother, the comte de Provence, and of the arts minister, the comte d'Angiviller. They were little noticed. Franklin, meanwhile, wrote his sister to say that "few Strangers in France have had the good Fortune to be so universally popular," noting, "My Face is now almost as well known as that of the Moon."[8]

In 1779 the VIR Portrait, or Fur Collar Portrait, as it is also called, was the property of Jacques Donatien Le Ray de Chaumont, a wealthy and energetic entrepreneur, a major supplier of goods to the American army, and a principal individual donor to the American cause. Franklin could hardly have refused his request for a likeness, but we know nothing else about the history of the painting and can assume only that it was retained by Le Ray at least until he was forced into bankruptcy in 1791. We have, however, been able to establish that sittings for the 1778 painting began with the pastel

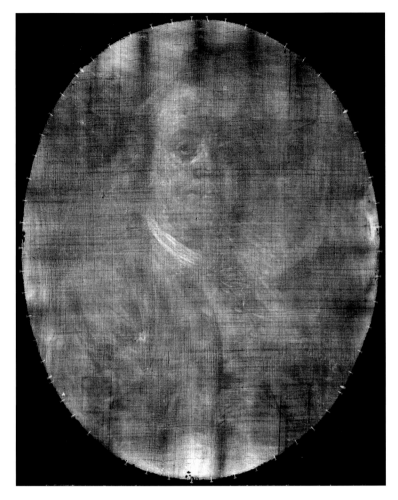

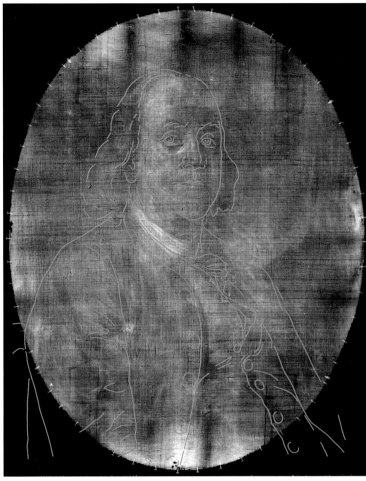

fig. 5 X-radiograph of VIR Portrait (fig. 1)

fig. 6 X-radiograph of VIR Portrait (fig. 1) overlaid with a tracing of Gray Coat Portrait (fig. 2) (green lines)

belonging to the New York Public Library,[9] which is often referred to as the Gray Coat Portrait. In accordance with the norms of the time, the artist would have presented himself to Franklin, a figure of importance, and it is likely that they met late in 1777 (previously Duplessis had been busy with the king's state portrait) or early in 1778 at the diplomat's residence in Passy. The pastel shows Franklin in a coat with a narrow collar worn over a waistcoat of the same pale color. Old labels on both the front of the nineteenth-century frame and the mounting on the reverse dating the portrait to 1783 have proved to be incorrect.[10] The X-radiograph (fig. 5) of the 1778 oil painting made in 2016 reveals that Duplessis began with the Gray Coat design, demonstrating that, as we suspected, the pastel preceded it and is the source image. The pastel was examined at the Metropolitan Museum and it became possible to document the relation between the two more precisely. When a tracing of the pastel was laid over the X-radiograph of the painting, the contours were found to match closely (fig. 6). At some intermediate stage of work on the VIR Portrait, Duplessis added the distinctive fur collar (which partly obscures the original narrow collar in the

X-radiograph) and replaced the buttons on the coat with frogs. Doubtless the pastel was taken from life, as it is the simplest, the most natural, and the most acutely observed, even though it was not brought to a high degree of finish in the details. Less well known than the Fur Collar Portrait, it has not been imprinted on the public imagination to such a degree. Those who find the Gray Coat image familiar may be remembering one of the iterations of the hundred-dollar bill (figs. 7, 8).

Although pastels (sticks of color combining pigment with a powdery white mineral and a gum binder) were widely admired in the second half of the eighteenth century, the Franklin portrait is one of only a handful of works by Duplessis in the medium. Pastels were employed almost exclusively for finished portraits, but this is a rare preparatory study. The materials were portable and the work could be carried out fairly quickly, which in the present case would have been a convenience given the sitter's dislike of posing. Its immediacy evokes a sense of rapid execution, though it was constructed according to customary procedures. Technical examination reveals that the artist worked up the composition directly, developing the preliminary stage

fig. 7 United States of America $100 Federal Reserve Note, first issued in 1929 (series 1928)

fig. 8 United States of America $100 Federal Reserve Note, first issued in 2013 (series 2009)

to her son Amédée Hureau de Sénarmont, and the pastel was held in the family until the death of the latter's son Henry in 1867. A year later it was purchased by John Bigelow, one of the founders of the New York Public Library. The agent was William Henry Huntington and the seller, a Monsieur de Sénarmont. Bigelow presented the work to the library in 1908, together with a manuscript copy of the statesman's autobiography and other related documents. The history of ownership is therefore uninterrupted and unimpeachable, which we wish were the case with our largely undocumented painting.

Early in 1777, in either February or March, Le Ray de Chaumont provided Franklin with a house on the property of his newly purchased Passy estate, the château de Valentinois.[11] The close professional and personal relationship that quickly developed between them suggests that Le Ray not only owned but also must have commissioned the 1778 portrait, particularly as he is listed as the owner in the checklist of the 1779 Salon. It may be imagined that the oval canvas was painted, in accordance with contemporary practice, in the artist's studio at the palais du Louvre. For help in rendering the likeness, Duplessis turned to the pastel, but, necessarily, he also scheduled one or more additional sittings, as there are differences not limited to the sitter's costume.

What type of portrait had Franklin chosen earlier in his life? Into his mid-sixties, he had worn a wig on formal occasions. The Scottish portraitist David Martin depicted him semiofficially in 1763, when, for example, he wore a well-groomed and powdered wig and an elaborate coat (The White House, Washington, D.C.). This was how he chose to appear two years after he began his service as commercial representative in London.[12] The following decade witnessed material differences in image making. Simplicity, while politically desirable, may also have afforded greater comfort to the aging diplomat. By all reports Franklin lived well, exercised little, and was healthy and quite vigorous for much of his final stay in France. In the course of the voyage over, however, he suffered from boils and an irritation of the skin, which spread from his head to his upper body and over time also afflicted his legs. He took warm baths regularly and consulted a physician who prescribed Belloste's Pills to alleviate these discomforts, but by October 1777 the pills had left him with a "Quantity of Water in [his mouth], and the Teeth . . . loosened."[13] Franklin noted that he had lost three teeth and he stopped taking the medication, but the afflictions continued to bother him intermittently.[14] Since his scalp was affected, he may have set his wig aside for reasons of health as well as of appearance. He was never again

of the likeness with a thin layer of green, carmine, and blue pastel. He enriched the palette with a range of closely related tints, which he rubbed and mixed with his fingers and a stump (a leather coil). The features and some other details were then delineated with the tips or broken edges of the colored sticks. It was perhaps in a spirit of experimentation that Duplessis chose parchment (animal skin prepared with lime) for the support. The artist may have selected the exceptionally large skin for its translucency; it also offered greater dimensions than handmade paper at the time. The skin was tacked to a stretcher and the pastel was applied to the napped, or suedelike, side. The artist did not use a fixative, which would have diminished the radiance of the scattered light reflected off the innumerable powdery particles.

Before Franklin departed for America in 1785, he presented the pastel to Louis Guillaume Le Veillard, who had been the mayor of Passy in the 1770s and was a close friend and neighbor with whom the diplomat played chess. Le Veillard accompanied the elderly statesman, much diminished in health, on the first stages of his journey. Franklin's friend was executed in 1794 during the exceptionally violent interval of the French Revolution known as the Terror, but he was survived by his wife and a daughter, who died unmarried in 1834. Through his first cousin, Marie, his estate passed

portrayed with a wig, although for his official appearances at Versailles he would have been expected to dress much more formally and to have worn one.

On balance, in the VIR Portrait Franklin looks hardier, heavier, and younger than he does in the pastel. The important circumstances of a Salon exhibition may have suggested these improvements. His face is full and his lips are well formed. But the receding upper lip indicates the loss of teeth in the intervening period.[15] The sitter's posture may have been poor, and he appears to lean forward: one of the few things about the painting that disturbed visitors to the Salon was that they could not tell whether he was seated or standing (the pastel indicates a chair, but the canvas, because of its oval shape, does not, and this may be the cause of the confusion).[16] While the first ten months of the year 1777 had been exceedingly difficult for both the elderly American patriot and the American cause, by 1778 the tide had turned. Red, the color of the coat, is an evocative, ennobling color, and for the French, fur was a reminder of the pioneering American spirit that they admired. Perhaps the collar and lining are intended to be red fox, which was hunted for its pelt in North America.

Among those who singled out the work for its nobility and truth to nature was Pierre Samuel Dupont, who also drew attention to the exceptional gilded and inscribed frame.[17] In the words of Dupont, Franklin was without equal in his time, manifesting the vigor of Hercules, a statement that surely addresses the qualities of the man and not those of the elderly sitter as Duplessis presented him.[18] On September 14 and 15, 1779, Elkanah Watson, a young American who had traveled to France to deliver dispatches to Franklin, visited the Salon at the Louvre to see the portrait; he presented a more realistic assessment. He found himself among what he described as "a prodigious current of human animals" on his way to see the "master piece of painting representing our Illustrious Patron Doctr. Franklin," and he noted that the work was "deposited (as a mark of particular respect) upon the left of his present Majesty."[19] In fact, the royal portrait by Duplessis to which Watson referred represented not the king but his brother, distinguished by a white satin costume with decorations, wearing a heavily powdered wig, and painted on a larger canvas as convention dictated. In the case of Duplessis's Franklin, while it is important to distinguish between what was admired about the picture and what was admired about the man, it is fair to say the artist's reputation benefited greatly from the latter.

The carved and gilded oval frame most likely dates to 1778 as well and, based on its design, may have been made by the celebrated designer and wood-carver François Charles Buteux.[20] The elaborate carving adds a further layer to the Franklin iconography and pays homage to his accomplishments as an American inventor and statesman. The ornament—including *rais de coeur* (lamb's tongue), *feuille enroulé* (twisted acanthus leaf and rod), and pearling—is characteristic of the Louis XVI style developed by Buteux while he was working as a wood-carver in the architectural bureau of the Crown. The oak base of the frame is gessoed and water-gilded with matte and burnished passages on ocher and red bole, or clay. The oval is surmounted by swags of olive, symbolizing peace and wisdom, and laurel, associated with a victor's crown. Above, branches of oak and American boxwood form a wreath. Entwined in the foliage is an undulating rattlesnake with a forked tongue. This reptile, indigenous only to North America, is the topic of a letter Franklin submitted anonymously to the *Pennsylvania Journal* in 1775. He elaborated on the animal's distinctive characteristics, noting that it portrayed "a strong picture of the temper and conduct of America."[21] The drop pendant forms a cartouche or shield that secures a muskrat pelt with snarling teeth, a protruding tongue, claws, and a ratlike tail. Opposite the animal's head there is a Phrygian cap, already a symbol of liberty eleven years before the onset of the French Revolution. In the creation mythology of native North Americans, the muskrat was thought to have brought forth the earth from the primordial mud. The pelt twists around a club, emblematic of Hercules—who embodied truth, heroism, and determination. In addition, the Fur Collar Portrait was provided with a laudatory inscription by Juste or Justus Chevillet Feutry, which was appended to the 1778 engraving by Juste Chevillet.[22]

There are no fewer than several dozen same-size replicas of Duplessis's VIR Portrait, and it is likely that many of them were painted while Franklin was in Paris and a subject of immediate interest. Visitors to the Salon who admired the work would have been among the first to seek out the artist to commission replicas. The American statesman understood the importance of circulating his image, and although he found himself obliged to give sittings to a number of painters, sculptors, and draftsmen while he was in France, he made it clear, as previously mentioned, that he did not enjoy doing so. He did not wish to sit for the same artist repeatedly, suggesting to at least one supplicant who applied for an original work that he should make do by commissioning a replica from Duplessis instead.[23] In general terms, Duplessis is reported to have worked slowly and to have had numerous helpers. Versions by

fig. 9 Workshop of Joseph Siffred Duplessis. *Benjamin Franklin*, 1779 or after. Oil on canvas, oval, 27⅝ × 22¼ in. (70.2 × 56.5 cm). The Metropolitan Museum of Art, Gift of George A. Lucas, 1895 (95.21)

him and by his studio assistants, and other versions, probably less expensive, by independent hands, were wanted for the same reason that someone might now display a photograph of a famous politician he or she admires. The Metropolitan Museum is fortunate enough to own an excellent replica of the VIR Portrait as well (fig. 9), and the two are so close that in reproduction it is difficult to distinguish between them.

The contours of the Museum's second version match those of the first so precisely that the design can only have been transferred directly from one to the other (fig. 10). Contemporary artists' manuals describe various methods for the common practice of replicating a design. The one most likely used by Duplessis and others working in his shop would have involved applying thin translucent paper to a glass covering the VIR Portrait, tracing the contours of the image, blackening the entire reverse of the translucent paper with charcoal or chalk (this is rather like using old-fashioned carbon paper), and incising the traced design onto another canvas with a stylus. Because there are hardly any changes in the palette, the replica must have been made

in the Duplessis studio. However, it remains impossible to say, other than as a matter of opinion, whether this replica is by the artist in its entirety or retouched by him, or (although in our opinion this is unlikely) whether it is by a talented imitator. Of the paintings and pastels that replicate the VIR Portrait, none is signed or dated. An inscription on the reverse of the replica at the Metropolitan Museum—*Peint par Duplessis pour obliger monsieur le vicomte De Buissy*[24]—provides a contemporary context, and an original owner belonging to the Buissy family has been tentatively identified. Other inscriptions of the kind have not been found (and probably will not be, because by now it is likely that all of the replicas have been relined with newer canvas).

There are many good replicas of the VIR Portrait in the United States, and as several are in public collections, we extended our study by seeking out other accessible examples of good quality, the contours of which might, with the help of colleagues, be traced. We applied to the North Carolina Museum of Art (fig. 11), Monticello, and the Huntington Library, which own replicas that we believe are contemporaneous. The first recorded owner of the replica in North Carolina was Isaac Cox Barnet, an American who moved to France in 1794 and died there in 1833.[25] Barnet was a commercial agent in Bordeaux and Le Havre and a consul in Brest and Paris. He married a French aristocrat, through whom he may have gained ownership of the North Carolina picture. We would argue that this painting could be by Duplessis himself. Another example of interest belonged to Thomas Jefferson and is at Monticello (fig. 12).[26] Jefferson bought the canvas in Paris on September 10, 1786, from Jean Valade, a little-known painter to the king, Academician, and art dealer.

fig. 11 Attributed to Joseph Siffred Duplessis. *Benjamin Franklin*, 1779 or after. Oil on canvas, oval, 27½ × 21½ in. (69.8 × 54.6 cm). North Carolina Museum of Art, Gift of the North Carolina Citizens Association (G.75.26.1)

It was sold to Jefferson as the work of Greuze, but in recent years it has been attributed to Valade himself. Eighteenth-century artists routinely made oil copies of oil paintings, but pastel replicas are few in number. We illustrate a pastel of high quality from the Huntington that is first recorded in New York in 1890 and has also been ascribed to Valade (fig. 13).[27] The Huntington and Monticello portraits have been associated owing to their identical, original, late eighteenth-century frames. Tracings of all three have been superimposed on the VIR Portrait: they all align closely (fig. 14). Since the coloring is so similar, all must have emerged from the Duplessis workshop.[28] It comes as no surprise to discover that Duplessis always retained a replica of his famous Franklin portrait: he sent the replica to the Salon of 1801. In the Anglophone world, Duplessis's Benjamin Franklin joins Hans Holbein's portrait of Henry VIII and Gilbert Stuart's of George Washington in maintaining its uniquely persistent vitality over the centuries.

fig. 12 Workshop of Joseph Siffred Duplessis (attributed to Jean Valade [French, 1710–1787]). *Benjamin Franklin*, 1779 or after. Oil on canvas, oval, 28¾ × 23³⁄₁₆ in. (73 × 58.9 cm). Thomas Jefferson Foundation at Monticello (1977-80)

ACKNOWLEDGMENTS

This project began as a dossier exhibition, with the single loan of the pastel from the New York Public Library, which was held at the Metropolitan Museum from August 22 through November 28, 2016. Katharine Baetjer offers her thanks for their help and interest to Anthony Marx, President and CEO of the New York Public Library; to Deborah Straussman, Head of Registrar Services, New York Public Library; and to her friend Emily K. Rafferty, President Emerita of the Metropolitan Museum. The authors express their warm appreciation to the designer of the show, Daniel Kershaw, as well as to the graphic designer, Constance Norkin. We acknowledge the important contributions of Evan Read, associate manager of technical documentation, Department of Paintings Conservation, for help with the images in the exhibition and in the present article. Carol Bergren Santoleri, research assistant in the Department of European Paintings, gathered material on the related works; Constance McPhee, curator, Department of Drawings and Prints, provided prints from her department for the exhibition. We are also

fig. 13 Workshop of Joseph Siffred Duplessis (attributed to Jean Valade). *Benjamin Franklin*, 1779 or after. Pastel on blue paper adhered to linen, oval, 28½ × 22½ in. (72.4 × 57.2 cm). The Huntington Library, Art Collections, and Botanical Gardens (53.4)

grateful to colleagues who took enormous trouble to supply tracings of works in their collections: David Steel of the North Carolina Museum of Art; Susan R. Stein at Monticello; Melinda McCurdy at The Huntington Library, Art Collections, and Botanical Gardens; and Michiko Okaya of the Art Galleries and Collections, Lafayette College.

KATHARINE BAETJER
Curator, Department of European Paintings, The Metropolitan Museum of Art

MARJORIE SHELLEY
Sherman Fairchild Conservator in Charge, Department of Paper Conservation, The Metropolitan Museum of Art

CHARLOTTE HALE
Conservator, Department of Paintings Conservation, The Metropolitan Museum of Art

CYNTHIA MOYER
Associate Conservator, Department of Paintings Conservation, The Metropolitan Museum of Art

fig. 14 Ghosted image of VIR Portrait (fig. 1) overlaid with tracings of three replicas: North Carolina Museum of Art (fig. 11; turquoise lines), Monticello (fig. 12; magenta lines), and Huntington Library (fig. 13; gold lines)

NOTES

1 Franklin's life is extensively documented, notably by the American Philosophical Society and Yale University in *The Papers of Benjamin Franklin*, digitized from 1988 to the present by Packard Humanities Institute, www.franklinpapers.org. An account of the sitter's years in France is Schiff 2005.

2 The terracotta bust of Franklin by Jean Jacques Caffiéri (1725–1792) (Bibliothèque Mazarine, Paris) was exhibited at the Salon of 1777 as number 218. Jean Antoine Houdon (1741–1828) showed a terracotta bust (location unknown) at the Salon of 1779 as number 221. A fine example by Houdon in marble, signed and dated 1778, is in the Metropolitan Museum (72.6).

3 Jean-Baptiste Nini (1717–1786), born in Urbino, moved to Paris no later than 1758 and in the 1760s began to make molded, circular terracotta medallions with profile bust portraits of famous contemporaries derived mostly from engravings, which circulated in the thousands. In 1771, Jacques Donatien Le Ray de Chaumont commissioned one of himself, and in 1772 entered into a contract with Nini whereby he sponsored the artisan's work. Nini was provided with facilities at the château de Chaumont, and profits were divided between the two men. Nini's first Franklin medallion was marketed in the spring of 1777. One of his models was based on a drawing by Thomas Walpole's son and another on a work by Anne Vallayer-Coster. See Schaeper 1995, pp. 24–26, 128–29. The Metropolitan Museum owns representations of Franklin by Nini in various materials; see www.metmuseum.org (83.2.170, 83.2.175, 83.2.178, 83.2.282, 01.31.4, 42.76.14), and a single roundel showing Le Ray de Chaumont (52.133.9).

4 See Augustin de Saint-Aubin (1736–1807), after Charles Nicolas Cochin II (1715–1790), *Benjamin Franklin*, etching, first state of five, 1777 (1986.1057); Marguerite Gérard (1761–1837), after Jean Honoré Fragonard (1732–1806), *The Genius of Franklin*, etching, first state of two, 1778 (83.2.230). Both may be seen at www.metmuseum.org/art/collection. For the third, Jean Claude Richard, Abbé de Saint-Non (1727–1791), after Jean Honoré Fragonard, *Le Docteur Francklin couronné par la Liberté*, aquatint, see www.philamuseum.org/collections/permanent/50127.html.

5 Munhall 1997, pp. 22–26, ill. (American Philosophical Society portrait). The Metropolitan Museum owns a miniature signed and dated 1777 by Charles Paul Jérôme de Bréa (ca. 1739–1820) after one of Greuze's Franklin portraits (68.222.9). Franklin and Greuze belonged to the same Masonic lodge, where they subsequently met.

6 For the portrait by the "pretty and talented" Rose Filleul, see Sellers 1962, pp. 281–84, pl. 23. Claude-Anne Lopez (1966, pp. 227–28) suggests that Filleul's personal charms rather than her ability as a painter secured her the commission. Anne Rosalie Filleul (1752–1794), born Bocquet, exhibited at the Académie de Saint-Luc in 1774. She married Louis Filleul, as his third wife, in 1777, and through him became *gardienne* of the neighboring château de La Muette. Franklin was fond of young women and enjoyed Rose's company in particular; her wedding invitation survives among his papers. She worked in watercolor, pastels, and oils, making several portraits of the children of the comte d'Artois, youngest brother of Louis XVI (three pastels are at the Musée National du Château de Versailles). Owing to her connection with the royal family, she died by the guillotine. For the print after her painting by Louis Jacques Cathelin (1739–1804) (MMA 83.2.227), see Portalis and Béraldi 1880–82, vol. 1, p. 331, no. 23 ii, and Roux 1940, pp. 36–37, no. 80.

7 The principal sources are Belleudy 1913 and Chabaud 2003; and, on the general subject of Franklin portraits and the relation between the pastel and the painting by Duplessis in particular, the comprehensive work of Sellers 1962, especially pp. 124–37, 246–67, pls. 24 (Duplessis: "Fur Collar," no. 1), 25 (Duplessis: "Gray Coat," no. 1). We have proven that the pastel came first, which is what Sellers believed to be the case.

8 Benjamin Franklin to his sister Jane Mecom, October 25, 1779, for which see www.franklinpapers.org (633242 = 030-582b.html).

9 Documentation provided by the New York Public Library is gratefully acknowledged. In general on the subject of Duplessis's pastels, which are rare, and with thanks to Neil Jeffares, consult Duplessis's work online at www.pastellists.com/Articles/Duplessis.pdf. Other important pastels, both ovals, represent the Abbé Jourdan (Salon of 1769, no. 197) and the composer Christoph Willibald Gluck (1714–1787), who moved to Paris in September 1773 and lived there for the balance of the decade. He sat to Duplessis for a portrait in oils in 1775 (Kunsthistorisches Museum, Vienna). The pastel is unlocated. See also Belleudy 1913, pp. 49, 324 no. 75, 325 no. 82.

10 With respect to the date, the small identifying label on the front of the frame follows that on the reverse, which reads in part "BENJAMIN FRANKLIN, / A 77 ANS, / Peint par Jh Sd Duplessis, / 1783. / Donné par lui-même" (that is, to M. Le Veillard, as discussed below).

11 See Martindale 1977. Le Ray de Chaumont bought the property in August 1776 and installed Franklin there at no charge in February or March 1777.

12 The portrait may have been intended to advance the career of David Martin (1737–1797). The sitter was pleased with it and ordered a replica to be sent to America, which was unusual in that he intervened, and must have paid, directly. See Sellers 1962, pp. 328–40, pl. 8 (Martin, no. 1).

13 I thank Carol Santoleri for her work on this subject and reference a note dictated by Benjamin Franklin dated October 17, 1777, "Franklin's Description of His Ailments"; see www.franklinpapers.org (628572 = 025-077a.html).

14 Journal entries by Benjamin Franklin are dated October 4, 1778, to January 16, 1780. "Franklin's Journal of His Health," www.franklinpapers.org (630725 = 027-496a.html). Stacy Schiff (2005, p. 90) states that he had been ingesting mercury.

15 Barrymore Laurence Scherer's review in the *Wall Street Journal* of September 6, 2016, drew attention to the change in Franklin's face. I have also benefited from the advice of Albert L. Ousborne, D.D.S.

16 Friedrich Melchior Grimm, letter, October 1779, in Tourneux 1880, p. 327: "Le portrait . . . serait le chef-d'œuvre de M. Duplessis si la position du modèle était mieux indiquée; on ne sait s'il est debout ou s'il est assis, il a l'air d'un homme qui tombe." All contemporary criticism known to us is referred to on www.metmuseum.org/art/collection/search/436236.

17 "On a mis au bas de son portrait cette laconique inscription: *Vir*. Il n'y a pas un trait de sa figure ni de sa vie qui la démente." Pierre Samuel Dupont, letter to Caroline Louise of Hesse-Darmstadt, margravine of Baden, in Dupont (1779) 1908, pp. 106–7.

18 ". . . qu'on n'en connaît pas de son âge qui lui soit égal. Toutes ses proportions annoncent la vigueur d'Hercule . . . ," ibid., p. 106.

19 "Journal no. 4, Travels in France," Elkanah Watson Papers, SC12579, box 1, New York State Library, quoted in Sellers 1962, p. 125.

20 For François Charles Buteux (1732–1788), see the discussion of a drawing in the Musée des Arts Décoratifs cited by Sarah Medlam in 2007.

21 John D. MacArthur, "Benjamin Franklin on the Rattlesnake as a Symbol of America," reproduces the letter, signed "An American Guesser," published in the *Pennsylvania Journal*, December 27, 1775, www.greatseal.com/symbols/rattlesnake.html.

22 Sellers 1962, p. 249, pl. 27 (Duplessis: "Fur Collar," no. 2). For an illustration of the engraving by the German-born Juste or Justus Chevillet (1729–?1802), see Library of Congress Prints and Photographs Division, Washington, D.C. (https://lccn.loc .gov/2003674085). The engraving is inscribed: *Benjamin Franklin / Né à Boston, dans la nouvelle Angleterre, le 17 Janv. 1706 / Honneur du nouveau monde et de l'humanité, / Ce Sage aimable et vrai les guide et les éclaire; / Comme un autre Mentor, il cache à l'œil vulgaire, / Sous les traits d'un mortel, une divinité. Par M. Feutry / Duplessis Pinxit, Parisiis 1778 / Chevillet Sculpsit / Tiré du Cabinet de M. Le Ray de Chaumont &ca*. The writer was Aimé Amboise Joseph Feutry (1720–1789).

23 John Clyde Oswald (1926, p. 10) provides a translation of an undated letter on the subject that was sent to a member of the Fournier family of type founders.

24 The inscription (*painted by Duplessis to / oblige monsieur the vicomte / de Buissy*) was photographed in 1931, before the painting was lined. In 2009 a three-quarter-length portrait by Duplessis of a seated man—said to have descended in the family of the sitter and inscribed on the stretcher *Peint par Duplessis* and *M de Buissy*—was acquired by the National Gallery of Canada, Ottawa. It may be dated about 1780 and perhaps represents Pierre de Buissy (1737/43–1787), a guards officer and master of the hunt to the comte d'Artois, who could be the individual referred to in the inscription on our replica. Many thanks for their help in this matter go to our colleagues Paul Lang and Christopher Etheridge of the National Gallery of Canada, Ottawa.

25 See North Carolina Museum of Art, "ArtNC," http://artnc.org /works-of-art/benjamin-franklin-1706-1790.

26 The painting was sold after Jefferson's death to the Boston Athenaeum, exhibited at the Museum of Fine Arts, Boston, and long identified as the primary version. In 1977 it was reacquired by the Thomas Jefferson Memorial Foundation for Monticello (1977–80). See www.monticello.org/site/research-and -collections/benjamin-franklin-painting.

27 Kimberly Chrisman-Campbell in Bennett and Sargentson 2008, pp. 381–83, no. 143, color ill., and especially n. 11, as attributed to Jean Valade (1710–1787).

28 Michiko Okaya recently provided a tracing of a version of the Benjamin Franklin portrait by Duplessis belonging to Lafayette College, Easton, Pennsylvania. Because the contours match and the coloring is similar, the painting must also be attributed to the Duplessis workshop.

REFERENCES

Belleudy, Jules
  1913 *J.-S. Duplessis, peintre du roi.* Chartres: Imprimerie Durand.

Bennett, Shelley M., and Carolyn Sargentson, eds.
  2008 *French Art of the Eighteenth Century at The Huntington.* New Haven: Yale University Press.

Chabaud, Jean-Paul
  2003 *Joseph-Siffred Duplessis, 1725–1802: Biographie.* Mazan: Etudes Comtadines.

Dupont, Pierre-Samuel
  1908 "Le Salon de 1779." In "Lettres sur les Salons de 1773, 1777 et 1779, addressées par Du Pont de Nemours à la Margrave Caroline-Louise de Bade," *Archives de l'art français,* n.s., 2, pp. 105–7.

Jeffares, Neil
  2016 "Duplessis, Joseph-Siffred." In *Dictionary of Pastellists before 1800.* Updated September 7. www.pastellists.com /Articles/Duplessis.pdf.

Lopez, Claude-Anne
  1966 *Mon Cher Papa: Franklin and the Ladies of Paris.* New Haven: Yale University Press.

Martindale, Meredith
  1977 "Benjamin Franklin's Residence in France: The Hôtel de Valentinois in Passy." *Magazine Antiques* 112, no. 2, pp. 262–73.

Medlam, Sarah
  2007 "Callet's Portrait of Louis XVI: A Picture Frame as Diplomatic Tool." *Furniture History* 43, pp. 143–54.

Munhall, Edgar
  1997 "Greuze's Portrait of Benjamin Franklin in the American Philosophical Society." In *Franklin and Condorcet: Two Portraits from the American Philosophical Society,* pp. 22–26. Exh. cat., Frick Collection, New York; Philadelphia Museum of Art. Philadelphia: The Society.

Oswald, John Clyde
  1926 *Benjamin Franklin in Oil and Bronze.* New York: W. E. Rudge.

Portalis, Roger, and Henri Béraldi
  1880–82 *Les graveurs du dix-huitième siècle.* 3 vols. Paris: D. Morgand et C. Fatout.

Roux, Marcel
  1940 *Inventaire du fonds français: Graveurs du XVIIIᵉ siècle.* Vol. 4, *Cathelin–Cochin Père (Charles-Nicolas).* Paris: Bibliothèque Nationale.

Schaeper, Thomas J.
  1995 *France and America in the Revolutionary Era: The Life of Jacques-Donatien Leray de Chaumont, 1725–1803.* Providence: Berghahn Books.

Scherer, Barrymore Laurence
  2016 "'Benjamin Franklin: Portraits by Duplessis' Review: How We Picture a Founder." *Wall Street Journal,* September 6, 2016.

Schiff, Stacy
  2005 *A Great Improvisation: Franklin, France, and the Birth of America.* New York: Henry Holt.

Sellers, Charles Coleman
  1962 *Benjamin Franklin in Portraiture.* New Haven: Yale University Press.

Tourneux, Maurice, ed.
  1880 *Correspondance littéraire, philosophique et critique par Grimm, Diderot, Raynal, Meister, etc.* Paris: Garnier frères.

KAREN M. KERN
YAEL ROSENFIELD
FEDERICO CARÒ
NOBUKO SHIBAYAMA

The Sacred and the Modern: The History, Conservation, and Science of the Madina *Sitara*

fig. 1 *Sitara*. Produced in the Warshat al-Khurunfish, Cairo, A.H. 1315/1897–98. Black silk, pink and green silk/cotton, white cotton lining; silver and silver-gilt metal wire thread, orange and white silk thread, orange and white linen thread; silver sequins; 110⅝ × 63 in. (281 × 160 cm). The Metropolitan Museum of Art, Gift of Professor Maan Z. Madina, in memory of his mother, Najiyya Khanum al-Kurdi, 2009 (2009.59.1)

This article examines the history and conservation and offers a scientific analysis of a *sitara* given to The Metropolitan Museum of Art in 2009. This *sitara*, one of only a small number known from published sources, is a late nineteenth-century Ottoman curtain that hung on the Bab al-Tawba (Door of Repentance) inside the Ka'ba in Mecca. Historical analysis situates this rare object within a centuries-old tradition of textile production for the most sacred sites in Islam. Examination of the yarns, dyes, weaving and embroidery techniques, metal wire thread, and other materials and processes that went into the production of this sacred and symbolic curtain presents it in the context of its manufacture in the globalized world of the late nineteenth century.

HISTORY

Textiles produced for the Ka'ba in Mecca, Islam's holiest site, represent the most sacred and iconic objects in

Islamic art. In 2009, Maan Z. Madina, professor emeritus in the Department of Middle Eastern, South Asian, and African Studies at Columbia University, New York, gave the Metropolitan Museum one of these, an interior curtain (*sitara*) that hung on the Bab al-Tawba (fig. 1).[1]

While the textiles that draped the exterior of the Ka'ba are well represented in museums and private collections,[2] Bab al-Tawba *sitara*s have generally been less known to the larger community of art historians, having appeared in public or private art collections only recently. The production of sacred textiles for the Ka'ba has a long history that dates back to the earliest years of Islam, and the custom of draping the exterior walls and interior spaces with these textiles is well established in the historical record. Responsibility for commissioning the Ka'ba textiles and transporting them to Mecca generally fell to the ruler who held sovereignty over the holy cities. The Ottoman sultans were the longest serving of these rulers, having conquered Egypt, Mecca,

and Medina in 1517. As rulers of Mecca and Medina, they thus acquired the title *Khadim al-Haramayn al-Sharifayn* (Custodian of the Two Noble Sanctuaries) and in this capacity held the privilege of ordering replacement of these textiles, an honor that continued until the end of the Ottoman dynasty in 1923. Throughout these centuries, the covering that draped the exterior walls of the Ka'ba (*kiswa*), the belt around the Ka'ba embroidered with Qur'anic inscriptions (*hizam*), and the curtain covering the door into the Ka'ba (*burqu'*) were seen by millions of pilgrims who performed the hajj.[3] Textiles hanging inside the Ka'ba, however, were seen only by the few dignitaries and special guests who were privileged to enter, or pilgrims who were present when the doors were opened for prayer. The Bab al-Tawba is the door to the stairway up to a mezzanine where the Prophet Muhammad is believed to have ordered the destruction of pagan idols as a ritual of repentance. This site later became a repository for

fig. 2 The four uppermost cartouches of the *sitara* in fig. 1 embroidered with the *basmala* and with Qur'anic *Ayat* 54 of *Sura* VI

fig. 3 The cartouche beneath the four cartouches in fig. 2, embroidered with the name of Sultan 'Abd al-Hamid II, who had the imperial prerogative of ordering the replacement of textiles for the Ka'ba

precious gifts sent to the Ka'ba by Muslim rulers from around the world. The Bab al-Tawba *sitara*s are much less well known in the long historical record of coverings for the Ka'ba, and their production is perhaps of more recent origin. Although the British explorer Richard Burton, visiting the Ka'ba in 1853, chronicled in detail the exterior coverings, his account of the interior described the Bab al-Tawba without a curtain.[4] The earliest extant curtain known from published sources dates to 1893.[5] More examples are likely to appear in the future, but their rarity may be due to the fact that they were more private, the personal offerings of rulers who wished to receive the *baraka* (blessing) associated with this sacred space. They were also protected from the elements so they did not need to be replaced as frequently as the outer coverings, which were traditionally made anew yearly and transported to Mecca at the time of the hajj.

The Bab al-Tawba *sitara*s that are known from published sources (see note 5) and the Madina *sitara* are of the same basic design and have the same Qur'anic verse, *Ayat 54* of *Sura VI* (*al-An'am*), embroidered on them. A variation occurs in only one of them, which is discussed below. In all of the examples, however, the fabric creates the structure that frames the textual message, making that message cohesive and coherent, one that calls to memory the underlying tenet of Islam. That tenet bids Muslims to remember the judgment day and reminds them of God's mercy for the repentant sinner, as well as proclaiming the authority and sovereignty of the rulers who commissioned and oversaw the production and transportation of the textiles. The primary decorative element is Arabic calligraphy in the *jali thuluth* script.[6] The top four cartouches of the Madina *sitara* (fig. 2) begin with an embroidered inscription of the *basmala* (In the name of God, the Most Gracious, the Most Merciful), an invocation focusing the believer on the glory and majesty of Allah. The inscription continues with the Qur'anic *Ayat 54* of *Sura VI* (*al-An'am*):

بسم الله الرحمن الرحيم وَإِذَا جَاءَكَ الَّذِينَ
يُؤْمِنُونَ بِآيَاتِنَا فَقُلْ سَلَامٌ عَلَيْكُمْ كَتَبَ رَبُّكُمْ
عَلَى نَفْسِهِ الرَّحْمَةَ أَنَّهُ مَنْ عَمِلَ مِنْكُمْ سُوءًا بِجَهَالَةٍ
ثُمَّ تَابَ مِنْ بَعْدِهِ وَأَصْلَحَ فَأَنَّهُ غَفُورٌ رَحِيمٌ

When those come to thee who believe in Our signs, Say: "Peace be on you: Your Lord hath inscribed for Himself (the rule of) Mercy: verily, if any of you did evil in ignorance, and thereafter repented, and amended (his conduct), lo! He is Oft-forgiving, Most Merciful."[7]

The connection between this verse and the Door of Repentance is clear: God will grant forgiveness and mercy to those believers who commit sins but repent with humility and without arrogance.

The fifth cartouche (fig. 3) contains an inscription naming Ottoman sultan 'Abd al-Hamid II (r. 1876–1909) as the ruler who held imperial prerogative and sovereignty over the holy cities of Mecca and Medina and who thus had the honor of ordering the replacement of the *sitara*:

امر بعمل هذه السارة الشريفة حضرت مولانا الاعظم السلطان عبد الحميد خان نصره
الله امين

Our great Master, Sultan 'Abd al-Hamid Khan, ordered the work of this noble curtain; God grant victory to him. Amen.

The inscription was a form of memorialization that symbolized the ruler's religious and political authority.[8]

The inscription in the lower three cartouches (fig. 4) designated 'Abbas Hilmi Pasha, governor, or khedive, of Egypt from 1892 to 1914, with the honor of overseeing the production and transportation of the *sitara* and asked for God's victory or glory, a tradition thought to bring blessings and good omens.

جدد مذه الستارة الشريفة حضرت مولانا
الاعظم افندينا عباس حلمي باشا خديوي مصر المحروسة
ابن المرحوم محمد توفيق باشا ادام الله عزه

Our great Master, our Effendi, 'Abbas Hilmi Pasha, Khedive of Egypt, the [divinely] protected, son of the late Muhammad Tawfiq Pasha, renewed this noble curtain; Lord make glory permanent with him.

The reign of this sultan and the rule of his governor overlapped, thereby narrowing the date of manufacture of the Madina *sitara* to the seventeen-year period

fig. 4 The three cartouches in the lower half of the *sitara* in fig. 1, embroidered with the name 'Abbas Hilmi Pasha, the governor of Egypt who oversaw production of the textile at the Warshat al-Khurunfish in Cairo and its transportation during the hajj

a

b

fig. 5 Paper at the bottom edge of the *sitara* in fig. 1, inscribed in ink سنة ٣١٥, identifying the date of production as the year A.H. 1315/1897–98. The paper is shown (a) in place between the black silk background fabric and the white cotton lining, and (b) in an X-radiograph showing the full size of the note, which is held in place with embroidery stitches.

between 1892, when 'Abbas Hilmi came to power in Egypt, and 1909, the end of 'Abd al-Hamid's rule as sultan. However, we can suggest a more precise date of production, for during conservation of the *sitara*, a piece of paper was discovered sewn among the layers of the curtain (fig. 5a). The paper is degraded and largely unreadable except for سنة ٣١٥ (A.H. 1315/1897–98). The inscription on the sitara also honors the Khedive's father, "the late Muhammad Tawfiq Pasha" (d. 1892). 'Abbas Hilmi Pasha was perhaps mourning his father's recent death and memorializing him in this inscription. But the same dedication appears on the *sitara* in the Topkapı Palace Museum, Istanbul, which is dated A.H. 1325/1907–8, thus late in 'Abbas Hilmi Pasha's governorship.[9] It seems that his custom of inscribing his late father's name was a practice he followed throughout his time in office, one by which he sought to bring blessings associated with the sacred space to his father. The convention of naming deceased rulers was not 'Abbas Hilmi Pasha's innovation, for the tradition of such dedications appears as early as the beginning of the eighteenth century on sacred textiles like the tomb covers for the Prophet Ibrahim and for the Prophet Muhammad in Medina. The tradition also appears on other Ka'ba textiles during the period of Sultan Abd al-Hamid II.[10]

Recent scholarship has suggested that the Bab al-Tawba's *sitara*s were replaced only upon the succession

of a new sultan.[11] However, a comparative examination of some of the complete *sitara*s made anew during the reign of Sultan 'Abd al-Hamid II and the governorship of 'Abbas Hilmi Pasha shows that they were replaced more frequently. In addition to the Madina *sitara*, there is a *sitara* in the Nasser D. Khalili Collection of Islamic Art, dated A.H. 1311/1893–94, and one in the Topkapı Palace Museum, dated A.H. 1325/1907–8, as well as two other *sitara*s recently seen at auction, one that was manufactured between 1892 and 1909, and the other inscribed with the year of A.H. 1321/1903–4.[12] This frequency of renewal suggests that this interior textile was replaced every few years as needed.

The *sitara*s that are alike are composed of a central rectangle containing the cartouches, the lower ones surrounded by floral embroidery. The border around the rectangle contains rosettes interspersed with an arabesque design (see fig. 1). The stylistic and textual exception is the late-Ottoman *sitara* dated A.H. 1321/ 1903–4 that was auctioned at Sotheby's London in 2007 (fig. 6). It is inscribed with the underlying message of God's forgiveness and mercy in the upper rectangular cartouche embroidered with a portion of Qur'anic *Ayat* 25 of *Sura* XLII (*al-Shura*), "He is the One that accepts repentance from His Servants."[13] The main cartouche contains Qur'anic *Ayat* 255 (Verse of the Throne) of *Sura* II.[14] This verse is one of the Qur'an's most beloved

fig. 6 Sitara, dated A.H. [1]321/
1903–4. Black and colored silk
ground embroidered with silver
and silver-gilt wire thread;
94½ × 70⅞ in. (240 × 180 cm).
Sold, Sotheby's, London, 2007,
lot 42

in its portrayal of God's incomparability and his all-powerfulness. But it does not have the same clear connection that Qur'anic 6:54 has to repentance and the Bab al-Tawba. The Verse of the Throne is, in fact, more often inscribed on the *burqu'* (the curtain for external door of the Ka'ba).[15] The roundels that flank the Verse of the Throne contain the names of the first four *Rashidun* (Rightly Guided) Caliphs, 'Abu Bakr, 'Umar, 'Uthman, and 'Ali, who ruled immediately after the death of Muhammad, as well as 'Ali's two sons and Muhammad's grandsons, Hasan and Husayn, who suc-

ceeded to rulership in the Shi'ite tradition. This convention is unique to this particular Bab al-Tawba *sitara*, for while the names of the Prophet Muhammad's grandsons do appear on his tomb covers in Medina, suggesting the close familial connection between Muhammad and his grandsons, their inscription on this *sitara* breaks from the tradition in the small number of known Bab al-Tawba *sitara*s that memorialize only sultans and khedives. In this case, the inclusion of the grandsons of the Prophet would remind the community (and particularly those dignitaries and believers who were privileged to enter the Ka'ba) of the sense of union in the pilgrimage and that in the most sacred sites of Islam unity of the community superseded sectarian Sunni-Shi'i divisions.

The Madina *sitara* and those discussed here were preserved intact, unlike the exterior *kiswa*s. The hangings on the exterior wall of the Ka'ba were commonly cut up and distributed when they were removed, a practice that was based on a hadith (tradition) from the Prophet Muhammad's wife 'A'isha', who said, "Sell those covers and spend the money you earn for the poor and the travelers who are on their way to Allah." Many of the textiles were returned to Istanbul to become holy relics in the imperial treasury, or they were repurposed as wall hangings or tomb covers for Ottoman royalty in their mausolea.[16] That the known Bab al-Tawba *sitara*s were left whole suggests that after their replacement their special baraka necessitated that they be given to dignitaries or followed the path of other textiles into the royal treasury or into use as tomb covers.[17]

The high quality of workmanship in the Madina *sitara* illustrated what was expected in such a sacred textile. In the 1860s, when seeing the Ka'ba textiles, the Ottoman historian Mustafa Naima was awestruck by the "majestic beauty" of the gold and silver embroidery.[18] Yet the Madina *sitara*, even though it hung in an interior space, was also sufficiently robustly made to have withstood long periods on view (see "Conservation, Materials, and Techniques" below). For most of the nineteenth century, textiles for the hajj were manufactured in Cairo at the Warshat al-Khurunfish (Khurunfish Workshop), established by the Ottoman governor Muhammad 'Ali in 1817.[19] This was, in fact, a complex of workshops that brought together European craftsmen and Egyptian trainees, and the machinery necessary for the production and embellishment of textiles. In addition to machinery, the men made tools for ironworking such as anvils and lathes, and added spinning wheels for producing silk thread and looms for weaving silk and cotton fabrics. There were facilities for dyeing, as well as studios for transfer-

fig. 7 Full-size design for a curtain for a door inside the Ka'ba, painted on paper. Nasser D. Khalili Collection of Islamic Art (MSS 1128.8). Areas to be embroidered in gold are colored yellow and those to be embroidered in silver are blue.

fig. 8 Photograph of Hajj Muhammad Hasan Amin Nada, veteran craftsman at the Warshat al-Khurunfish, Cairo, ca. 1900. In his right hand he holds a spool of metal-wire thread; with his left hand, under the panel he is embroidering, he brings the needle up through the fabric and then back down to couch the metal thread. Nasser D. Khalili Collection of Islamic Art

ring patterns to the fabric and for embroidery. In these studios, craftsmen cut, sewed, lined, and tightly stretched the background cloth on tension tables. They then transferred the designs to the cloth by pouncing and finally executed the labor-intensive and skillful embroidery (figs. 7, 8).[20]

Textile workshops throughout the Ottoman Empire, like the Warshat al-Khurunfish, were affected by the influx of European imports and the introduction of modern techniques and materials. The conventional view has long held that the decline of the Ottoman textile industry was a chronic condition that led to massive unemployment and impoverishment over the course of the nineteenth century. During the flood of European products from the 1820s through the 1850s, many Ottoman industries did indeed decline. Even workshops like the Warshat al-Khurunfish, with its highly specialized production of sacred textiles, retrenched during this period. About 1880, 'Ali Pasha Mubarak, an Ottoman-Egyptian reformer and modernizer, wrote that although the workshop was still functioning it had fallen into disrepair and was making only the *kiswa*.[21] The Warshat al-Khurunfish, however, withstood these challenges, was restructured, recovered, and, like other textile industries, managed to regain its position by the late nineteenth century. Success depended on a number of factors including the adaptation of textile workshops to new materials and technologies coming from Europe.[22] Not all materials were necessarily imported from Europe, however, for although artificial dyes were developed in England and Germany in the 1850s and 1860s, they did not displace the Ottoman dyestuff industry. That industry transformed from a labor-intensive operation, dependent on gathering and preparing vegetable dyes and subject to the vagaries of nature, to a less expensive mechanized industry with dyes that were reliably produced and easier to apply. By the 1870s, the Ottomans were importing synthetic dye-stuffs, but by the end of the nineteenth century they were also producing high-quality alizarin and cheaper but photosensitive aniline dyes, though they were not as fast as European dyes (see "Analysis of Metal Wires and Dyes" below).[23]

Although the history of producing silver and silver-gilt metal wire thread used for embroidering these sacred textiles is well documented from as early as 1540 in Bursa through the mid-eighteenth century in Istanbul, the status of the wire industry in the nineteenth century is not well known.[24] Archival documents from the Warshat al-Khurunfish, however, show that this facility had the capacity to draw and gild the silver wire they used in the embroidery process.[25] Other important industries throughout the nineteenth century included reeling silk and weaving cloth, with workshops employing more than 400,000 people throughout the Ottoman Empire. Silk products from Ottoman factories were particularly desirable after French and Italian cocoons were devastated by the silkworm disease epidemic in 1853. Bursa's silk industry, for example, remained competitive as a result of the establishment of steam-powered spinning mills in the 1840s and 1850s.[26] The disease eventually affected the Ottoman silk industry as well, and led European manufacturers to look for markets in East Asia after the opening of the Suez Canal in 1869, though the Ottoman silk industry recovered after the disease was brought under control.

From 1880 onward the Ottomans more easily adapted to the demands of the world economy and the silk industry expanded with new mills opening in Bursa, Edirne, and Lebanon.

The Warshat al-Khurunfish was part of this late nineteenth-century expansion, with its capacity for spinning, dyeing, and weaving, including special looms for weaving silk cloth.[27] Over the course of the nineteenth century, this process of expansion was uneven, but ultimately workshops such as the Warshat al-Khurunfish were able to continue a long-standing tradition of sacred textile production within the late-Ottoman globalized world.

KMK

CONSERVATION, MATERIALS, AND TECHNIQUES

The Madina *sitara* is a black silk curtain appliquéd with pink and green silk/cotton cartouches that contain Arabic calligraphy (see figs. 1–4). It is further embellished throughout with arabesques and scrolling vines. Text, arabesques, and scrolling vines are embroidered in silver and silver-gilt metal wire thread (see fig. 9a). Sequins adorn the centers of the large rosettes around the border of the *sitara* (fig. 10). The metal-thread embroidery was executed skillfully and meticulously over padding to create a raised effect that was achieved by laying down layers of linen thread over which metal wire was applied by couching. Beneath the areas embroidered with silver-gilt wire thread, orange-colored linen padding thread was used; for the silver areas, white linen padding thread was used. Padding

fig. 9 Photomicrography (10x) of a detail of the obverse and reverse of the *sitara* in fig. 1. The obverse (a) shows embroidery with silver-gilt wire thread couched with orange silk thread in the middle, and with silver wire thread couched with white silk thread above and below. The reverse (b) shows the double back stitch in orange silk threads supporting the silver-gilt wire embroidery and in white silk threads supporting the silver.

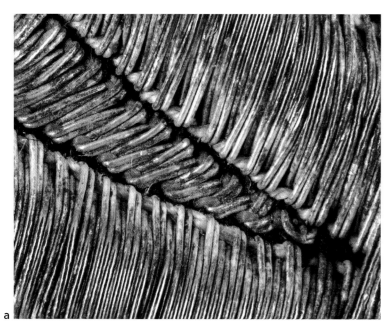

a   b

fig. 10 Sequins that border the centers of the rosettes in the border of the *sitara* in fig. 1

threads are clearly visible on the front of the *sitara* in areas where there is loss of metal thread. On the reverse of the embroidery, there is visual evidence that the bundles of padding threads were carried over from one motif to the next, a clear footprint of the original workmanship (see fig. 11). This also indicates that the padding threads penetrated the ground fabric from obverse to reverse and vice versa. In contrast, the metal wire was simply couched to the surface of the background fabric, not carried to the back where it would be unseen and thus wasted. Precious-metal wire was costly and by this method a significantly smaller amount of it was used. Metal embroidery was often raised this way because it better reflects light, adding a vibrant shimmer to the surface of the panel. This would have been even more dramatic and opulent when the *sitara* was first produced, at the end of the nineteenth century, before oxidation and corrosion marred the original sheen of the wire.

The metal thread was couched with silk thread, orange for the silver-gilt wire and white for the silver wire.[28] On the back, the couching appears in herringbone stitch, but on the front the metal thread is held in place at the edges of the motif with double back stitches (fig. 9a).[29] This stitch was used because of its strength and stability, as seen on the reverse where interlacing silk threads support the metal wires (fig. 9b).

The *sitara*, which weighs about 25 pounds, is composed of four layers of fabric (described here from the front toward the back), needed to support the heavy metal wire. The embroidery was executed through the black silk background fabric and a layer of white cotton muslin. The next layer is an additional lining of white cotton fabric coated with white pigment on the outer side, attached to the back with webbing around the edges. The final layer, the back of the *sitara*, is a green fabric, a color that was traditionally used to line *sitara*s. That this same fabric was also used for the green cartouches confirms that the green lining is original to the Madina *sitara*, not a later addition. The curtain was designed to be hung on the Bab al-Tawba inside the Ka'ba by five loops: three along the top and two at the bottom corners.

When acquired by the Metropolitan Museum in 2009, the *sitara* was in fragile condition, which has prevented its display. Though it was strong structurally because of its multilayered composition, its decoration, both the metal-thread embroidery and the appliquéd cartouches, was damaged and weakened, requiring considerable conservation. Textiles made of precious silk fabric with valuable metal-thread embroidery were usually made for religious purposes and for royalty and have therefore been better preserved. Nevertheless

fig. 11 Detail of the reverse of the *sitara* in fig. 1 illustrating the way the orange padding threads, in the middle of the photograph, are carried from one motif to another

fig. 12 A rosette in the border of the *sitara* in fig. 1 before conservation (a) and after conservation (b)

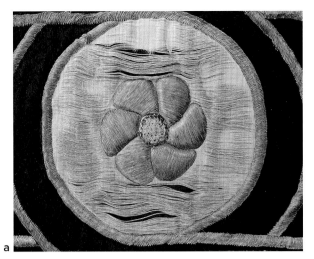

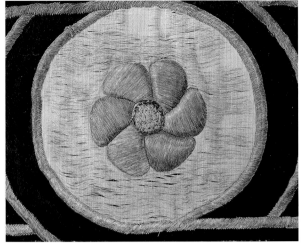

such textiles often endured stresses related to their composition and use: metals corrode and can accelerate the aging process of textiles, and the sharp edges of metal wire can damage delicate silk fabric. As for the use of *sitara*s and the other hajj textiles, their considerable significance and status meant that they would have been preserved. However, little is known about the provenance of this *sitara* before it was acquired by Professor Maan Z. Madina in 1988 (see note 1) to explain the damage it incurred.

The most obvious deteriorated areas on the *sitara* are the pink and green fabrics of the appliquéd cartouches and rosettes. These fabrics are composed of thin silk warps and thicker cotton wefts, woven in a warp-faced satin weave.[30] Large areas display loss of warps, leaving behind long weft floats. These fabrics are also extremely faded, as demonstrated by areas uncovered during conservation that had not been exposed to light and thus retained some of their vibrant color.

Treating these fabrics, a priority, involved stabilizing the weft thread floats using conservation couching stitches (fig. 12a, b).[31] The types of dyes on the cartouche fabrics, discussed in "Analysis of Metal Wires and Dyes" below, will help interpret the origin of these fabrics and contribute to our understanding of their deteriorated condition.

The initial stage of the conservation treatment was to separate the layers of fabric making up the *sitara*. The white cotton lining covered in white pigment features a round blue trademark stamp reading "Standish Mayflower Bleach" (see fig. 13). Standish, a town in Lancashire, northwest England, was home to Standish Bleach Works, an industrial mill complex that operated from 1886 until 1998.[32] The presence of this stamp reinforces the date the *sitara* was produced, 1897–98, and the fact that the Cairo workshop imported this lining for the *sitara* from England, illustrating an example of trade relations between the Cairo workshop and England in the late nineteenth century.

During the close inspection and treatment of an object, exciting and unexpected discoveries are often made. Such was the case when a piece of paper annotated in ink, described in "History" above, was found attached to the bottom edge of the *sitara* between the black silk background fabric and its muslin lining (fig. 5a). One area of the note, on which is written سنة ٣١٥ (A.H. 1315/1897–98), was exposed, analyzed, and conserved; the rest of the paper is inaccessible and may contain more writing. An X-radiograph of the area shows a shadow of the full note and its location (fig. 5b).[33] Unfortunately this technique did not show writing, probably because the ink used was carbon based rather than metal based, the latter more likely to be visible using X-ray.[34] Reflected infrared photography was experimented with in an attempt to read the concealed

fig. 13 Standish Mayflower Bleach stamp on the pigment-coated cotton lining of the *sitara* in fig. 1

inscription, but that, too, was unsuccessful.[35] Transmitted visible light infrared photography, which has shown some positive results, may prove successful.[36]

ANALYSIS OF METAL WIRES AND DYES

Insights into the production process of the Madina *sitara* can also be obtained from the scientific study of its constituent materials, such as the metal wires and the dyed threads, that were available to the Cairene workshop. While little is known about the techniques of manufacturing silver-gilt wire thread in the late Ottoman Empire, its production is documented at least until the mid-eighteenth century in Istanbul, and in Cairo in the nineteenth and twentieth centuries.[37] In Europe at the end of the nineteenth century, the manufacture of plain and worked drawn metal wires was fully industrialized, and metallic filaments of different composition were exported worldwide to serve a wide variety of applications. In *A Treatise upon Wire, Its Manufacture and Uses*, published in 1891, silver and silver-gilt wire are said to be "chiefly used for filigree, embroidery, and decorative work, as well as for some scientific instruments."[38] Belgium, Great Britain, France, and Germany are often cited as the leading producers of such wires.

Four wires from the *sitara*, one silver and three silver-gilt, were analyzed. One of the gilt-wire samples was taken from an area of embroidery hidden among the layers of padding threads. A single lacquered metal sequin was collected from the center of one of the large rosettes around the border. The wires and the sequin were first examined under a stereomicroscope, later mounted on carbon stubs and analyzed by scanning electron microscopy (SEM) and energy dispersive spectroscopy (EDS).[39] Fragments of the silver-gilt wires, the silver wire, and the sequin were also embedded in epoxy resin, cross sectioned, and investigated by SEM coupled with energy and dispersive X-ray spectroscopy (EDS-WDS) and electron backscattered diffraction analysis (EBSD).[40]

The wires all show clear signs of the drawing process used in their manufacture in the form of continuous parallel marks along the length of the wire (figs. 14, 15a). Die marks occasionally scratched the gilding of the silver-gilt wire and exposed the metal beneath (fig. 14a), which indicates that the wire was drawn after the gold was applied, most likely to a preliminary silver rod of a diameter larger than the final product.[41]

In cross section, the four wires that were tested appear very similar in diameter and shape (fig. 14). They all have an approximately circular section and a diameter of 230–240 micrometers. This size is very similar to British Standard Wire Gauge (SWG) number 34 of 0.0092 inch; the Standard Wire Gauge is a legal standard introduced in Great Britain in 1883.[42]

fig. 14 Backscattered electron (BSE) images of the surfaces and cross sections of the three typologies of wires tested: (a) silver-gilt wire with traces of copper; (b) silver-gilt wire with traces of lead and copper; and (c) the ungilded silver wire. The width of the top three images measures 600 μm; the width of the bottom three images measures about 350 μm.

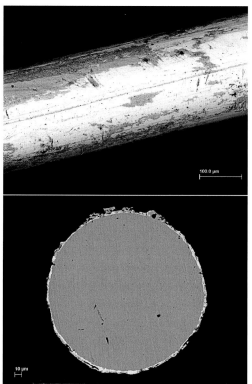
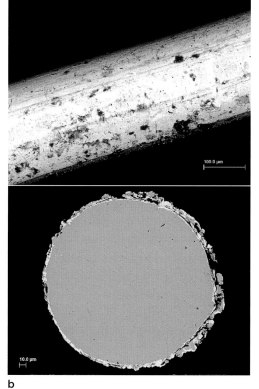
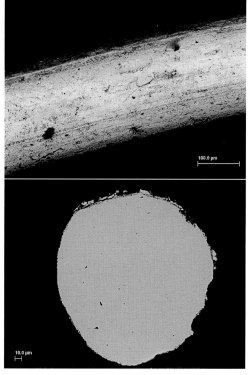

a

b

c

KERN / ROSENFIELD / CARÒ / SHIBAYAMA 83

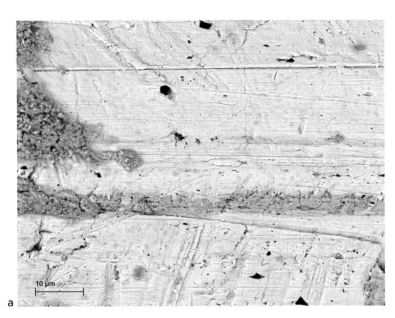
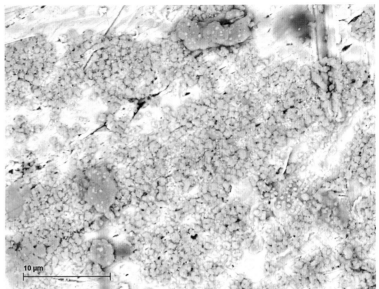

fig. 15 Backscattered electron (BSE) images of the surfaces of wires, showing (a) die marks and corrosion products on the surface of the silver-gilt wire in fig. 14a; and (b) abundant silver chlorides on the surface of the silver-gilt wire, in fig. 14b that was concealed behind the embossed embroidery

fig. 16 Backscattered electron (BSE) image of the cross section of the silver-gilt wire with traces of lead and copper, showing uneven gold thickness and metal fines

Close observation of the wire surfaces in cross section reveals the presence of abundant metal fragments (fines) resulting from a combination of abrasive and adhesive wear,[43] which are limited to the sides of the wire with thinner gilding (fig. 16). These deformed metal flakes are both silver and silver-gilt, supporting the fact that the wires were drawn after gilding.

The wires and the sequin are all made of fine silver alloy,[44] containing trace amounts of copper and lead. Similar drawn silver-gilt wires with slightly higher copper content (up to 1% in weight) and variable sizes have been identified in five sixteenth- to nineteenth-century embroidered Ka'ba curtains in the Topkapı Palace Museum.[45] The slightly different composition and characteristic inclusions of the Madina *sitara*'s wires suggest that they were created from at least three different batches of silver of high purity.

The gilding thickness of each wire is extremely variable, from approximately 500 nanometers to 5.3 micrometers. There is no clear evidence of the gilding technique that was used, but the absence of elements other than gold and silver, the interdiffusion of gold and the underlying silver, and the considerable gilding thickness might indicate that a gold foil or leaf was attached to the silver rod, possibly by heating.[46]

An EBSD orientation map of a longitudinal cross section of the wire shows equi-axed grains and no preferred crystallographic orientation (fig. 17), a microstructure consistent with a final annealing treatment applied after the wire was drawn.[47] Annealing of silver wire was commonly done multiple times at intermediate stages of the manufacture,[48] and was necessary to restore the ductility of the metal to be drawn and to reduce the brittleness of the final product.

The sequin, measuring about 4.9 millimeters in diameter, was punched from a sheet of almost pure silver,[49] and the central hole, about 0.8 millimeter in diameter, was pierced at the same time. Before punching, the silver sheet was coated with an organic colored layer, as testified by the circular mark on the red layer of the pierced metal (fig. 18). Fourier transform infrared micro-spectroscopy (FTIR) of the sequin substrate identified proteinaceous matter consistent with the use of gelatin,[50] which was stained in red with eosin, as identified by EDS and HPLC (high performance liquid chromatography) analysis.[51] SEM investigation shows how corrosion products, consisting of silver chloride and sulfide crystals up to a few microns in size, are

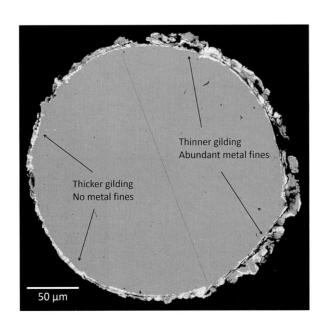

Thinner gilding
Abundant metal fines

Thicker gilding
No metal fines

50 μm

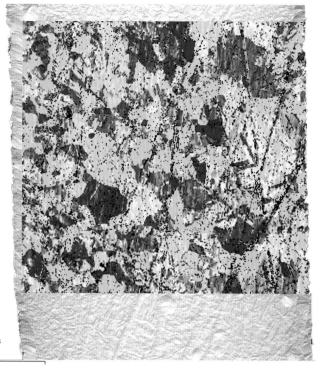

fig. 17 Inverse pole figure map of a longitudinal section of the ungilded silver wire, showing microstructure and crystallographic orientation of grains in respect to the transverse direction. The black points in the color map are unsolved points, which are mostly concentrated along major surface scratches that were not removed by ion milling.

limited in gilded wires to clusters of elongated islands parallel to the wire axis and tend to concentrate in the die marks (figs. 14, 15).

The characteristics of the *sitara*'s wires are consistent with late nineteenth- to early twentieth-century technical descriptions of wire making found in European and American treatises. The specific size of

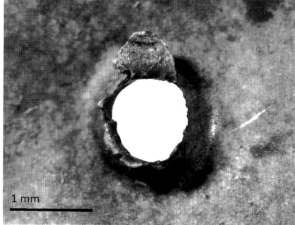

fig. 18 Front and back of the sampled sequin, with a detail of the pierced hole

the wires suggests that they were drawn according to the British standard introduced at the end of the nineteenth century. The millesimal fineness of the *sitara*'s silver wires (close to 999) is particularly high when compared with other standard productions of the time and is consistent with the values documented in the archival record of the Warshat al-Khurunfish.[52] This last result suggests that the wires were produced in the Cairene workshop.

Dyes used on the various yarns and the colorant used on the red sequins of the *sitara* were analyzed by high performance liquid chromatography–photodiode array detection (HPLC–PDA).[53] The summary of this analysis is found in the table in the Appendix.[54] Those dyes are primarily early synthetic organic dyes, developed in the second half of the nineteenth century. More than one type of dye was used on several of the yarns. Indigo, a main colorant of indigo dye, was detected on the black background fabric. Whether the indigo was from a plant source or was synthesized has not been determined. Synthetic indigo was available on a commercial scale from 1897 from a German chemical company, BASF.[55] Therefore, based on the date of the *sitara*, 1897–98, the indigo used on the background fabric could be either synthetic or natural indigo. The same types of dyes were used on both the warps and the wefts of each appliquéd cartouche, with an additional dye that was used only on the warps (see the table in the Appendix). The extra dye for the warps of the pink cartouche tested, eosin Y, and for the warps of the green cartouche tested, diamond green B, may have been added because of the weaving structure of the cartouches, in which the warps are more visible than the concealed wefts (see "Conservation, Materials, and Techniques" above). That the same types of dyes were found in the warps and wefts of each cartouche and that the extra dyes were added to the more visible warps may suggest that the choice of dyes was deliberate and was part of the dyeing process used on the *sitara*. This may indicate that dyeing of yarns for the *sitara* was planned as a part of the production process.

Ellagic acid was detected on both the silk warps and the cotton wefts of the cartouches, but not on the other yarns. Ellagic acid is derived from hydrolysable tannins found in various plants,[56] so plant extracts containing hydrolysable tannins were likely to have been used on the yarns along with the early synthetic dyes.

The tannins on the silk warps were probably used for weighting,[57] as well as to improve the strength and the drape of the silk.[58] Since the Middle Ages, perhaps even earlier, tannin has been considered an agent used for weighting, and weighting with tannin alone is known not to damage silk.[59] Tannin-containing plants used for tanning fibers include gall nuts, sumac, and myrobalans.[60] Weighting using metal salts instead of tannins, in particular weighting with tin, began at the end of the nineteenth century, although it was soon found that tin-weighted silk would rapidly deteriorate.[61] Other mineral salts for weighting, such as lead acetate and zinc, were also used but to a lesser extent.[62] Elements of warps and wefts from the *sitara* were analyzed by SEM-EDS.[63] However, tin, the most used metal for weighting silk, was not detected on the silk warps. In addition, the use of other, lesser used metal elements known as weighting agents at that time appears to be unlikely, suggesting that the silk was probably weighted with tannins alone. In terms of tannins that were found on cotton wefts, they were probably used as mordant in order to fix dyes.[64] It is known that a tannin mordant was applied to cotton prior to its dyeing with basic dyes, the same ones that were used on the cotton wefts.[65]

Qualities of lightfastness and wash fastness of most early synthetic dyes are known to be poor, in particular those basic dyes that were used on the cartouches, although the fastness depends on the individual or class of dye, depth of shade, and substrates.[66] Indigo dye, used on the black background fabric, is known to be relatively fast to both light and washing.[67] The cartouches' current shades of pink, green, and yellow are most likely the colors that have faded to some extent.

Dyes used on the *sitara* appear to reflect the period when early synthetic organic dyes had become more popular than natural dyes because of their bright color, ease of application, and low cost.[68] Those early synthetic dyes were discovered in England and Germany in the mid-nineteenth century and then mass-produced and exported to the rest of the world,[69] indicating the influence of the globalized dye market on the *sitara*. However, the silks seem to have been weighted with tannins alone, a rather traditional technique, at a time when most European silks were weighted with tin salts.[70]

FC AND NS

CONCLUSION

This analysis of the Madina *sitara*, which once hung on the Bab al-Tawba (Door of Repentance) inside the Ka'ba in Mecca, examines it as an object of centuries-old religious symbolism and political memorialization as well as an object of material culture in the globalized world of the late nineteenth century. The information gathered during the *sitara*'s conservation and the

scientific analysis of metals and dyes used in its production are consistent with scholarship on the late nineteenth-century economic history of the Ottoman Empire, where textile workshops were forced to reorganize after the onslaught of European imports, and to update their production methods with the latest materials and techniques. The artisans in the Warshat al-Khurunfish in Cairo, which specialized in producing textiles for the Ka'ba, utilized machinery and materials borrowed from or influenced by up-to-date manufacturing techniques. The choice of materials that went into the Madina *sitara* demonstrates the importance of the international market in the production of this sacred object: the precious-metal wires were drawn according to current technology, using high-purity silver alloy, while the yarns woven into fabrics were colored using the latest innovative synthetic organic dyes. Conservation was aided by the scientific analysis that revealed deterioration of the fabric elements and embroidery threads in relation to their proximity to the corroded silver wire. The colors of the pink and green cartouches had faded because of the inherently unstable nature of early synthetic organic dyes. The background fabric, dyed with the naturally more stable indigo, remained closer to its originally vibrant color.

The discovery during conservation of the dated note sewn among layers of the *sitara* was serendipitous, and more comprehensive analysis of the note is planned. Further, discovering the trademark stamp on one of the linings established a direct connection between the Cairo workshop and an industrial bleach mill in northwest England, a relationship based on the cotton trade between Egypt and England that has long been recognized in the historical record. The Metropolitan Museum's *sitara* is thus representative of late nineteenth-century global interactions involved in its production as well as an object that illustrates the extraordinary work of artisans carrying on a centuries-long tradition of embroidering inscriptions in precious-metal wire thread that convey the themes and messages most sacred to the religion of Islam.

ACKNOWLEDGMENTS

The authors extend their appreciation to Sheila Canby, Patti Cadby Birch Curator in Charge, and Marilyn Jenkins-Madina, curator emerita, Department of Islamic Art at the Metropolitan Museum; Richard M. Keresey, senior vice president, Antiquities Department, Sotheby's; Nahla Nassar, curator and registrar, Nasser D. Khalili Collection of Islamic Art; Janina Poskrobko, acting conservator in charge, and Florica Zaharia, conservator emerita, Department of Textile Conservation at the Metropolitan Museum. In addition, they thank Angela Campbell, Caterina Cappuccini, Cristina Carr, Minsun Hwang, Laura Peluso, Adriana Rizzo, Ruth Rosenthal, Marina Ruiz Molina, and Midori Sato.

KAREN M. KERN
Associate Professor of Ottoman and Modern Middle East History, Department of History, Hunter College, The City University of New York

YAEL ROSENFIELD
Associate Conservator, Department of Textile Conservation, The Metropolitan Museum of Art

FEDERICO CARÒ
Associate Research Scientist, Department of Scientific Research, The Metropolitan Museum of Art

NOBUKO SHIBAYAMA
Research Scientist, Department of Scientific Research, The Metropolitan Museum of Art

APPENDIX

High-performance liquid chromatography–photodiode array detection (HPLC–PDA) analysis of dyes on some fabrics and threads used in making the Madina *sitara*

TESTED FABRICS AND THREADS IN THE *SITARA*		COLOR	MATERIAL	SUGGESTED MAJOR DYES AND AUXILIARY AGENTS	COLOUR INDEX (C.I.) GENERIC NAME OF THE DYE AND ITS YEAR OF DISCOVERY
Pink cartouche	Warp	Pink	Silk	Safranine T	C.I. Basic Red 2, 1859-
				Eosin Y	C.I. Acid Red 87, 1871-
				New Fuchsin	C.I. Basic Violet 2, 1889-
				Tannins	
	Weft	Pink	Cotton	Safranine T	C.I. Basic Red 2, 1859-
				New Fuchsin	C.I. Basic Violet 2, 1889-
				Tannins	
Green cartouche	Warp	Green	Silk	Diamond Green B	C.I. Basic Green 4, 1877-
				Thioflavin T	C.I. Basic Yellow 1, 1888-
				Quinoline yellow	C.I. Acid Yellow 3, 1882-
				Tannins	
				A small amount of natural yellow dye (flavonoid dye)	
	Weft	Yellow	Cotton	Thioflavin T	C.I. Basic Yellow 1, 1888-
				Quinoline yellow	C.I. Acid Yellow 3, 1882-
				Tannins	
Padding under the metal-thread embroidery		Orange	Bast fibers	Orange II	C.I. Acid Orange 7, 1876-
Sewing thread		Orange	Silk	Orange II	C.I. Acid Orange 7, 1876-
				Metanil yellow	C.I. Acid Yellow 36, 1879-
Background fabric		Black	Silk	Indigo	
Sequin		Red		Eosin Y	C.I. Acid Red 87, 1871-

NOTES

1 Professor Madina was a well-known collector and benefactor. At a Sotheby's auction in New York in 1988, he acquired a textile identified in the catalogue (lot 284) as a late eighteenth- to early nineteenth-century Mughal tomb covering. Knowing that it was misidentified, he assigned one of his graduate students, this author, to identify the textile, and she discovered that it was a *sitara* that had hung on the Bab al-Tawba. Professor Madina later donated the *sitara* to the Metropolitan Museum in memory of his mother, Najiyya Khanum al-Kurdi.

2 See, for example, İpek 2011.

3 The hajj is one of the Five Pillars of Islam. It is obligatory for all Muslims to make the pilgrimage to Mecca at least once in their lifetime, if they are able to physically and financially.

4 Burton (1893) 1964, vol. 2, pp. 207–16.

5 This earliest-known confirmed extant Bab al-Tawba *sitara* is in the Khalili Collection described below; see Porter 2012, p. 258, fig. 196. There is a *sitara* dated earlier, about 1880, that was auctioned in 2003 at Bonhams London (lot 105). This *sitara* was described as a Bab al-Tawba curtain similar to one auctioned at Christie's London in 1999 (lot 21), which was also labeled as having hung on the Bab al-Tawba. Both the Bonhams and Christie's catalogue descriptions cite a *sitara* in the collection of the Tareq Rajab Museum in Kuwait that is dated to the nineteenth century but not designated as a Bab al-Tawba curtain; see Safwat 1997, pp. 114–15. Although these three curtains and the Madina *sitara* are from the period of Sultan 'Abd al-Hamid II, the three differ from the Madina *sitara* iconographically and in choice of Qur'anic text. These three curtains are also significantly smaller in size than the Madina *sitara*, which indicates that further research needs to be conducted to confirm whether they were produced to drape the Bab al-Tawba or were intended to hang elsewhere.

6 *Jali thuluth* script originated with Ibn al-Bawwab (d. 1031), the celebrated medieval calligrapher from Baghdad; Khalili 2006, p. 43.

7 Qur'an 6:54, translation Ali (1934) 1946, vol. 1, pp. 302–3.

8 Stillman and Sanders 2000, p. 536.

9 For the *sitara* in the Topkapı Palace Museum, see Tezcan 1996, pp. 64–65. A dedication to Muhammad Tawfiq Pasha is also inscribed on the *sitara* auctioned at Christie's London 2005, lot 48, dating to 1892–1909.

10 See, for example, the covers for the Shrine of the Prophet Ibrahim (Christie's London 2005, lot 49, and Sotheby's London 2007, lot 41); and the curtain for the tomb of the Prophet Muhammad in Medina (Sotheby's London 2007, lot 40). For other Ka'ba textiles from the Hamidian period, see Bonhams London 2003, lot 105; Christie's London 1999, lot 21; and Safwat 1997, pp. 114–15.

11 Porter 2012, pp. 262–63.

12 For the *sitara* in the Khalili Collection, see ibid., p. 258; for the one in the Topkapı Palace Museum, see Tezcan 1996, pp. 64–65; for the curtain made between 1892 and 1909, see Christie's London 2005, lot 48; and for the one dated by Sotheby's as A.H. [1]321/1903–4, see Sotheby's London 2007, lot 42. Three other *sitara*s, the present locations of which are unknown, are recorded in publications; see Rif'at 1925, vol. 1, p. 264, ill.; Aḥmad 1937, p. 81, ill.; and Gouda 1989, p. 264, ill.

13 Qur'an 42:25, translation Ali (1934) 1946, vol. 2, p. 1313.

14 Qur'an 2:255, translation Ali (1934) 1946, vol. 1, pp. 102–3: "God! There is no god but He,—the Living, the Self-subsisting, Eternal. No slumber can seize Him nor sleep. His are all things in the heavens and on earth. Who is there [who] can intercede in His presence except as He permitteth? He knoweth what (appeareth to His creatures as) Before or After or Behind them.

Nor shall they compass aught of His knowledge except as He willeth. His Throne doth extend over the heavens and the earth, and He feeleth no fatigue in guarding and preserving them. For He is the Most High, the Supreme (in glory)."

15 See, for example, the *burqu'* auctioned at Christie's London 2005, lot 46.

16 İpek 2011, pp. 59–60.

17 Porter 2012, p. 265; Tezcan 2007, pp. 229–30.

18 Cakir, Simsek, and Tezcan 2006, pp. 503, 510n3.

19 The Warshat al-Khurunfish is also known by the name Dar al-Kiswah al-Sharifa, which it received in 1953 and retained until its closing in 1962. In 2011 the Nasser D. Khalili Collection of Islamic Art acquired an important collection of hajj artifacts, including archival material from the Cairo workshop. This collection consists of many objects that shed light on the production process, including photographs of artisans at work, documents, embroidery templates, tools, and raw materials. Yael Rosenfield traveled to London to research *sitara*-related objects in the Khalili Collection and arranged for permission to publish their photographs, and this author would like to thank her for her contribution to this section.

20 Nassar 2013, pp. 175–83.

21 Ibid., p. 176.

22 Quataert 1994, p. 87.

23 Quataert 1993, pp. 30, 32; Quataert 1994, pp. 87–88, 100.

24 Cakir, Simsek, and Tezcan 2006, p. 504.

25 Nassar 2013, p. 176.

26 Quataert 1993, p. 29; Quataert 1994, pp. 87–88, 100.

27 Thompson 1999, pp. 30–34; Nassar 2013, p. 176.

28 The orange silk thread showed extensive signs of deterioration, causing the silver-gilt wire to come loose from the background.

29 The double back stitch, also known as the crossed back stitch, is used mainly for shadow-work embroidery; see Thomas 1989, p. 47. A similar technique can be found in Indian metal embroidery; see Morrell 1994, p. 104, fig. 92, sample i.

30 In this warp-faced satin weave, the cotton wefts are concealed by the silk warps; the fabric thus appears shiny and silk-like. According to Irene Emery (1966, p. 108), satin weave is one of the three basic weave structures (plain, twill, and satin). It is a simple float weave structure, with long floats in one set of elements, in this case the warps. In addition to this weave structure, satin also denotes a smooth lustrous fabric. The black silk ground fabric is also a satin weave.

31 For this couching, we used the thread Gutermann Skala 100% Polyester, 5000 m., which was strong and blended well with the ground fabric.

32 "Mayflower, Standish Conservation Area Appraisal, April 2010," www.wigan.gov.uk/Docs/PDF/Resident/Planning-and-Building -Control/Conservation-areas/April2010MayflowerCAA1199kb .pdf. According to section 3.1, "History: Modern Period," Standish Bleach Works "used the Mayflower ship as their trademark, an allusion to Captain Myles Standish."

33 Cristina Carr, conservator in the Department of Textile Conservation of the Metropolitan Museum, conducted the X-radiography.

34 O'Connor and Brooks 2007, p. 278.

35 Marina Ruiz Molina, associate conservator in the Department of Paper Conservation of the Metropolitan Museum, performed reflected infrared photography and shared her expertise with the process.

36 Thompson and Halliwell 2005.

37 Cakir, Simsek, and Tezcan 2006, p. 504; Nassar 2013, p. 180.

38 Smith 1891, p. 112.

39 Imaging and surface analysis of the wires and the sequin were realized in variable pressure mode at 20kV and 40 Pa, using a FE-SEM Zeiss Σigma HD, equipped with an Oxford Instrument X-MaxN 80 SDD detector.

40 Wires were sectioned both orthogonally and tangentially to the axis. After mechanical polishing with Micro-Mesh® and Buehler® MicroCloth down to ¼ μm, samples were milled with a Hitachi IM400 argon gun, ion mill system, and coated with 12 nm carbon. SEM-EDS analysis was realized in high vacuum mode at 20kV, WDS with an Oxford Instrument Inca Wave spectrometer at 30kV, and EBSD with a Nordlys Nano detector at 20kV. EBSD data were processed with Oxford Instrument Aztec software.

41 Smith 1891, p. 25; Brenni 1930, pp. 14–17. These two texts, from the late nineteenth and the early twentieth century, report that the wire fabrication started with a silver rod of about 35–38 mm in diameter. This was heated before gold leaf was applied and then the two metals were drawn together.

42 Pöll 1999.

43 Abrasive wear and adhesive wear develop during drawing of wires through a die with asperities and from contact with other metal surfaces during the manufacturing process.

44 According to J. Bucknall Smith (1891, p. 11), the silver used for wire making was occasionally above standard purity, such as 992/1000 silver (i.e., 99.2% in weight). In the *sitara*, ungilt wire alloy is approximately 99.7% silver, 0.29% copper, with traces of lead, iron, and zinc about 0.01%, as determined by WDS. Iron and zinc are present in diffuse, discrete inclusions of oxides. The gilded wires were drawn from almost pure silver. One wire is 99.87% silver and 0.13% copper, while the other two, one of which is the hidden wire, are approximately 99.89% silver and 0.11% lead, with traces of copper below 0.02%. Discrete inclusions of lead with traces of gold and the mineral altaite, a lead telluride, were identified by EDS and EBSD in the latter two wires.

45 Cakir, Simsek, and Tezcan 2006.

46 Lechtman 1971.

47 Cho et al. 2006.

48 Smith 1891, p. 114.

49 The sequin is approximately 99.91% silver, with traces of copper about 0.09%, as determined by WDS.

50 FTIR was performed by Caterina Cappuccini and Adriana Rizzo, using a Hyperion 3000 Microscope interfaced to a Tensor 27 (Bruker Optics), equipped with a 15x FTIR objective and a MCT detector (mercury cadmium telluride), liquid nitrogen cooled. The FTIR spectra were acquired as 64 scans in the range of 4000 to 600 cm⁻¹ and 4 cm⁻¹ resolution.

51 EDS analysis identified the presence of bromine, while HPLC analysis identified eosin Y, an organic colorant having bromine in its structure.

52 Nassar 2013, p. 180.

53 Small yarn samples were taken from the textile, extracted with a mixture of 0.01 M aqueous oxalic acid, pyridine, and methanol (3/3/4, v/v/v) assisted with heat; the extract was dried in a vacuum desiccator. The residue was dissolved in a mixture of methanol and 1% aqueous formic acid (1/1, v/v). The solution was centrifuged; the supernatant was injected into the HPLC system. The analytical system used consisted of a 1525μ binary HPLC pump, 2996 PDA detector, 1500 series column heater, in-line degasser, and a Rheodyne 7725i manual injector with 20 μl loop (Waters Corporation, Milford, Mass.). An Xterra RP18 (3.5 μm-particle, 2.1 mm I.D. x 150.0 mm) reversed-phase column was used with a guard column (Xterra RP18 3.5 μm-particle, 2.0 mm I.D. x 10.0 mm) (Waters Corporation, Milford) with a flow rate of 0.2 ml/min. The column pre-filter (Upchurch Ultra-Low Volume Precolumn Filter with 0.5 μm stainless steel frit, Sigma-Aldrich, Saint Louis, Mo.) was attached in front of the guard column. Column temperature was 40° C. The mobile phase was eluted in a gradient mode of 1% formic acid in de-ionized water (v/v) (A) and methanol (B). The gradient system was 90% (A) for 3 min → to 60% (A) in 7 min. in a linear slope → to 0% (A) in 24 min. in a linear slope, and then back to 90% (A) in 1 min. and held at 90% (A) for 10 min. The operation and data processing software was Empower Pro (2002).

54 Although there were a few color components detected but not identified, they are also likely color components of early synthetic dyes because the UV-visible absorption spectra of the unknown color components were similar to those of the identified components of synthetic dyes. Also, those components do not match any known natural dyes. The Colour Index is a reference database of dyes and pigments, and it lists colorants using dual classification, Colour Index Generic Name and Colour Index Constitution Numbers. The *Colour Index* (1971, vol. 1, pp. 1001, 1607) states that basic dyes are dyes that in aqueous solution yield colored cations and that acid dyes are water-soluble anionic dyes that are applied to nitrogenous fibers such as wool, silk, nylon, and modified acrylic fibers from acid or neutral baths.

55 Balfour-Paul 1998, p. 82.

56 Haslam 1966, pp. 91–92.

57 Tannins are reported to have been used for weighting silk in order to compensate for a weight loss caused by the degumming process; this was for economic reasons because silk was expensive and was sold by weight; Hacke 2008, p. 3; Hofenk de Graaff 2004, p. 336; Matos 1915, p. 41; and Knecht, Rawson, and Loewenthal 1893, vol. 1, pp. 181–83. Raw-silk fibers are composed of two different types of proteinaceous materials: fibroin (the structural core) and sericin (the gum that coats fibroin). Sericin is removed by the degumming process in order to separate fibroin filaments and to make the silk more lustrous; Hacke 2008, p. 3.

58 Weighted silk is usually heavier with better draping quality; Hacke 2008, p. 3. Also, it is said that tanning strengthens the silk fibers; Bogle 1979, p. 4; Matos 1915, p. 41; Knecht, Rawson, and Loewenthal 1893, vol. 1, p. 181.

59 Hacke 2008, p. 4; Bogle 1979, p. 4.

60 Knecht, Rawson, and Loewenthal 1893, vol. 1, pp. 181–83, Matos 1915, p. 41.

61 Hacke 2008, p. 7; Bogle 1979, pp. 5–6.

62 Hacke 2008, p. 6.

63 The SEM-EDS analysis was performed using the same instrument and experimental conditions reported in note 39 above. EDS analysis of several selected yarns from the *sitara* identified various metal elements. Traces of Na, Mg, Al, Si, S, Cl, K, Ca, and Fe were detected in most of the samples. In some cases, specific elements were detected in discrete particles found at the surface of the threads, such as Cr in the pink warp, Pb in the yellow and pink wefts, as well as in the white weft lining. These findings are perplexing because dyeing manuals instructed that those basic and acid dyes were to be applied to silk directly without metal salts, and applied to cotton with either tannins or metal salts of aluminum or tin; *Colour Index* 1971, vol. 1, pp. 1001, 1607–9; Knecht, Rawson, and Loewenthal 1893, vol. 2, pp. 451–55, 456, 505–6, 509. Considering the complex history of the *sitara*, it is

challenging to interpret such findings and exclude unintentional contamination by the manufacturing process or airborne particulates or from manipulation of the textile before it entered the Museum's collection. In a few cases, material intentionally added to the surface of the threads was recognized, such as abundant barite (Ba, S) found in small, dispersed particles on the white weft lining and on the sewing thread; a kaolinitic clay (Al, Si) was found on the sewing thread, together with barite. Often, corrosion products of the metal wires have been found on both warp and weft threads, as well as on the sewing thread, in the form of silver chlorides and sulfides associated with traces of gold.

64 Knecht, Rawson, and Loewenthal 1893, vol. 1, p. 176. While cotton shows little power to retain dyes, cotton attracts tannins from aqueous solutions to form insoluble compounds with dyes.

65 Ibid., vol. 2, pp. 451–55; *Colour Index* 1971, vol. 1, pp. 1607–9.

66 *Colour Index* 1971, vol. 1, pp. 1004, 1017, 1075, 1153, 1607, 1611, 1633, 1649, 1680; Barnett 2007, p. 70. Some metal salts were also spoken of as having been used with tannins in order to improve wash fastness of early synthetic dyes, both on silk and cotton, from the end of the nineteenth century. Those metals were mainly antimony for light shades, and iron or tin for dark and dull shades; Scharff 1999, p. 657; Steelman 1922, p. 662; Matos 1915, p. 42; Knecht, Rawson, and Loewenthal 1893, vol. 2, p. 452. However, those metal elements typically used for light shades, the colors of the colored cartouches, were not detected by SEM-EDS analysis.

67 *Colour Index* 1971, vol. 3, p. 3775; Padfield and Landi 1966, pp. 183–89.

68 Barnett 2007, p. 74.

69 Ponting 1981, pp. 161–71.

70 Hacke 2008, p. 6.

REFERENCES

Aḥmad, Yusuf
1937 *Al-Maḥmal wa-al-ḥajj* (The ceremonial palanquin and the pilgrimage). Al-Qahirah: Maṭbaʻat Ḥijazi.

Ali, Abdullah Yusuf
1946 *The Holy Qurʾan: Text, Translation and Commentary by Abdullah Yusuf Ali*. [3rd ed.] 2 vols. New York: Hafner Publishing Company. First published 1934.

Balfour-Paul, Jenny
1998 *Indigo*. London: British Museum Press.

Barnett, Jennifer C.
2007 "Synthetic Organic Dyes, 1856–1901: An Introductory Literature Review of Their Use and Related Issues in Textile Conservation." *Reviews in Conservation* 8, pp. 67–77.

Bogle, Michael M.
1979 *The Deterioration of Silks through Artificial Weighting*. Textile Conservation Center Notes, 11. North Andover, Mass.: Merrimack Valley Textile Museum.

Bonhams London
2003 *Islamic and Indian Art*. Sale cat., Bonhams London, May 1.

Brenni, Luigi
1930 *L'arte del battiloro e i filati d'oro e d'argento: Cenni storico-tecnici*. Milan: The author.

Burton, Sir Richard F.
1964 *Personal Narrative of a Pilgrimage to Al-Madinah & Meccah*. Edited by Isabel Burton. 2 vols. Reprint of the 1893 memorial ed. New York: Dover.

Cakir, A. F., Gülsu Simsek, and Hülya Tezcan
2006 "Characterisation of Gold Gilt Silver Wires from Five Embroidered Silk Qaaba Curtains Dated between the 16th and 19th Centuries." *Applied Physics A: Materials Science & Processing* 83, no. 4, pp. 503–11.

Cho, Jae-Hyung, K. H. Oh, A. D. Rollett, J.-S. Cho, Y.-J. Park, and J.-T. Moon
2006 "Investigation of Recrystallization and Grain Growth of Copper and Gold Bonding Wires." *Metallurgical and Material Transactions A: Physical Metallurgy and Materials Science* 37, no. 10 (October), pp. 3085–97.

Christie's London
1999 *Islamic, Indian and Armenian Art and Manuscripts*. Sale cat., Christie's London, October 12.
2005 *Islamic Art and Manuscripts*. Sale cat., Christie's London, April 26.

Colour Index
1971 Society of Dyers and Colourists and American Association of Textile Chemists and Colorists. *Colour Index*. Vols. 1, 3. 3rd ed. Bradford, Yorkshire: Society of Dyers and Colourists.

Emery, Irene
1966 *The Primary Structures of Fabrics: An Illustrated Classification*. Washington, D.C.: Textile Museum.

Gouda, Abdulaziz
1989 "Die Kiswa der Kaʻba in Makka." PhD diss., Freie Universität, Berlin.

Hacke, Marei
2008 "Weighted Silk: History, Analysis, and Conservation." *Reviews in Conservation* 9, pp. 3–15.

The Hajj
2013 *The Hajj: Collected Essays*. Edited by Venetia Porter and Liana Saif. London: British Museum.

Haslam, Edwin
1966 *Chemistry of Vegetable Tannins*. London and New York: Academic Press.

Hofenk de Graaff, Judith H.
2004 *The Colourful Past: Origins, Chemistry and Identification of Natural Dyestuffs*. Riggisberg: Abegg-Stiftung; London: Archetype Publications.

İpek, Selin
2011 "Dressing the Prophet: Textiles from the *Haramayn*." *Halı: Carpet, Textile and Islamic Art*, no. 168, pp. 59–61.

Khalili, Nasser D.
2006 *Islamic Art and Culture: A Visual History*. Woodstock and New York: Overlook Press.

Knecht, Edmund, Christopher Rawson, and Richard Loewenthal
1893 *Manual of Dyeing: For the Use of Practical Dyers, Manufacturers, Students, and All Interested in the Art of Dyeing*. 3 vols. London: Charles Griffin and Co.

Lechtman, Heather N.
1971 "Ancient Methods of Gilding Silver: Examples from the Old and New Worlds." In *Science and Archaeology*, edited by Robert H. Brill, pp. 2–30. Fourth Symposium on Archaeological Chemistry, 1968, Atlantic City. Cambridge, Mass.: MIT Press.

Matos, L. J.
1915 "Vegetable Weighting of Silk." *American Silk Journal* 34, no. 12 (December), pp. 41–42.

Morrell, Anne
1994 *The Techniques of Indian Embroidery*. London: Batsford.

Nassar, Nahla
2013 "Dar al-Kiswa al-Sharifa: Administration and Production." In *The Hajj* 2013, pp. 175–83.

O'Connor, Sonia A., and Mary M. Brooks
2007 *X-Radiography of Textiles, Dress and Related Objects*. Oxford: Elsevier Butterworth-Heinemann.

Padfield, Tim, and Sheila Landi
1966 "The Light Fastness of the Natural Dyes." *Studies in Conservation* 11, no. 4, pp. 181–96.

Pöll, J. S.
1999 "The Story of the Gauge." *Anaesthesia* 54, no. 6 (June), pp. 575–81.

Ponting, Kenneth G.
1981 *A Dictionary of Dyes and Dyeing*. London: Bell and Hyman.

Porter, Venetia
2012 "Textiles of Mecca and Medina." In *Hajj: Journey to the Heart of Islam*, edited by Venetia Porter et al., pp. 256–65. Exh. cat. London: British Museum Press.

Quataert, Donald
1993 *Ottoman Manufacturing in the Age of the Industrial Revolution*. Cambridge Middle East Library 30. Cambridge and New York: Cambridge University Press.
1994 "Ottoman Manufacturing in the Nineteenth Century." In *Manufacturing in the Ottoman Empire and Turkey, 1500–1950*, edited by Donald Quataert, pp. 87–121. SUNY Series in the Social and Economic History of the Middle East. Albany: State University of New York Press.

Rifʻat, Hilmizade İbrahim
1925 *Mirʾat al-Ḥaramayn wa al-Riḥlat al-Ḥijaziya wa-al-Ḥajj wa-mashaʻiruhu al-diniya, muḥalla bi-miʾat al-ṣuwar al-shamsiya* (A mirror of the sacred town of Mecca and Medina; a geographic, historic and social account of a journey to the Hidjaz and of the sacred pilgrimage, illustrated by maps, plans and portraits). 2 vols. Al-Qahira: Dar al-Kutub al-Miṣriya.

Safwat, Nabil F.
1997 *The Harmony of Letters: Islamic Calligraphy from the Tareq Rajab Museum*. Singapore: National Heritage Board.

Scharff, Annemette Bruselius

1999 "Synthetic Dyestuffs for Textiles and Their Fastness to Washing." In ICOM Committee for Conservation, *12th Triennial Meeting, Lyon, 29 August–3 September 1999: Preprints*, edited by Janet Bridgland, vol. 2, pp. 654–60. London: James and James.

Smith, J. Bucknall

1891 *A Treatise upon Wire, Its Manufacture and Uses, Embracing Comprehensive Descriptions of the Constructions and Applications of Wire Ropes*. London: Offices of "Engineering"; New York: J. Wiley and Sons.

Sotheby's London

2007 *Arts of the Islamic World Including Fine Carpets and Textiles*. Sale cat., Sotheby's London, October 24.

Sotheby's New York

1988 *Indian, Himalayan and Southeast Asian Art and Indian Miniatures*. Sale cat., Sotheby's New York, March 16–17.

Steelman, James

1922 "Mordants and Mordanting." *Textile Colorist* 44, no. 526 (October), pp. 661–63.

Stillman, Yedida K., and Paula Sanders

2000 "Ṭirāz: Development of the Ṭirāz Institution." In *The Encyclopaedia of Islam*, edited by P. J. Bearman et al., vol. 10, pp. 535–38. New ed. Leiden: Brill.

Tezcan, Hülya

1996 *Astar al-Haramayn al-Sharifayn* (Curtains of the two holy shrines). Edited by Ahmad Mohammad Issa; translated by Tahsin Ömer Tahaoğlu. Istanbul: Research Centre for Islamic History, Art, and Culture; Markaz al-Abhath lil-Tarikh wa-al-Funun wa-al-Thaqafah al-Islamiyah.

2007 "Ka'ba Covers from the Topkapı Palace Collection and Their Inscriptions." In *Word of God, Art of Man: The Qur'an and Its Creative Expressions; Selected Proceedings from the International Colloquium, London, 18–21 October 2003*, edited by Fahmida Suleman, pp. 227–38. Oxford: Oxford University Press in association with the Institute of Ismaili Studies.

Thomas, Mary

1989 *Mary Thomas's Dictionary of Embroidery Stitches*. New ed. by Jan Eaton. New York: Crescent Books. First published 1934.

Thompson, Elizabeth

1999 *Colonial Citizens: Republican Rights, Paternal Privilege, and Gender in French Syria and Lebanon*. New York: Columbia University Press.

Thompson, Karen N., and Michael Halliwell

2005 "An Initial Exploration of the Benefits of Using Transmitted Visible Light and Infrared Photography to Access Information Concealed within Multilayered Textiles." In *Scientific Analysis of Ancient and Historic Textiles: Informing Preservation, Display and Interpretation: Postprints*, edited by Rob Janaway and Paul Wyeth, pp. 177–84. AHRC Research Centre for Textile Conservation and Textile Studies, First Annual Conference, July 13–15, 2004. London: Archetype.

ANNE MONAHAN
ISABELLE DUVERNOIS
SILVIA A. CENTENO

"Working My Thought More Perfectly": Horace Pippin's *The Lady of the Lake*

The first monograph devoted to an African American artist was Selden Rodman's *Horace Pippin: A Negro Painter in America*, published in 1947.[1] Perhaps even more surprising than its lateness is its subject: a self-taught painter from West Chester, Pennsylvania, whose meteoric public career lasted only nine years. Horace Pippin (1888–1946) made his debut in a local art show in 1937, less than a decade after he had started painting, and was soon attracting curators, collectors, critics, and dealers across the country with his depictions of World War I, in which he had been grievously wounded; daily life in and beyond rural Pennsylvania; nature, often domesticated in still lifes and gardens; and heroes of various stripes, including Jesus Christ, John Brown, Abraham Lincoln, Marian Anderson, and Major General Smedley Butler.[2] By the time of his unexpected death, he had more than seventy-five national and international exhibitions to his

fig. 1 Reverse of Horace Pippin (American, 1888–1946). *The Lady of the Lake*, ca. 1936–39. Oil on canvas, 20½ × 36 in. (52.1 × 91.4 cm). The Metropolitan Museum of Art, Bequest of Jane Kendall Gingrich, 1982 (1982.55.1) (fig. 2)

credit, including solo shows in West Chester (1937), Philadelphia (1940, 1941), New York (1940, 1944), Chicago (1941), and San Francisco (1942); the monograph under way; and gallery representation in Philadelphia, New York, and Los Angeles. This attention was part of an interwar fascination with autodidacts, mostly European Americans, who were championed for fusing abstract form and homey subjects.[3] The combination was seen as a gateway to modernism for viewers wary of avant-garde styles and politics, and the artists' life stories resonated with the democratic populism widespread during the Great Depression.

Owing to Pippin's laborious technique and abbreviated career, his oeuvre comprises fewer than 140 burnt-wood panels, paintings, and drawings, which can be divided into those produced before and after 1937, when exhibition and sales records begin.[4] The Metropolitan Museum of Art owns nine works of art by Pippin, having purchased the painting *Victorian Interior II* (1945, 58.26) from Rodman in 1958 and received the rest in a bequest of 1982 from Jane Kendall Gingrich, who had begun assembling her collection in 1943. Then known as Mrs. John D. M. Hamilton and a fixture of the society pages, Gingrich lived near Pippin in Chester

County, entertained him at her impressive home, and acquired his paintings *Asleep* (1943, 1982.55.3), *Self-Portrait II* (1944, 1982.55.7), and *Victorian Interior I* (1945, 1982.55.5) during his lifetime. The group includes one of the African American family scenes for which he is celebrated and one of the floral still lifes, sometimes in elaborate interiors, which he increasingly produced for a voracious market. Pippin also gave Gingrich *The Den* (1945, collection of halley k. harrisburg and Michael Rosenfeld, New York), which she omitted from the bequest. After the artist's death, Gingrich, perhaps inspired by her own art making and patronage, assembled a parallel collection centered on his creative process.[5] That set includes the preparatory drawing *After Supper* (ca. 1935, 1982.55.8); the unfinished paintings *Family Supper* (1946, 1982.55.4), *Chairs* (1946, 1982.55.6), and *Holy Mountain IV* (1946, 1982.55.2); and the early composition *The Lady of the Lake* (ca. 1936–39, fig. 2), the initial elements of which can be seen on the reverse, where the paint soaked through the unprimed canvas (fig. 1). That original design is one of two thus far identified in Pippin's oeuvre; the other, *The Getaway* (1939, figs. 3, 4), was published by Rodman as a "preliminary study" and "sketch on the back of the Canvas."[6]

fig. 2 Horace Pippin (American, 1888–1946). *The Lady of the Lake*, ca. 1936–39. Oil on canvas, 20½ × 36 in. (52.1 × 91.4 cm). The Metropolitan Museum of Art, Bequest of Jane Kendall Gingrich, 1982 (1982.55.1)

The reverse of *The Lady of the Lake* casts new light on an image that has long puzzled art historians.[7] The composition is an ambitious and fairly large one for Pippin, whose combat injury restricted his right arm's range of motion. As his only nude, it depicts a lighter-skinned, brunette woman reclining on a patterned blanket in a quirky, waterside garden. A log cabin and canoe sit to the left, mountains fill the horizon, and long shadows indicate either early morning or late afternoon. Rodman surmised that the image had been "suggested if not copied direct from insurance calendars," and Lynda Roscoe Hartigan and Jacqueline Francis have perceived a debt to the widely reproduced nudes in nature by Maxfield Parrish (1870–1966), but specific quotations have yet to be identified.[8] Likewise, Hartigan and Francis posit a connection to Walter Scott's poem "The Lady of the Lake" (1810), set in sixteenth-century Scotland, and the silent film it inspired in 1928. The poem accords with the painting insofar as Scott's titular heroine is a raven-haired beauty who boats on a lake and lives in a log house with a "rustic bower"; however, Pippin's passive figure, curious plant stands, and vaguely Native American blanket and canoe are difficult to square with a narrative dedicated to a heroic Highland

lass.[9] As Francis notes, that discrepancy was not lost on the painting's original audience, judging from an early review describing the canvas as "somehow more American Indian than Sir Walter Scottish in atmosphere and makeup."[10] In 1942 the painting acquired the subtitle *The Sunbath*, confusing matters further.[11]

The position of *The Lady of the Lake* in Pippin's chronology has also proved troublesome, as have the dates of much of his early work.[12] The catalogue for his 1941 solo show at the Arts Club of Chicago dates the painting to 1936, which Rodman later adopted in his monograph. A newly discovered checklist for Pippin's 1942 exhibition at the San Francisco Museum of Art dates the painting to 1939.[13] The artist's dealer and agent, Robert Carlen, supplied the cataloguing data for both shows, and it is unclear if the later date is a correction or mistake. Those three years are significant. In 1936 Pippin was working in relative obscurity, showing and selling his art informally to friends and neighbors. By 1939 he had been cultivating relationships with local art mavens for a few years, and those friendships seem to have influenced his work.[14] Whatever Carlen's intentions, the year 1939 better fits the painting's exhibition history, which began in January 1940 with Pippin's first

fig. 3 Horace Pippin. *The Getaway*, 1939. Oil on canvas, 24 ⅝ × 36 in. (62.5 × 91.4 cm). Philadelphia Museum of Art, Bequest of Daniel W. Dietrich II (2016-3-3)

fig. 4 Reverse of *The Getaway* (fig. 3)

solo show at Carlen's gallery in Philadelphia.[15] Were *The Lady of the Lake* ready in 1936, it might have turned up in one of the local shows in which Pippin took part in the late 1930s or among the works he shipped to the New York dealer Hudson Walker in 1939.[16]

The Lady of the Lake invites the kind of technical art history study—a combination of visual, scientific, and archival analyses—that is rarely accorded the work of self-taught artists. Building on Mark Bockrath and Barbara Buckley's pioneering 1993 survey of Pippin's materials and techniques, we shift the interpretative frame from Scott's poem to argue that *The Lady of the Lake* indexes Pippin's mounting ambition in the late 1930s, when he engaged and experimented with aesthetic conventions informing the art alongside which his own was increasingly exhibited. The resulting study opens the discursive horizon for *The Lady of the Lake* in particular and for Pippin's sometimes recondite imagery in general; challenges the primacy of texts, including his titles and oft-quoted statements, in interpretations of his art; and complicates assumptions about the relation of art's margin and mainstream for him and his peers.[17]

Pippin's statements began in earnest in 1938, when he introduced himself to a national audience via the exhibition and catalogue *Masters of Popular Painting: Modern Primitives of Europe and America* at the Museum of Modern Art (MoMA), New York. The show included four of his paintings, and Dorothy Miller's catalogue entry quoted at length from a statement he had supplied:

> *How I Paint.* . . . The colors are very simple such as brown, amber, yellow, black, white, and green. The pictures which I have already painted come to me in my mind, and if to me it is a worth while [*sic*] picture, I paint it. I go over that picture in my mind several times and when I am ready to paint it I have all the details that I need. I take my time and examine every coat of paint carefully and to be sure that the exact color which I have in mind is satisfactory to me. Then I work my foreground from the background. That throws the background away from the foreground. In other words bringing out my work. The time it takes to make a picture depends on the nature of the picture. For instance the picture called *The Ending of the War, Starting Home* [*sic*] which was my first picture. On that picture I couldn't do what I really wanted to do, but my next pictures I am working my thought more perfectly. . . . To me it seems impossible for another to teach one of Art.[18]

In a 1941 interview, Pippin distilled that explanation as "pictures come to my mind." He continued,

"I think my pictures out with my brain and then I tell my heart to go ahead."[19] By 1944, critics like Rosamund Frost of *Art News* were relaying the message:

> Pippin's style is simply the result of an inner vision of burning intensity. Lack of teaching has less to do with it than a determination to come as close to that vision as possible.
>
> To attain this end Pippin will take unlimited pains, firmly convinced that he is copying the world exactly as it is. When an ultra-sensitive sense of tone and placement tell him that an object or a color doesn't "set" in the picture, he paints it over, building up the pigment to the thickness of impasto—a kind of triumph of the trial and error system.[20]

His fellow painters later recalled conversations that emphasized this realism. Romare Bearden remembered, "what impressed me most though was . . . especially how positive he was that his paintings were completely realistic."[21] Edward Loper reported, "He said, 'Ed, you know why I'm great? . . . Because I paint things exactly the way they are. . . . I don't do what these white guys do. I don't go around here making up a whole lot of stuff. I paint it exactly the way it is and exactly the way I see it.'"[22]

Coupled with long-standing preconceptions about autodidacts' guileless transparency, such comments have engendered a sense of Pippin's work as an unmediated transcription of a fully realized vision, be it imagined or observed, and one that is immune to the influence of the academic tradition. That impression has been reinforced by the rarity of preparatory studies like *After Supper* (fig. 5) and affirmed in the titles of his retrospectives: "Horace Pippin: The Way I See It," at the Brandywine River Museum of Art, Chadds Ford, Pennsylvania (2015), and "I Tell My Heart: The Art of Horace Pippin," which finished its national tour at the Metropolitan Museum (1995).[23] By demonstrating how comprehensively Pippin reconceptualized his work in progress—changes that go far beyond just replacing an object or color—*The Lady of the Lake*, like *The Getaway*, evinces a gap between his rhetoric and practice that makes space for new perspectives on his project.

The Lady of the Lake evolved from a composition that analogizes woman to nature in an organic arrangement of extended horizontals and sweeping curves to one that domesticates woman *and* nature in a more symmetrical, static, and staged design. On the verso the black-haired nude reclines at twilight on a bare, brown shore, silhouetted against dark blue water that reflects

fig. 5 Horace Pippin. *After Supper*, ca. 1935. Graphite on cardboard, 14 × 22⅛ in. (35.6 × 56.2 cm). The Metropolitan Museum of Art, Bequest of Jane Kendall Gingrich, 1982 (1982.55.8)

fig. 6 Horace Pippin. *After Supper*, ca. 1935. Oil on fabric, 19 × 23½ in. (48.3 × 59.7 cm). Collection of Leon Hecht and Robert Pincus-Witten, New York

a dark blue sky, with rolling green hills in the distance. On the recto every element but the nude's body is transformed, along with the image's implicit narrative. The same figure, now in broad daylight, acquires trappings of civilization that include a cabin, canoe, blanket, lawn, garden, and a modern hairstyle in a lighter color. The lighter sky, sparkling white water, and shadows cast across the foreground are in keeping with the new time of day. The far shoreline disappears under a higher waterline, the hills grow into stark mountains, and tall evergreens frame the composition like a proscenium.

The final painting's bright palette, especially its red punctuations, marks another departure from the initial version and Pippin's work to date, which Rodman noted "had not yet used color with any more ambitious intent than to pick out the tongue of a buffalo, a wound, or a rusty leaf."[24] The revisions for *The Getaway* are fewer but similarly significant, as they shift the painting's tone and narrative from static to dynamic: the standing gray canid (a wolf? dog? fox?) morphs into a red fox making off with a crow in its mouth, as the red barn fades to dark gray.[25] The pair of paintings makes plain that Pippin was, at least occasionally, less interested in realizing preconceived compositions than in experimenting with imagery, themes, narratives, and solutions at the easel. The drawing for *After Supper* (fig. 5) does likewise in its erasures (which do not register in reproduction) and distance from the finished painting.

———

To understand how Pippin developed and altered his picture, we examined it in normal and raking light and in comparison with his other work of the 1930s and with X-radiography, infrared reflectography (IRR), X-ray fluorescence (XRF) imaging, and Raman spectroscopy.[26] He painted *The Lady of the Lake* on a medium-weight, two-over-one basket-weave cotton canvas.[27] Bockrath and Buckley identified a similar support in four paintings; in at least three, including *The Lady of the Lake*, the canvas was not primed with a ground layer.[28] Of those, only *The Lady of the Lake* has retained its original strainer, which does not appear to be a commercial product. It is made of spruce wood and crudely constructed, with four unusually thick and rough-cut wood members devoid of beveled edges and butt-jointed with plain joint fasteners. The artist could have made the strainer with available, local wood.[29] It is unclear how often Pippin made his own strainers because most of his early paintings have been restretched for conservation purposes. By 1940,

fig. 7 Horace Pippin. *Holy Mountain IV*, 1946. Oil on canvas, 26 × 36 in. (66 × 91.4 cm). The Metropolitan Museum of Art, Bequest of Jane Kendall Gingrich, 1982 (1982.55.2)

fig. 8 X-radiograph of *The Lady of the Lake* (fig. 2). The presence of the stretcher is digitally reduced for clarity.

he had switched to commercial stretchers, canvases, and canvas boards.

Pippin typically started a painting by outlining, first in pencil, then black paint, a technique also seen in unfinished canvases in the Gingrich bequest such as *Holy Mountain IV* (fig. 7). Infrared examination did not reveal any pencil outlines in *The Lady of the Lake*; however, painted outlines of his original composition are clearly visible on the canvas's reverse, where the paint penetrated the unprimed fabric.[30] Microscopic examination revealed that he mostly used two colors: the foreground figure in dark blue, the middle-ground riverbank in dark blue and black (used separately), and the hills and far riverbank in black. That variety may indicate that the outline colors in the initial design relate to an element's depth in the pictorial field. On the recto outlines of the rolling hills and middle-ground riverbank are visible as a combination of thick, scoring marks and ridges wholly unrelated to the finished composition.

Pippin filled in his initial outlines using a restricted palette typical of his work prior to 1937. Visual and microscopic examination of the canvas's reverse indicates that his preliminary color scheme largely follows the list in the statement he gave MoMA: earth colors such as ocher and umber, black, white, and dark green—plus lots of blue, which he had been using since the early 1930s.[31] The blues visible on the reverse are Prussian blue, either pure or modulated with white.[32] Initially, the water was painted with a combination of

blue and earth-colored pigments, and the sky was constructed as alternating, irregular strips of dark blue and turquoise that follow the hills' curving topline. The overall tonality of the image suggests twilight, much as the gray cast in *After Supper* (fig. 6) suggests dusk, extending the artist's interest in times of day; moreover, that painting's elongated clouds resemble the banded sky of *The Lady of the Lake*.

Pippin produced *The Lady of the Lake* in a set of painting campaigns of uncertain sequence and duration, but the paint layers offer some clues. For example, one can identify the canoe as a very late addition because it sits on top of the white water and white railing, which were already dry. He consistently waited for his paint to dry before adding new elements, suggesting that his revisions transpired over an extended period.

Early on, Pippin added the gray cabin and staircase atop a fully developed landscape, as is clear in the X-radiograph (fig. 8). They are only partly visible on the reverse because the oil medium seeped through the light-colored, probably thinly applied paint in the sandy foreground (at the bottom of the composition) and not through the darker, more thickly applied paint for the shore and trees in the middle ground. Despite this difference, both areas were painted on top of the same underlying ocher layer (the first one that he applied to the canvas), as demonstrated by examination and analysis of two cross-section samples removed from paint passages at the middle and bottom of the cabin (fig. 9).[33] The cabin's staircase and railing, both visible on the reverse, are outlined carefully in the same dark blue used at the outset for the female figure, indicating that Pippin continued the blue/black color scheme for his outlines as his picture evolved.[34] At some point, he balanced the cabin by painting in the rocky peninsula at right and later the large evergreens at both edges of the canvas, additions that restrict the initial composition's panoramic view without altering the canvas's dimensions. Late in the painting's development, he revisited the area of the staircase to reorganize the handrail, paint the stairs white, and add the yellow canoe, enlivening that quadrant of the composition. Presumably about the same time, he filled in the space between the railings in bright green but never added the individual blades of grass that cover the rest of the lawn.

Pippin also used multiple campaigns to transform the body of water from relatively narrow and predominantly blue to wide and silvery, silhouetting the figure's head and chest against a light field and shifting the tonality of the composition to cool. First, he covered the water and distant shoreline with a unifying layer of gray paint made with titanium white, an opaque pigment that neutralized the underlying colors of blue, umber, and ocher. Then, after revising the foreground, he returned to scumble over the gray with white. The silvery areas are zinc white, the semiopacity of which created thin, modulated highlights, and the thicker ones are likely titanium.[35] His use of artist's paints, particularly these white pigments, demonstrates his familiarity with their properties and hints at how he conceived the image: the zinc white is painted around the foliage in the planter at right (which had already been painted atop the gray undercoat) but under the canoe and trellis, which came even later.[36]

Presumably about the time that Pippin reshaped the body of water, he completely reworked the top half of the picture by replacing the dark blue sky and brown hills with a lighter blue sky, gray mountains, and a strip of trees separating them from the water below.[37] The changes redefine the composition in a few ways. Formally, the similar values of the blue and gray unify the top of the composition in a lighter block that aligns with the silvery color of the lake. Conceptually, the mountains fill the horizon, creating a sense of enclosure and perhaps security for the nude woman, who is dwarfed by their size, even as they further restrict the initial design's expansive view. Narratively, the blue sky, clouds, and birds signal daylight, instead of romantic twilight.

Microscopic examination indicates that Pippin executed the revisions in a few ways, the techniques and sequence of which are not entirely clear. He painted the strip of trees directly over a dark umber, like that of the hills visible through the back of the canvas. He blocked in the mountains with a thick, off-white layer, which shows a partial black outline at far right, then scumbled over it in various shades of gray to define their volume. For the sky, he neutralized the original, deep blue with a layer of middle gray, as he had done with the water below, then painted in a smaller sky by scumbling over the gray with two formulations of light blue. The paint above the mountain at right is more transparent: not only does the gray show through in places (see frontispiece), but also the dark band in that area on the X-radiograph indicates less radiopacity.

This brightening corresponds with an overall tendency in Pippin's work of the late 1930s that Edwin Alden Jewell of the *New York Times* observed in a review of 1940: "Whereas in his [Pippin's] first oil, upon which he says he spent three years, the forms are actually and laboriously built up in low relief by means of layer upon layer of thick, dark, enamel-like paint; in subsequent work the paint is smoothly, more thinly applied and the palette is wont to be a great deal brighter."[38] Pippin's growing preference for or access to bright whites

fig. 9 Photomicrographs of cross-section samples removed from *The Lady of the Lake,* from the cabin at middle (a) and bottom (b), as indicated by arrows on the detail of the painting, acquired with visible illumination and a 200x original magnification

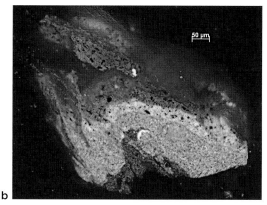

a

b

fig. 10 Infrared photograph of the reverse of *The Lady of the Lake* (fig. 1)

apparently motivated him to repaint much of two works about this time. By spring 1939 he had retouched *The Country Doctor* (ca. 1933–39, Museum of Fine Arts, Boston) to send to his dealer in New York. By 1940 he had reworked *Highland Dairy Farmhouse, Winter* (ca. 1925–30) and renamed it *The Old Mill* (1940, collection of Merrill Wright, Seattle), probably to meet demand after his Philadelphia debut.[39] Pippin acknowledged the pressure at the time, happily explaining to a local reporter: "The way things look now it will be a sell-out, and I won't have any pictures to bring back after the show's over. . . . I've been running back and forth to Philadelphia so much I haven't had much time to do any work in the past two weeks. I've got to get busy and get enough pictures together for another show, maybe in New York."[40]

fig. 11 Detail of the blanket fringe of *The Lady of the Lake* (fig. 2)

Visual examination of the front and X-radiography of *The Lady of the Lake* reveals that Pippin reworked the foreground extensively: changing the shoreline; overlaying the brown soil with green grass; creating, then reducing and recoloring a blanket; inserting, then reworking plants and planters; and, finally, experimenting with cast shadows in several places. The additions mostly signal the nude's increasing distance from pristine nature, even as the figure itself remains fairly consistent. Her very pale, slightly pink hue is at odds with the stark white or gray Pippin often used for lighter skin tones in the 1930s (e.g., *After Supper*) and fits the somewhat warm coloration of *Major General Smedley Butler, USMC* (1938, collection of Philip Jamison, West Chester) and *A Chester County Art Critic (Portrait of Christian Brinton)* (1940, Philadelphia Museum of Art).[41]

Visual examination, X-radiography, and infrared photography of the reverse indicate that Pippin made repeated attempts to resolve the anatomy of the right shoulder before hiding the problem under the figure's restyled hair, a change that contributed to the image's iconographic reorientation from nature to culture (fig. 10). At first, the nude had long, black hair, maybe pulled into a braid or ponytail, which draped over her right shoulder, counter-gravitationally across her breast, and down along her side. To cover his painting difficulties, Pippin reworked the hair to fall partway down the figure's back in gentle waves, lightened it to brown, and shortened it to preserve a view of the torso. The result traded the long, black tresses' romantic or exotic associations for those of contemporary fashion in the 1930s.

Initially, the nude reclined on a brown shore, which Pippin shifted to a grassy lawn fairly early, perhaps to complement the cabin as a sign of human alteration of the landscape. He reinforced that theme with the blanket, a literal intervention between the figure and the natural world. The textile originally extended almost to the stairs and the bottom framing edge, before Pippin overpainted the left and bottom edges with blades of grass. (In raking light, this area appears somewhat embossed and slightly more saturated in color than does the surrounding lawn.) Microscopic examination has revealed a partial, black outline along the blanket's top and bottom. After filling in and revising the blanket, Pippin covered its edges (and outline) with individual blades of grass.

Now bright white and green, the blanket was first rendered as an ocher and grayish-white field.[42] That field was bordered by a symmetrical set of undulating rose and spring green stripes, the colors of which survive in the fringe (fig. 11). That design evokes the toddler's blanket in *After Supper*, which commemorates the artist's childhood neighborhood in Goshen,

New York, and so constitutes a buried, autobiographical reference to the pleasures of domesticity.[43] Francis posits that the blanket may be Navajo in style, presumably on the basis of the large central diamond shape that marks the white-and-green version.[44]

The odd planters, an obvious sign of domesticated nature, are among the last and most reworked additions to the composition. They began as flare-shaped, ocher stands, which Pippin repainted gray, partially obscured with red flowers and pendulous foliage, then decorated with suits from a deck of playing cards (fig. 12).[45] Presumably about the same time, he added plants elsewhere to resolve compositional difficulties. Flowering plants fill the gap behind the stairs, and a trellised rosebush hides what may have been a tree stump like those in *Teacher's College Powerhouse* (ca. 1925–30, Harmon and Harriet Kelley Foundation for the Arts, San Antonio), *Abraham Lincoln and His Father Building Their Cabin at Pigeon Creek* (ca. 1934–37, Barnes Foundation, Philadelphia), and *The Getaway*.[46] This promiscuous display of flowers marks an early engagement with the floral subjects that he would come to favor heavily in the 1940s, as in *Victorian Interior I* and *Victorian Interior II*.[47] It also animates the lower half of the image with a

fig. 12 Elemental maps acquired by XRF imaging of the front of *The Lady of the Lake*. White indicates the distributions of (a) calcium, (b) zinc, (c) chrome, and (d) iron in the composition.

fig. 13 Horace Pippin. *Mountain Landscape (Lush Valleys)*, ca. 1936–39. Oil on fabric, 23 × 29½ in. (58.4 × 74.9 cm). Myron Kunin Collection of American Art, Minneapolis

rhythmic distribution of red, a color that Pippin rarely used with such enthusiasm in other works of the 1930s.[48]

X-ray fluorescence imaging indicates that Pippin used two visually identical but chemically distinct dark green, chrome-based paints: a formula with calcium for the two tall evergreens framing the composition, and one without for everything else, including late additions like the planters' foliage and trellis, which were inserted before and after, respectively, the lake's white scumbling (fig. 12a, c).[49] The distinct formulae indicate that Pippin used different tubes (and probably different brands) of the same paint color, perhaps because he made the additions at different times. This data, coupled with the shadows' inconsistent execution (all but one is positioned on the same diagonal), suggests that he devised the image's lighting scheme fairly late in his process and probably in more than one campaign. Rare in Pippin's oeuvre, shadows cast by natural light also appear in *Birmingham Meeting House* (1940, Myron Kunin Collection of American Art, Minneapolis) and *Mountain Landscape (Lush Valleys)* (ca. 1936–39, fig. 13).[50] The latter painting bears other commonalities with *The Lady of the Lake*:

gray mountains, a similar palette, its status as an anomalous subject in Pippin's work, and a supposed execution date of 1936.[51] Even so, *Mountain Landscape (Lush Valleys)* is darker in tone, its mountains are more dramatic, and shadows are more intrinsic to the composition.

Finally, Pippin signed *The Lady of the Lake* twice in his preferred location, the bottom right corner, and in his characteristic combination of upper and lower case letters, "H. PiPPiN" (fig. 14).[52] First, he signed on the grass in black in his standard block print, and later all but covered those letters with ornate ones in white paint akin to that of the stair and railing. Not only is the white hypervisible against the dark field, but the script is also eye-catching, with the ends of each letter embellished with small, branching points that evoke twigs or trees. Pippin used the distinctive style occasionally throughout his career, from *Shell Holes and Observation Balloon, Champagne Sector* (ca. 1931–37, Baltimore Museum of Art), to *A Chester County Art Critic: Portrait of Christian Brinton*, a gift to his first mentor, and finally to the *Barracks* (1945, Phillips Collection, Washington, D.C.), the only canvas for which an oil study survives.[53]

Pippin rarely superimposed signatures.[54] On the contrary, in the late 1930s, he painted carefully around existing signatures on *Major General Smedley Butler, USMC* and *The Country Doctor* when brightening the pictures' sky and snow, respectively (changes that affect their tonalities, not compositions). In that light, might the superimposed signatures of *The Lady of the Lake* correlate with its extended evolution? The initial, black signature would represent a point at which Pippin prematurely considered the canvas finished, and the final, white one would follow subsequent revision(s), perhaps to the troublesome area around the stair. That the stair, railing, and signature are painted a similar white (titanium), perhaps for formal balance, raises the possibility of a connection.

———————

Attention to the facture of *The Lady of the Lake* opens new lines of inquiry regarding the painting's importance, Pippin's process, and the methods by which his project has been understood. A particularly rich vein of investigation is the relationship between his title and Scott's poem, given that the initial composition lacked the cabin, garden, and boat that would seem to justify a debt to the text. That gap raises broader questions about the value of Pippin's titles as interpretive guides, since his own choices often differ from the names under which the works were shown and sold. For example, he

fig. 14 *The Lady of the Lake,* details of signature (top) and XRF maps (bottom) showing the distribution of calcium (white) and titanium (red) originating in the black and white paints respectively. The black pigment is a carbon-based black, such as bone black, and the white is titanium white.

used *After Supper* for an image of Goshen, New York, that was long misnamed *After Supper: West Chester*.[55] Even more telling, *Mountain Landscape* bears a fragmentary label in Pippin's handwriting, probably from the 1930s, that indicates he named the painting *Lush Valleys*.[56] Discrepancies persist throughout his career and affect his most celebrated works; for example, he used *The Domino Game* for the painting now known as *The Domino Players* (1943, Phillips Collection, Washington, D.C.) and *The Knowledge of God* for at least one work in the series now known as *The Holy Mountains I–IV* (1944–46).[57] In that light, the title of *The Lady of the Lake*, which seems only superficially related to the image and plays on a literary or popular cultural reference legible to sophisticated viewers, prompts speculation about the influence of Pippin's social and professional network in its selection.

If Pippin's first pass at *The Lady of the Lake* has less to do with Scott's poem than with analogizing a black-haired woman to nature, the painting's assessment as "more American Indian than . . . Scottish" merits a second look.[58] As experts of vintage illustrations Rick Martin and Charlotte Martin have observed, "Indian maidens" were ubiquitous in Pippin's day (about 1910 to 1940) in almanacs, posters, sheet music, cigar boxes, and especially calendars, where the figuration of Native Americans as attractive, seemingly defenseless, young women alone in the wilderness in waning light represented "a last gasp attempt at romanticizing the closing of the Old West at the end of the nineteenth century" (fig. 15).[59] Made by a host of artists less celebrated than Parrish, the illustrations sited their comely subjects in nature, often near water and under an evening sky, and the sometimes scantily clad women were consistently identified by long, black braids and maybe a canoe. In light of the iconographic parallels with *The Lady of the Lake*, Rodman's assertion that the work is based on an unidentified calendar image raises new possibilities. Tellingly, as Pippin eliminated his initial composition's relatively subtle signifiers of Native American identity—namely, the figure's long black hair, pristine landscape, and twilight setting—he introduced more obvious ones in the canoe and patterned blanket. Given that no direct quotations have yet been identified, the painting may synthesize multiple print sources, as does *John Brown Going to His Hanging* (1942, Pennsylvania Academy of the Fine Arts [hereafter PAFA], Philadelphia).[60] *The Buffalo Hunt* (1933, Whitney Museum of American Art, New York), another painting with a Native American theme that Rodman credited to an unidentified print source, may share a similar genesis and sentiment.

fig. 15 R. Atkinson Fox (Canadian American, 1860–1935). *In Meditation, Fancy Free,* ca. 1920s. Chromolithograph(?), 11 × 14 ¼ in. (27.9 × 36.2 cm)

Like the embedded blanket's reference to Goshen, *The Lady of the Lake* may also encode a personal connection in that Pippin grew up near the Pocono Mountains of eastern Pennsylvania, the site of an early iteration of the legend of Winona.[61] In that version, set as the Dutch were surrendering their colony to the English in the seventeenth century, the chief's daughter (an "Indian princess") leaped to her death from Winona Cliff, Pennsylvania, when her Dutch beloved announced his return to the Netherlands.[62] It is tempting to see parallels in that landscape (fig. 16) with the rolling hills and river of the initial design of *The Lady of the Lake.*

If *The Lady of the Lake* began as a Native American subject, how does its cabin relate to Pippin's sustained interest in the motif? By the late 1930s, he had already included cabins in his burnt-wood panels *The Bear Hunt II* (ca. 1925–30, Chester County Historical Society, West Chester), *Untitled (Winter Scene)* (ca. 1925–30, ex. coll. Anne Strick), and *Autumn Scene Near Durham, North Carolina* (ca. 1925–30, private collection, San Diego) as well as the paintings *Cabin in the Cotton* and *Abraham Lincoln and His Father Building Their Cabin at Pigeon Creek*—a group notable for its subjects' diversity. He continued in the 1940s, adding interior views like the unfinished *Family Supper (Saying Grace).*

The artist's interest in the cabin motif probably started as a canny exploitation of the formal conso-

nance between the wood buildings and his wood panels; however, its persistence in his oil paintings suggests a deeper investment, as he used the cabin to signify home or security for historical and contemporary hunters, farmers, pioneers, and African American and European American families.[63] Individually, the cabin in *The Lady of the Lake* marks human encroachment on the natural landscape, but collectively might Pippin's cabins hint at a transhistorical, transracial commonality within the American experience?

On another level, the cabin draws attention to Pippin's self-described practice of "work[ing] my foreground from the background." That opaque phrase is usually taken to mean his practice of indicating depth by painting pictorial elements in layers, one atop the last. His earliest paintings, like *The Ending of the War: Starting Home* (1930–33, Philadelphia Museum of Art) and *Cabin in the Cotton,* are so heavily worked that they are effectively bas-relief. Although Pippin scaled back as the decade progressed, *The Lady of the Lake* retains some dimensionality in the figure's profile and tree leaves. Perhaps more important, its reverse demonstrates both compositional approaches that Pippin outlined in the MoMA catalogue. First, he blocked in the nude, lake, and hills together in a unified base layer, as if he had worked out their interrelationship in advance. He then added the cabin, blanket, and other elements on top in a process that seems to correspond with his foreground-from-background technique.[64] The initial version of *The Getaway* evinces a similar process, with the gray animal, red barn, and surrounding snow blocked in together, to which Pippin later added the fox on top of the snow.

Pippin's use of the terms "foreground" and "background" signals his familiarity, if not felicity, with the specialized language of pictorial composition. Their deployment in a catalogue devoted to autodidacts telegraphs his desire to position himself in a more sophisticated register than the one usually accorded self-taught artists. Notably, this ambition coincides with Pippin's first formal exhibitions at the Chester County Art Association (CCAA) and ties to boosters like painter N. C. Wyeth (1882–1945) and modernist critic and curator Christian Brinton, who midwifed the artist's debut in 1937 and subsequent entry in *Masters of Popular Painting.* (It would still be a couple of years before Pippin met Carlen and enrolled at the Barnes Foundation, Merion, Pennsylvania, where his exposure to art history and theory is usually thought to have begun.[65])

It would seem that seeing his work interpolated in exhibitions alongside that of Wyeth and other local painters had a profound influence on Pippin. His initial take on *The Getaway* tracks closely with Wyeth's *The Fox*, now known as *Fox in the Snow* (ca. 1935, fig. 17), with which it appeared in the CCAA Annual of 1937, and he made at least one visit to the Wyeth family's studio.[66] This informal art education, which probably also included CCAA stalwarts like Brinton, seems to have spurred an interest in academic painting conventions that colored Pippin's work of the time. For example, his production of the late 1930s often seems designed to tick boxes on the hierarchy of genres by which academic art had been structured since the seventeenth century, as he augmented his record of history and genre paintings with the figure study of *The Lady of the Lake*, several portraits, *Mountain Landscape (Lush Valleys)*, the animal painting of *The Getaway*, and the still life of *The Warped Table* (1940, PAFA).[67] Even more telling, the short-lived attention to cast shadows evident in *The Lady of the Lake* and *Mountain Landscape (Lush Valleys)* bespeaks an engagement with the illusionistic representation of light that has characterized Western painting since the Renaissance.

Another hint at Pippin's burgeoning interest in art history is his substitution, probably in spring 1939, of a running red fox for the original gray animal of *The Getaway*.[68] The revision is usually credited to the influence of Winslow Homer's *Fox Hunt* (1893, PAFA), in which a desperate fox, beset by crows, crosses a snowbound coast.[69] *The Getaway* borrows Homer's figures, palette, and diagonal composition but inverts his grim narrative by giving the victorious fox a crow for dinner. If Pippin saw the *Fox Hunt* in person at PAFA, might he also have absorbed lessons from other mainstays of the collection? It would have been difficult to ignore John Vanderlyn's *Ariadne Asleep on the Island of Naxos* (1809–14, fig. 18), a lifesize, female nude with pale skin and dark hair, reclining waterside on a blanket, with woods and a dramatic peak behind her, especially if Pippin were already considering or working on his own nude composition.

Regardless of Pippin's exposure to or interest in *Ariadne*, the evidence of his paintings in the late 1930s, especially *The Lady of the Lake*, suggests that they functioned as self-reflexive object lessons by which he engaged and internalized fundamental elements of the Western tradition. The programmatic aspect of his project has gone largely unrecognized owing in no small measure to Pippin's closing sentence in the MoMA catalogue, "To me it seems impossible for another to teach one of Art."[70] Although the sentiment has often been taken as his dismissal of art education *tout court*, his sentence might be just as easily read as a full-throated avowal of self-education.

It is a small irony that Pippin's initial success coincided with (and maybe prompted) his experimentation with the very academic conventions that he was lauded for ignoring—an engagement evident in *The Lady of the Lake*, *Mountain Landscape (Lush Valleys)*, and *The Getaway*. He was sufficiently taken with this new direction in his work to submit *Mountain Landscape (Lush Valleys)* to a CCAA annual and send *The Getaway* to his dealer Hudson Walker, but nothing came of those efforts.[71] No evidence survives of similar plans for *The Lady of the Lake*, but its bright, elaborate, second signature may bespeak his pride. The three paintings debuted in early 1940 in his first solo show in Philadelphia, for which a glowing review reproduced an image of the nude and described it as "fascinating."[72] Even so, the painting found no buyer, while *Mountain Landscape (Lush Valleys)* and *The Getaway* went to a pair of sisters from Philadelphia's Main Line who became the artist's lifelong friends.[73]

By Pippin's first solo show in New York that October, the anomalies of *The Lady of the Lake* were plain to critic Edwin Alden Jewell, whose nonetheless favorable reviews dismissed the "whimsical" canvas as "no more than quaint—quite sincere, no doubt, but obscurely fanciful rather than creatively imaginative."[74] Undeterred,

fig. 16 J. H. Stall (active early 1900s). *Delaware Water Gap*, ca. 1911. Gelatin silver print, 7 × 32½ in. (17.8 × 82.6 cm). Library of Congress, Prints and Photographs Division, Washington, D.C.

Carlen sent the painting to Pippin's solo shows at the Arts Club of Chicago in 1941 and the San Francisco Museum of Art in 1942, then to the Downtown Gallery, where it remained unsold at Pippin's death. The next year, Rodman listed it among the artist's "least successful canvases" and omitted it from the memorial exhibition he mounted in New York; it was likewise absent from Carlen's memorial show in Philadelphia.[75] The dealer sold Gingrich the painting sometime thereafter, but her attachment to it had already begun to wane by 1953, as she wrote him: "Sorry I wouldn't part with 'the den' at *any* price and don't want to sell the other [*Victorian Interior I*]. I would consider selling The Lady of the Lake at a good price. What do his things bring now? You're a super-salesman so work on your client about the beauties of The Lady of the Lake. George [Abell, her then-husband] hates it so! I of course love *all* Horace's things."[76]

Gingrich's 1955 divorce saved her the trouble of selling the painting, but its persistently ambivalent reception is telling. What do viewers find so off-putting? Jewell's complaints about its whimsy and opacity offer clues, since those traits fit uneasily with the perceived authenticity of Pippin's firsthand views of World War I and African American family life that initially brought him national attention.[77] Melville Upton, in another favorable review of Pippin's first New York show, distilled that appeal for his readers in the *New York Sun*:

To the art lover perhaps somewhat jaded by the sophistication and sameness of so much contemporary art, the painting of Horace Pippin will likely come as a welcome relief. . . . Getting his idea expressed so that it is clear to

him seems to have satisfied him, and although he has worked for years over a single canvas it never seems to have occurred to him to consult the work of others to see how they met certain technical problems. Such detached simplicity of outlook is rare and an asset in itself. But it doesn't by itself make an artist. Happily, he "has rhythm" as the stock phrase goes, and as most of his race, for he is a Negro, always seem to have. In addition he seems to have an instinctive feeling for color and design and a happy faculty in "spotting" his lights and darks, a heritage perhaps from savage ancestors not too far removed in point of time. And above all he has a driving sincerity that gives his works a certain validity irrespective of their indifference to, or ignorance of, the niceties of technical expression.[78]

Almost certainly informed by Pippin's statement in the MoMA catalogue, Upton made his enthusiastic case for Pippin by using his modernist style as a screen on which to project racist assumptions about his heritage, motivations, and meanings. While the text may palliate the artist's formal innovation for viewers weary of "sophistication" and qualify him for a market that valorizes autodidacts on the basis of a marginalized social or cultural position, it also institutionalizes racial meanings, identities, and stereotypes in and beyond the visual arts, a field where quality is supposedly indifferent to extra-aesthetic considerations like race.[79] As is clear from Upton's omission of *The Lady of the Lake*, which was included in that show, the painting has no place in such a calculus. Not only does its dialogue with academic tradition undo the critic's characterization of Pippin as willfully immune to outside influence, but also its instantiation of African American agency in an interracial context (namely, a black man asserting his right to paint a nude, white woman) also counters the racial stereotypes on which such compromised analyses rest. Moreover, it does so at a time when black men were being lynched in the United States on the pretext that they posed a threat to the purity of white women.[80]

Pippin's supposed immunity to influence proved to be a remarkably durable interpretative model, partly because his paintings of the 1940s synthesize their references so adroitly that obvious experiments like *The Lady of the Lake* and *Mountain Landscape (Lush Valleys)* are essentially confined to his commissions.[81] As a result, Pippin's sources can be hiding in plain sight.[82] In recent decades, scholars have worked to unmake a model predicated on Pippin's isolation by theorizing his debt to popular culture or current events, as in the 1928 silent film of *The Lady of the Lake*. Our attention to Pippin's facture indicates that identifying his sources and references can

fig. 17 N. C. Wyeth (American, 1882–1945). *Fox in the Snow (The Fox)*, ca. 1935. Oil on hardboard, 28½ × 41 in. (72.4 × 104.1 cm). Arkell Museum at Canajoharie, New York, Gift of Bartlett Arkell, 1940

fig. 18 John Vanderlyn (American, 1775–1852). *Ariadne Asleep on the Island of Naxos,* 1809–14. Oil on canvas, 68½ × 87 in. (174 × 221 cm). Pennsylvania Academy of the Fine Arts, Philadelphia, Gift of Mrs. Sarah Harrison (The Joseph Harrison, Jr. Collection) (1878.1.11)

be tricky, as the initial image of *The Lady of the Lake* leads in a different interpretative direction than its title would suggest. By demonstrating how carefully and thoughtfully he reworked that picture, how that development conflicts with his own discussions of his process, and how the result connects across his works of the 1930s, this object-based study sheds light on the scope of Pippin's ambition and agency at a transitional moment in his career and models a productive methodology for coming to terms with his complex, sometimes confounding project that might be extended to the work of his peers. Arguably more important, this new understanding of Pippin's process illuminates how porous the boundary between the art world's so-called outsiders and insiders can be.

ACKNOWLEDGMENTS
We extend our thanks to Mark Bockrath and Barbara Buckley; Robert Gober and Donald Moffett; Mimi Gross; Carter Lyon; Rick and Charlotte Martin; Zenia Simpson; Judith Stein; Suzan Friedlander, Arkell Museum at Canajoharie, New York; Mary Sebera, Baltimore Museum of Art; Audrey Lewis, Brandywine River Museum of Art, Chadds Ford, Pennsylvania; Jacquelyn Francis, California College of the Arts, San Francisco; Rachel Middleman, California State University, Chico; Pam Powell, Chester County Historical Society, Pennsylvania; Lily Zhou, D. C. Moore Gallery, New York; Randall Griffey, Evan Read, and Sylvia Yount, The Metropolitan Museum of Art; Rita Berg, Midwest Art Conservation Center, Minneapolis; Rebecca Shearier, Minneapolis Institute of Art, Minneapolis; Charlotte Ameringer, Museum of Fine Arts, Boston; Charlotte Barat, Museum of Modern Art, New York; Jenny Sponberg, Myron Kunin Collection, Minneapolis; Lynne Cooke, National Gallery of Art, Washington, D.C.; Hoang Tran, Pennsylvania Academy of the Fine Arts, Philadelphia; and Alexandra A. Kirtley and Jessica T. Smith, Philadelphia Museum of Art. The research for this article was supported by fellowships from The Metropolitan Museum of Art and the National Endowment for the Humanities and a grant from the Society for the Preservation of American Modernists.

ANNE MONAHAN
Independent Scholar

ISABELLE DUVERNOIS
Conservator, Department of Paintings Conservation, The Metropolitan Museum of Art

SILVIA A. CENTENO
Research Scientist, Department of Scientific Research, The Metropolitan Museum of Art

NOTES

1 Rodman 1947.

2 John Brown (1800–1859) and Abraham Lincoln (1809–1865) were instrumental in abolishing slavery in the United States, Brown as a radical abolitionist and Lincoln as commander-in-chief of the Union Army during the Civil War. Marian Anderson (1897–1993), a native Philadelphian, was one of the most celebrated singers of the twentieth century. By the time Pippin painted two portraits of her in the early 1940s, she had already given her famous 1939 concert on the steps of the Lincoln Memorial, arranged after she was denied permission to sing at Constitution Hall. Major General Smedley Darlington Butler (1881–1940) was a native of West Chester, Pennsylvania, and the most highly decorated marine in history at his death. By the time Pippin painted Butler's portrait in 1938, the retired general had supported the 1932 Bonus Army march on Washington, D.C., and published and promoted *War Is a Racket* (1935), an attack on the business interests that profit from warfare.

3 In Pippin's day, Henri Rousseau (1844–1910) of France and John Kane (1860–1934), a Scots American from Pittsburgh, were arguably the most celebrated autodidacts in the United States and much better known than Pippin's African American contemporaries Bill Traylor (1854–1949) of Montgomery, Alabama, and William Edmondson (1874–1952) of Nashville, Tennessee, even with the latter's solo show at the Museum of Modern Art (hereafter MoMA), New York, in 1937.

4 Rodman 1947, "Pippin's Works," pp. 82–88. Pippin's exhibition history and sales records are uneven. Documentation of his shows is nonexistent before 1937, when he made his debut in the Chester County Art Association (hereafter CCAA) Annual exhibition, and spotty before 1940, the year of his debut show in Philadelphia at the Carlen Galleries. Essentially no sales records survive from Carlen, but the Downtown Gallery, New York, which sold much of his work in the mid-1940s, kept excellent records. See Downtown Gallery Records, 1824–1974, bulk 1926–1969, Archives of American Art, Smithsonian Institution, Washington, D.C. (hereafter Downtown Gallery Records, AAA).

5 According to Denise Jacques (2003, pp. 4, 20–21), Gingrich studied art in Paris and reportedly studied sculpture with Isamu Noguchi, who was a friend; she also built a sculpture studio in her house in Havana in the 1920s and sponsored Cuban artists and artisans.

6 Rodman 1947, p. 22. One example, *The Ending of the War: Starting Home* (1930–33, Philadelphia Museum of Art), survives only in a documentary photograph made when the canvas was relined. The other relined canvases were not documented. *Paul Dague, Deputy Sheriff of Chester County* (1937, Chester County Historical Society, West Chester) and *Coming In* (1939, private collection, courtesy of D. C. Moore, New York) appear to have been painted over abandoned compositions. Three paintings that might fit this study were unavailable for examination— *Portrait of My Wife* (ca. 1936–39, Harmon and Harriet Kelley Foundation for the Arts, San Antonio), *After Supper* (ca. 1935, collection of Leon Hecht and Robert Pincus-Witten, New York), and *Gas Alarm Outpost, Argonne* (ca. 1931–37, private collection)—so their supports and canvas preparations are unknown.

7 The initial design of *The Lady of the Lake* was discovered during a conservation examination in 2014.

8 See Rodman 1947, pp. 13–15, for discussions of Pippin's use of print sources and an illustration of the printed prototype for *Christ and the Woman of Samaria* (1940, Barnes Foundation, Philadelphia). For Parrish, see Hartigan 1993, p. 92, and Francis 2015, pp. 7–12. For Pippin's quotations of printed sources in other works, specifically the John Brown series, see Monahan 2015.

9 For the painting's relationship to Scott's poem, see "The Lady of the Lake," canto 1, verses 15–19, 25–26 (Scott 1908, pp. 13–16, 21–22); see also Hartigan 1993, pp. 92–93, and Francis 2015, pp. 11–13.

10 *Philadelphia Inquirer* 1940.

11 Stockbook, Downtown Gallery Records, AAA.

12 Dating Pippin's early work is problematic, partly because his own narratives about that early production are inconsistent. Pippin's earliest statement on the subject describes making seven burnt-wood panels, starting in 1925 and finishing before taking up canvas in 1930; thus, we assign them a date of about 1925–30; see "The Story of Horace Pippin as Told by Himself" [March 1938], Museum Exhibition Files, *Masters of Popular Painting* (MoMA Exh. #76, April 27–July 24, 1938), Department of Painting and Sculpture, MoMA. The early paintings are more complicated. He almost always cited *The Ending of the War: Starting Home* as his first painting, but its inscription, September 15, 1930–December 21, 1933, puts the painting after *The Buffalo Hunt* (Whitney Museum of American Art, New York), which was inscribed October 30 (31?), 1933. In the absence of inscriptions or other period documentation, we date the early paintings in line with their first appearance, usually in the form of a date range.

13 Exhibition Checklist, *Paintings by Horace Pippin*, April 14–May 3, 1942, Exhibition Records, San Francisco Museum of Modern Art Archives, box 16, file 33.

14 After Pippin's successful submission to the CCAA Annual of 1937, its director, Christian Brinton, and his compatriots organized a solo show for the artist, included him in succeeding CCAA shows, and helped him obtain gallery representation in New York and Philadelphia.

15 Carlen Galleries 1940.

16 In addition to the solo show at the West Chester Community Center (1937), Pippin took part in the CCAA's annuals (1937–40) and the exhibition "Flowers in Art" (1938). The full extent of his participation in CCAA's projects is unknown as its archives have yet to be processed.

17 Bockrath and Buckley 1993. Francis (2015, p. 11) reads *The Lady of the Lake* as a demonstration of Pippin's "knowledge of landscape painting formulae" and recognition of the nude as "a standard by which Western artists measured themselves."

18 Horace Pippin, quoted in Cahill et al. 1938, pp. 125–26 (emphasis in original).

19 Blitzstein 1941, p. 12.

20 Frost 1944, p. 21. Frost was Pippin's only buyer from a show at the Bignou Gallery, New York, in 1940.

21 Bearden 1976, p. [1].

22 Edward Loper, oral history interview with Marina Pacini, AAA, May 12, 1989, transcript pp. 34–35.

23 See Lewis 2015 and Stein et al. 1993.

24 Rodman 1947, p. 13.

25 Switching the barn from red to gray makes sense compositionally and locally: red barns are conventional in New York, where Pippin was reared, but not in Chester County, Pennsylvania, where they were commonly white or weathered wood. Without removing a paint sample for cross-section analysis, it is impossible to know if Pippin darkened the sky in the final composition.

26 X-ray fluorescence (XRF) imaging of *Lady of the Lake* was carried out using a Bruker M6 Jetstream instrument. The front and the back of the painting were imaged at 90 msec/pixel, with the X-ray source operated at 50 kV and 0.5 mA. For acquiring maps of the front of the picture, a 500 micron spot size and a 750 micron step size were used, and for the back, a 700 micron spot size and a 700 micron step size. A detail of the area on the front with the signature was scanned with a 400 micron spot size and a 400 micron step size at 120 msec/pixel. Raman spectroscopy measurements were carried out in two paint cross sections removed from the front of the picture and in five sample scrapings removed from the back using a Renishaw Raman 1000 Microscope System, with a 785 nm laser excitation.

27 The raw canvas is amply visible on the reverse. Now discolored, it would have been off-white originally. The tacking edges in direct contact with the wood strainer have yellowed from wood lignin staining. The canvas's reverse has also yellowed due, in part, to the oil medium (not pigment) penetrating the fibers, which has oxidized over time.

28 Bockrath and Buckley 1993, pp. 171–72. The four paintings are *Dogfight over the Trenches* (ca. 1939, Hirshhorn Museum and Sculpture Garden, Smithsonian Institution, Washington, D.C.), *Portrait of My Wife*, *The Getaway*, and *Coming in. Dogfight over the Trenches* is painted on a black priming layer.

29 *Mountain Landscape (Lush Valleys)* (ca. 1936–39, Myron Kunin Collection of American Art, Minneapolis) has a stretcher that appears similar in construction. Stretchers, unlike strainers, can be expanded to tighten a loose canvas by tapping the small keys into the slots cut into the inner corners.

30 That does not necessarily mean that pencil outlines are absent, only that they cannot be detected because of the thickness of the paint layers. Dark pigments, such as carbon-based blacks and some blues, inherently block infrared wavelength penetration, which can render graphite marks invisible in the infrared reflectogram.

31 See, for example, the panel *Autumn Scene Near Durham, N.C.* (ca. 1925–30, private collection, San Diego) and painting *Cabin in the Cotton* (ca. 1931–37, Art Institute of Chicago).

32 The front of the painting was noninvasively analyzed by XRF imaging, except for two samples removed from the cabin for cross-section analysis. To identify the blue pigment on the front, a sample for Raman spectroscopy analysis would be necessary.

33 The two samples revealed similar stratigraphy and pigment combinations, including titanium white, a carbon-based black and some barium white, in addition to the chrome yellow and Prussian blue in the sample from the bottom spot. Raman-spectroscopy analysis has identified that the ocher paint is mainly composed of chrome yellow, a carbon-based black, and iron earth pigments.

34 The dark blue pigment was identified as Prussian blue by Raman spectroscopy.

35 Titanium white in its anatase form and zinc white were identified by Raman spectroscopy in paint samples and mapped throughout the overall composition by XRF imaging. It is difficult to say which pigment was used for thick highlights because the three white pigments (lead, titanium, and zinc) show some distribution in that area. It may have been Permalba brand, an opaque combination of zinc and titanium whites produced by F. W. Weber that Pippin was known to use in the 1940s (Bockrath and Buckley 1993, p. 174).

36 By early 1938 Pippin was using Weber paints, a brand of artist's paints made in Philadelphia; see his statement "How I Paint" [March 1938], Museum Exhibition Files, *Masters of Popular Painting* (MoMA Exh. #76, April 27–July 24, 1938), Department of Painting and Sculpture, MoMA.

37 There are no clues as to the timing of this revision beyond the fact that it lies under late additions to the evergreen foliage framing the sky on the right and left.

38 Jewell 1940a.

39 The degree of repainting in *The Country Doctor* is evident from the box Pippin reserved around his signature. The painting was among three that Pippin had sent to the dealer Hudson Walker in New York; see Hudson D. Walker Papers, 1920–1982, AAA. *The Old Mill* was first recorded in Pippin's solo show at the Bignou Gallery, New York, September 30–October 12, 1940. As indicated by the partly overpainted sticker at lower right, it was exhibited as entry "15," *Highland Dairy Farmhouse, Winter* (ca. 1925–30) in his solo show at the West Chester Community Center, June 8–July 5, 1937.

40 See Straley 1940 quoted in Stein 1993, p. 19.

41 Likewise, the figures' skin in *Cabin in the Cotton* is charcoal gray, and that of the figures in *Paul Dague, Deputy Sheriff of Chester County* and *Coming In* is stark white.

42 The blanket's initial coloration is partly visible under a microscope in some areas of the figure's shadow.

43 See Pippin's letter to "My dear friends," about June–July 1946 (Goshen Public Library, New York), which explains that he made *After Supper* after finding the neighborhood torn down on a visit to the town in 1935.

44 Francis 2015, p. 11.

45 The planters are particularly visible in the iron-distribution map obtained by XRF imaging, which reflects the presence of ocher pigments that contain iron oxides as the main colorants.

46 The object under the rosebush is discernible as a gray shape through visual examination and in the X-radiograph and as a vaguely cruciform shape in the calcium-distribution map obtained by XRF imaging (fig. 12a).

47 Other early examples include *The Admirer* (1939), now lost and never photographed, which supposedly depicted a baby in a garden, and the fantastical *Giant Daffodils* (1940, Pennsylvania Academy of the Fine Arts [PAFA], Philadelphia), which combines the oversize flowers with a realistically rendered spaniel.

48 The plentiful red brick of *Coming In* and poppies of *Dogfight over the Trenches* represent exceptions, as would red flowers if they appear in the garden depicted in *The Admirer*.

49 The chrome-based green pigment is either chrome oxide or viridian, which is a hydrated chrome oxide, and is mixed with a yellow iron earth pigment. The rest of the green paints in the composition include variable amounts of calcium, an element often present as filler in paint-tube formulations.

50 The shadows in *Portrait of Marian Anderson* (1940–46, Schomburg Center for Research in Black Culture, New York Public Library) seem to mimic studio lighting conditions. Shadows produced by fire- or candlelight appear occasionally: *Amish Letter Writer* (1940, collection of the Davidsons, Los Angeles), *Six O'Clock* (1940, collection of Eddie C. and C. Sylvia Brown, Baltimore), *John Brown Reading His Bible* (1942, Myron Kunin Collection of American Art, Minneapolis), *Interior* (1944, National Gallery of Art, Washington, D.C.), *Abe Lincoln's First Book* (1944, Carnegie Museum of Art, Pittsburgh), and *Barracks* (1945, Phillips Collection, Washington, D.C.).

51 The painting was not exhibited with a date in Pippin's lifetime, and Rodman gives no evidence for the one he assigns. See Rodman 1947, p. 2.

52 See Bockrath and Buckley 1993, p. 176, for Pippin's signatures.

53 Similar signatures appear on *Dogfight over the Trenches*, *Christ and the Woman of Samaria*, *The Trial of John Brown* (1942, Fine Arts Museums of San Francisco), *West Chester, Pennsylvania* (1942, Wichita Art Museum, Kansas), *Mr. Prejudice* (1943, Philadelphia Museum of Art), and *Abraham Lincoln, the Good Samaritan* (1943, PAFA).

54 Pippin superimposed a bright green signature on a dark green one in *My Backyard* (1941), which was reportedly destroyed.

55 Pippin used *After Supper* in his letter to "[his] dear friends" in Goshen in 1946, by which point Carlen had already shown and sold the painting as *After Supper, West Chester* and inscribed that name on the face of the drawing.

56 The label fragment indicates only the title's first letters, but the whole text appears in the checklist, Delaware Art Museum 1974, unpaginated.

57 The series comprises *The Holy Mountain I* (1944, collection of Camille O. and William J. Cosby Jr.), *The Holy Mountain II* (1944, collection of Leslie Anne Miller and Richard Worley, Bryn Mawr, Pennsylvania), *The Holy Mountain III* (1945, Hirshhorn Museum and Sculpture Garden, Smithsonian Institution, Washington, D.C.), and *The Holy Mountain IV*. Carlen and Rodman seem to be largely responsible for the changed titles, as in the case of *After Supper*. For *The Domino Game*, see Pippin's letter to Carlen, February 1, 1943, and for *The Knowledge of God*, see Pippin's letter to Carlen, February 5, 1945, both Carlen Galleries, Inc., Records, 1775–1997, bulk 1940–1986, AAA. Until 2017, Pippin's preferred title, *The Ending of the War, Starting Home*, had been supplanted by the variant *End of the War—Starting Home*, which appeared in exhibition checklists starting in 1937. For other examples of multiple titles assigned to a given work, see Monahan 1993, pp. 194–203.

58 *Philadelphia Inquirer* 1940.

59 Martin and Martin 1997, p. 186. Among the artists known for such work are Edward M. Eggleston (1882–1941), R. Atkinson Fox (1860–1935), F. R. Harper (1876–1948), and Henry (Hy) Hintermeister (1897–1972). The Land O'Lakes logo is a survival of that period.

60 Charlotte Martin, email to Anne Monahan, October 26, 2016.

61 Pippin also made an early panel titled *Hunting Lodge, Pocono Mountains* (ca. 1925–30, location unknown), which may be *Untitled (Winter Scene)* (ca. 1925–30, ex. coll. Anne Strick).

62 For the Winona story, see Brodhead 1870 and "The Legend of Lover's Leap," February 2010, Monroe County Historical Association, Stroudsburg, Pennsylvania, www.monroehistorical .org/articles/files/021410_loversleap.html.

63 For example, *Cabin in the Cotton* depicts a black family and *Abraham Lincoln and His Father Building Their Cabin at Pigeon Creek* depicts a white one.

64 Bockrath and Buckley 1993, p. 167.

65 Pippin apparently met Carlen not long before his show opened at the gallery in January 1940 and began attending classes at the Barnes Foundation on January 16, 1940; Barnes Foundation archivist Barbara Beaucar, email to Anne Monahan, August 9, 2016.

66 Chester County Art Association 1937; Wyeth 1971, p. 803.

67 Pippin's portraits include *Portrait of the Artist's Wife*, *Paul Dague*, *Major General Smedley Butler, USMC*, and *Coming In*. His earliest animal painting is probably *The Moose I* (1936), which is unlocated and apparently undocumented.

68 According to Elizabeth Sparhawk-Jones's undated letter to Hudson Walker of late March or early April 1939 (Carl Zigrosser

Collection, Archives, Philadelphia Museum of Art), Pippin sent *The Getaway* to the dealer even though it was unfinished.

69 That relationship is reinforced by the possibility that Pippin's chosen name for the painting was *The Fox*. On the other hand, Hartigan (1993, p. 83) reads the subject as a reference to life in Chester County.

70 Cahill et al. 1938, p. 126. The impression is compounded by reports like that of Romare Bearden, who recalled that "Pippin paid little attention to paintings of other artists hanging on the walls" of the Downtown Gallery in 1942; see Bearden 1976, p. [1].

71 Affixed to the backing board of *Mountain Landscape* is a fragment of a CCAA submission label, but no record of the painting in a CCAA annual has come to light.

72 *Philadelphia Inquirer* 1940, p. 14. The exhibition (Carlen Galleries 1940) comprised twenty-two paintings and five burnt-wood panels.

73 They are Mrs. Edmund C. Evans and Miss Ellen Winsor of Paoli, Pennsylvania, who lived about a mile down the road from Jane Kendall Gingrich in the early 1940s.

74 Jewell 1940a and 1940b, reviewing Bignou Gallery 1940.

75 Rodman 1947, p. 13. M. Knoedler and Co. 1947 and Art Alliance 1947.

76 Jane Kendall Abell [later Gingrich] to Robert Carlen, November 27, 1953; Carlen Galleries Records, AAA.

77 Prior to Pippin's show at the Bignou Gallery, New York, critics would have known him from the three war scenes and *Cabin in the Cotton* on view in "Masters of Popular Painting." *Cabin in the Cotton* was erroneously presumed to represent his childhood memories of the American South. For more on the correlation between the perception of authenticity and value in the field of self-taught art, see Fine 2003.

78 Upton 1940, p. 15.

79 Omi and Winant 2015.

80 For the racial implications of Pippin's subject, see Francis 2015, p. 11.

81 For *Mr. Prejudice* as a commission that attempts to synthesize diverse sources, see Rodman 1947, p. 4, and Puchner 2015.

82 Monahan 2015.

REFERENCES

Art Alliance, Philadelphia
  1947 *Horace Pippin Memorial Exhibition*. Exh. cat. Philadelphia: Art Alliance, April 8–May 4.
Arts Club of Chicago
  1941 *Exhibition of Paintings by Horace Pippin*. Essay by Albert C. Barnes. Exh. cat. Chicago: Arts Club of Chicago, May 23–June 14.
Bearden, Romare
  1976 "Horace Pippin." In Phillips Collection 1976, [pp. 1–2].
Bignou Gallery
  1940 *Paintings by Horace Pippin*. Exh. cat. New York: Bignou Gallery, September 30–October 12.
Blitzstein, Madelin
  1941 "The Odds Were Against Him." *U.S. Week* 1, no. 7 (April 26), pp. 12–13.
Bockrath, Mark F., and Barbara A. Buckley
  1993 "Materials and Techniques." In Stein et al. 1993, pp. 166–83.
Brodhead, Luke W.
  1870 *The Delaware Water Gap: Its Scenery, Its Legends, and Early History*. Philadelphia: Sherman & Co.
Cahill, Holger, Maximilien Gauthier, Jean Cassou, Dorothy C. Miller, et al.
  1938 *Masters of Popular Painting: Modern Primitives of Europe and America*. Exh. cat. New York: Museum of Modern Art in collaboration with the Musée de Grenoble, April 27–July 24.
Carlen Galleries
  1940 *Horace Pippin*. Exh. cat. Philadelphia: Carlen Galleries, January 19–February 18.
  1941 *Recent Paintings by Horace Pippin*. Exh. cat. Philadelphia: Carlen Galleries, March 21–April 20.
Chester County Art Association
  1937 *Sixth Annual Exhibition*. Exh. cat. West Chester, Pa.: The Art Centre, May 23–June 6.
Delaware Art Museum, Wilmington
  1974 *Four Delaware Valley Primitives: Henry Braunstein, Ida E. Jones, Edward Charles Kimmel, Horace Pippin*. Essays by Susan E. Strickler and Cynthia Bell. Exh. cat. Wilmington: Delaware Art Museum, February 22–March 24.
Fine, Gary Alan
  2003 "Crafting Authenticity: The Validation of Identity in Self-Taught Art." *Theory and Society* 32, no. 2 (April), pp. 153–80.
Francis, Jacqueline
  2015 "All the Details I Need: Horace Pippin's Sources." In Lewis 2015, pp. 7–21.
F[rost], R[osamund]
  1944 "Pippin: Through Eyes of Innocence." *Art News* 43 (March 1–14), pp. 20–21.
Hartigan, Lynda Roscoe
  1993 "Landscapes, Portraits, and Still Lifes." In Stein et al. 1993, pp. 82–123.
Jacques, Denise
  2003 *The Tiled Mansion*. Havana: Ponton Caribe.
Jewell, Edwin Alden
  1940a "Pippin Has Display at Bignou Gallery." *New York Times*, October 1, p. 33.
  1940b "Art Week Takes Shape: Local Shows." *New York Times*, October 6, p. 137.
Lewis, Audrey, ed.
  2015 *Horace Pippin: The Way I See It*. Exh. cat., Brandywine River Museum of Art, Chadds Ford, Pa., April 25–July 19. New York: Scala Arts Publishers.

M. Knoedler and Co., New York
  1947 *Memorial Exhibition: Horace Pippin, 1888–1946*. Exh. cat. New York: M. Knoedler and Co., September 29–October 11.
Martin, Rick, and Charlotte Martin
  1997 *Vintage Illustration: Discovering America's Calendar Artists, 1900–1960*. Portland, Ore.: Collectors Press.
Monahan, Anne
  1993 "Resources and References." In Stein et al. 1993, pp. 186–207.
  2015 "Witness: History, Memory, and Authenticity in the Art of Horace Pippin." In Lewis 2015, pp. 35–55.
Omi, Michael, and Howard Winant
  2015 *Racial Formation in the United States*. 3rd ed. New York and Oxford: Routledge.
Philadelphia Inquirer
  1940 "Primitives by Pippin." *Philadelphia Inquirer*, January 21, p. 14.
Phillips Collection, Washington, D.C.
  1976 *Horace Pippin*. Essay by Romare Bearden. Exh. cat., Phillips Collection, Washington, D.C., February 25–March 1977; Terry Dintenfass Gallery, New York, April 5–30, 1977; Brandywine River Museum, Chadds Ford, Pa., June 4–September 5, 1977. Washington, D.C.: Phillips Collection.
Puchner, Edward
  2015 "Winning the Peace over *Mr. Prejudice*: Horace Pippin, the Social Gospel, and the Double V." In Lewis 2015, pp. 57–71.
Rodman, Selden
  1947 *Horace Pippin: A Negro Painter in America*. New York: Quadrangle Press.
Scott, Walter
  1908 *The Lady of the Lake*. Edited and with notes by William J. Rolfe. Rev. ed. Cambridge, Mass.: Houghton Mifflin.
Stein, Judith E.
  1993 "An American Original." In Stein et al. 1993, pp. 2–43.
Stein, Judith E., et al.
  1993 *I Tell My Heart: The Art of Horace Pippin*. Exh. cat., Pennsylvania Academy of the Fine Arts, Philadelphia, January 21–April 17, 1994; Art Institute of Chicago, April 30–July 10, 1994; Cincinnati Art Museum, July 28–October 9, 1994; Baltimore Museum of Art, October 26, 1994–January 1, 1995; MMA, February 1–April 30, 1995. Philadelphia and New York: Pennsylvania Academy of the Fine Arts in association with Universe Publishing.
Straley, George
  1940 "Pippin's Paintings Create a Sensation in Philadelphia." [*West Chester Daily Local News*, January 26]. Carlen Galleries, Inc., Records, 1775–1997, bulk 1940–1986, Archives of American Art, Smithsonian Institution, Washington, D.C.
Upton, Melville
  1940 "Some October Art Shows." *New York Sun*, October 5, p. 15.
West Chester Community Center
  1937 *Horace Pippin: Paintings and Burnt Wood Panels*. Exh. cat. West Chester, Pa.: West Chester Community Center, June 8–July 5.
Wyeth, Betsy James, ed.
  1971 *The Wyeths: The Letters of N. C. Wyeth, 1901–1945*. Boston: Gambit.

ANDREA BAYER
DOROTHY MAHON
SILVIA A. CENTENO

An Examination of Paolo Veronese's *Alessandro Vittoria*

Paolo Veronese's (1528–1588) portrait of a sculptor entered The Metropolitan Museum of Art's collection in 1946, and was presented in the Museum's *Bulletin* by Margaretta Salinger as a depiction of the painter's great contemporary Alessandro Vittoria (1525–1608) cradling a version of one of his most significant works, the bronze statuette *Saint Sebastian*, also in the Museum's collection (figs. 1, 2).[1] Since that time, the painting has been admired as one of Veronese's most refined portraits, but there have been persistent questions about its condition, quality of execution, meaning, and date. In addition, scholars have queried the identification of both the sitter and the statuette. We undertook an examination using only noninvasive means of analysis to understand the technique and surface of the painting more accurately before attempting a new consideration of these issues. Our study utilized X-radiography and macro-X-ray

fig. 1 Paolo Veronese (Italian, 1528–1588). *Alessandro Vittoria*, ca. 1575. Oil on canvas, 43½ × 32¼ in. (110.5 × 81.9 cm). The Metropolitan Museum of Art, Gwynne Andrews Fund, 1946 (46.31)

fluorescence (MA-XRF), with the aim of explaining the oddly unsatisfying pattern of the table covering, often assumed to be an Eastern carpet; determining the condition of the sitter's proper left hand, and other areas that appear weakly painted; and clarifying the prominent but indistinct markings at the upper left quadrant of the painting. Unanticipatedly, we also learned about the original composition on the canvas and, above all, changes in the painting that have led to an appearance that is far less colorful than originally intended. Overall, we have recovered information that leads to a more secure grasp of the artist's intentions for this important canvas.

TECHNICAL EXAMINATION

X-radiography revealed that Veronese painted the composition on top of another portrait that depicted a bearded man (fig. 3). He began by turning the canvas support upside down and canceling the earlier image by applying sweeping strokes of radiopaque lead white,

which are visible in the X-radiograph. Reusing a previously painted support was a common practice, and examples such as this one are frequently discovered through X-radiography, as artists painted over their own compositions, as well as those begun by other artists. When reusing a canvas, artists often turned the painting upside down and painted out the earlier image as Veronese did here. In this case, the sweeping strokes are confined to the head and torso area of the earlier portrait, suggesting that it was not entirely finished, as this was the only portion that required canceling. We set out to determine whether Veronese or another artist painted the first portrait. A comparison of the two portrait heads demonstrates a very different application of paint. The earlier portrait head is much smaller and overall exhibits a significantly more dense appearance in the X-radiograph (fig. 4b). This effect is due to the way in which the artist began to model the forms of the subject's head and face with fussy, dappled applications of lead-rich paint to create the flesh. The portrait head of Alessandro Vittoria (fig. 4a) was constructed from the beginning in an entirely different manner, with a more economical touch, and with the application of lead white concentrated on the highlights of the nose, cheekbones, and forehead to skillfully establish the forms with a sureness of mind from the start. A comparison to X-radiographs of other heads by Veronese

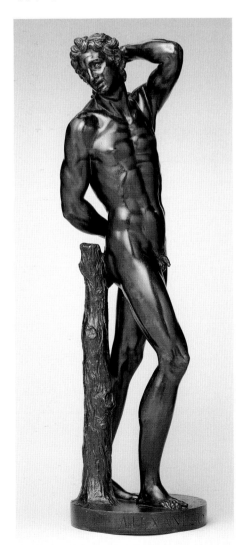

fig. 2 Alessandro Vittoria (Italian, 1525–1608). *Saint Sebastian*, 1566. Bronze, 21⅜ × 6¾ × 6¼ in. (54.3 × 17 × 16 cm). The Metropolitan Museum of Art, Samuel D. Lee Fund, 1940 (40.24)

fig. 3 X-radiograph of *Alessandro Vittoria* (fig. 1), revealing that Veronese used a canvas on which there was a partially painted portrait depicting a bearded man. The first portrait appears at the bottom, upside down, because the canvas was turned 180 degrees before the artist began the portrait of Alessandro Vittoria.

fig. 4 X-radiograph details of fig. 1, showing the head of Alessandro Vittoria (a) and the portrait below the paint surface (b). The head in (b) has been rotated 180 degrees for comparison. The random strokes sweeping across the head illustrated in (b) are applications of lead white that Veronese used to cancel out the earlier image before proceeding to paint. The head below the paint surface is smaller in scale, and overall the image appears dense (white). Conversely, the X-radiographic image of Veronese's portrait head of Vittoria (a) reveals a head that was constructed in an entirely different manner, less dense (darker). This comparison of the X-radiographs, which reveals starkly different techniques used to construct the two heads, indicates the hands of two different artists at work.

a

b

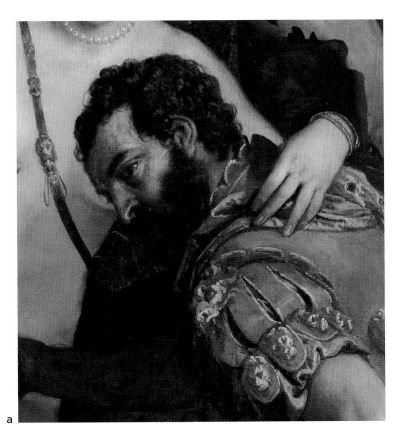

a

b

fig. 5 Paolo Veronese. Detail of *Mars and Venus United by Love*, 1570s. Oil on canvas, 81 × 63⅜ in. (205.7 × 161 cm). The Metropolitan Museum of Art, John Stewart Kennedy Fund, 1910 (10.189). Detail (a) and X- radiograph, detail (b). The X-radiographic detail of the head of Mars, from a painting firmly attributed to Veronese, demonstrates characteristics of a painting technique that are similar to those revealed in the X-radiograph of Vittoria (fig. 4a). The skillful and economical applications of lead white on the eyebrow, eye, cheekbone, and nose result in a strongly modeled form.

confirms his characteristic and consistent clarity of mind with regard to modeling the form (figs. 5a, b). The painting beneath this portrait was surely not painted by Veronese but may have been done by another artist working in his studio.

The portrait was also subjected to macro-X-ray fluorescence (MA-XRF). While point XRF analysis provides only the capacity to obtain the elemental composition of pigments in discrete spots, the MA-XRF scanner developed relatively recently allows the possibility of obtaining maps of the elemental composition of large areas by means of a moving stage.[2] The resulting maps of elements frequently provide broader insight into significant technical aspects.[3] For example, when the portrait by Veronese is viewed in normal light, the sitter's jacket or doublet appears to be black and rather lacking in detail and form (fig. 1). The XRF distribution map for copper provides a clearer image of the original forms and details, and strongly indicates that this garment was largely painted using the copper-based blue pigment azurite, and had a pattern (fig. 6a).[4] The discoloration or blackening of the blue pigment azurite when used in an oil medium, or in egg tempera when affected by later oil coatings, is well known.[5] Here the discoloration, which has led to the apparent diminishment of form and detail, is possibly exacerbated because the artist used azurite in

combination with smalt, another blue pigment that is also prone to discolor to an ashy gray or brownish hue.[6] Indeed, the XRF distribution map for cobalt, the primary element of the blue pigment smalt, reveals that a significant amount of this pigment is present (fig. 6b). It is probable that Veronese used this combination of azurite and smalt for specific reasons, as he did in other paintings. The pigment azurite tends to shift to a more greenish hue over time when used in an oil medium, while smalt has a cooler, more intensely blue color and frequently has been used as a substitute for the preferred but prohibitively expensive pigment ultramarine.[7]

The XRF mapping results also raised questions about the patterning of the textile laid across the table. While the XRF distribution map for mercury (fig. 7), which indicates the red pigment vermilion, confirms that the base color of the fabric was intended to be red, the full range of colors of the pattern are no longer apparent. Looking at the same time at the XRF distribution map of cobalt (fig. 6b), it is possible to assert that smalt was used extensively in this section of the painting, and, oddly, its distribution seems to coincide with areas of pattern that now appear red. Examination of the surface with a stereomicroscope reveals that the textile underwent extensive restoration before entering the collection in 1946, likely prompted by the appearance of the

fig. 6 Elemental distribution maps acquired by XRF imaging of *Alessandro Vittoria* (fig. 1): copper (a) and cobalt (b). While the color of the sitter's doublet is black in normal light (fig. 1), the XRF map of copper on the left (a) indicates an abundant use of the blue pigment azurite, and the XRF map of cobalt on the right (b) indicates an abundant use of the blue pigment smalt. These two blue pigments used in combination confirm that the doublet was intended to be blue. Degradation of the two pigments has resulted in a significant change of appearance. The XRF images also reveal that much of the doublet's form and detail is no longer apparent to the naked eye. The XRF image (b) also reveals that parts of the pattern of the textile laid across the table contain a significant amount of the blue pigment smalt, indicating that here too a color change has occurred.

degraded smalt. Nevertheless, microscopic inspection, as well as close inspection of the surface of the painting with the unaided eye, reveals fragmentary evidence of the original paint layer consisting of a blue pigment combined with lead white. This mixture was applied in a thin layer on top of the red, resulting in a hazy purplish hue in order to effectively achieve a subtle fabric texture. Furthermore, in reviewing this information, carpet expert Walter Denny noted that the textile's pattern does not reflect any Islamic carpets of the types known to have circulated in Venice in the sixteenth century. Two possibilities have emerged from this reconsideration. The textile represented may be a cut velvet, the color of which has changed, and the patterns of which have been distorted during restorations that misinterpreted the original fabric. Alternatively, it could be a velvet or silk with embroidery and appliqué produced in Italy and France during this period.[8]

XRF mapping has in general provided clear elemental distributions that reveal locations where there is a complete loss of the original paint layers. Damage has

occurred around the perimeter, which has most notably affected the knuckles of the sculptor's proper left hand. The present restoration completed these digits in a clumsy manner, which has falsified the quality and form of the original. The XRF distribution map of iron provides a better-defined image of the original strength of form in this hand (fig. 8). Iron is a primary component of earth pigments, such as ochers, sienna, and other brown and red earths, which are used in paint mixtures to deepen tones and model forms.

The small black spots that pepper the XRF distribution map of lead reveal the small losses in the paint film and ground of a painting that is generally in good condition (fig. 9). The XRF distribution map of lead also provides a stronger image of the feature in the upper-left background, the identification of which was part of the genesis of this investigation. Despite surface abrasion and the increased transparency of the lead white–containing paint that has resulted in the diminishment of the form, XRF mapping helped to gain a better visual understanding of this passage. It is a statue, depicted

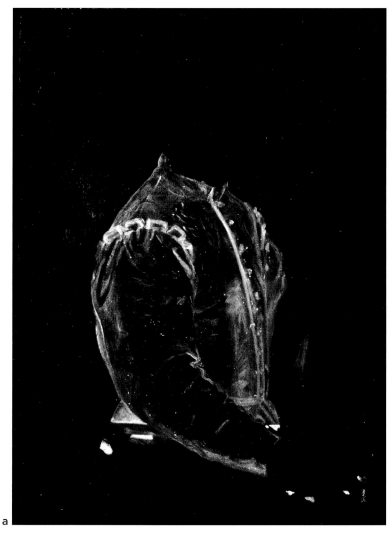
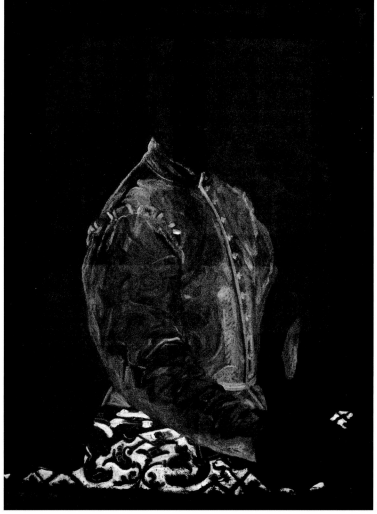

a
b

fig. 7 Mercury distribution map acquired by XRF imaging of *Alessandro Vittoria* (fig. 1). Mercury, a component of the red pigment vermilion, was used in mixtures to paint the flesh. It was also used as the base color for the fabric laid across the table. Details of the fabric pattern were applied on top of the base color to effectively achieve the subtle colors and texture of a cut velvet or an embroidered and appliqué surface.

from the waist down, with a weight-bearing left leg, a bent right knee, and drapery gathering on the pedestal base. This subject makes sense here, as statues appear in the background of other works by Veronese, perhaps as a reference to his training in Verona by his stonecutter father, as well as an attribute to enhance the depiction of a sculptor (see below, and fig. 11).[9] Following the completion of this study, consideration will be given to cleaning the portrait of its discolored varnish and extensive repainting, in order to regain the colors, forms, and original intentions of the artist to the extent possible.

INTERPRETATION OF THE PAINTING

The changes described above demonstrate that the viewer must imagine a more vivid surface, with a more subtle cloth (perhaps crimson-purplish in tone) swung over the table, a greater articulation of the position of the statuette within the sculptor's curling fingers, and a better-defined statue in the left background. All would have added to the success of the painting. With this new understanding of the condition and quality of the painted surface in mind, we can review the debates about the work's meaning and date.

The identification of the sitter and statuette has been the subject of some deliberation, to which we add our observations here. As noted earlier, Alessandro

Vittoria has generally been considered its subject, posed with his own statuette. However, in 1972, Wladimir Timofiewitsch proposed that the sitter is the considerably younger Veronese sculptor Girolamo Campagna (1549–1625), basing his analysis on the strong similarity between the statuette in the Museum's portrait and Campagna's large sculpted Atlas found at one side of a great fireplace in the Sala dell'Anticollegio in the Palazzo Ducale, Venice, and other factors.[10] This identification would force a dating of the picture to the last year of Veronese's life, as that sculpture was dated by the author to 1587/88, and would make it the last of his portraits. The sitter would have been in his late thirties. While the Museum did not adopt this new identification, many experts on the painter did, with the tide turning only in the context of recent studies of Vittoria.[11] These investigations added to the previous arguments by focusing on the importance of the design of the Saint Sebastian figure to Vittoria, as he referred to it repeatedly in his wills and owned one cast of it at his death; and of the significance of his own portraits to his professional self-presentation. Posthumous inventories list five portraits done at different times and by various artists. Vittoria kept them in a room of his home next to his small studio and near his garden: those who visited would see the artist represented by masterful portraitists in the context of his own studio.[12]

In addition, Veronese and Vittoria had a professional relationship, the strength of which seems reflected in this portrait. The two worked alongside each other in the Venetian church of San Geminiano about 1560, when Vittoria produced a marble bust of the dynamic parish priest Benedetto Manzini (Ca d'Oro, Venice), while Veronese used Manzini's features for the figure of Saint Severus in the church's organ shutters (Galleria Estense, Modena). The visual comparison between Veronese's painting and Vittoria's sculpture must have been striking.[13] In the Museum's portrait, Veronese creates another dynamic between the two arts, presenting—in paint—a nuanced description of sculpture's diverse qualities. The Saint Sebastian statuette is not identical in form to the finished bronze, but more interestingly, seems to be a model for it, possibly in terracotta washed with a white clay slip, a technique often used by Venetian sculptors.[14] To the other side of the sitter an antique torso—perhaps a variation of the upper half of the *Belvedere Torso*—is displayed on the table with its truncated head placed pointedly outward, toward the viewer. It recalls Veronese's great scene *The Martyrdom of Saint Sebastian* (San Sebastiano, Venice) (fig. 10), in which the living saint is posed directly above

fig. 8 Iron distribution map acquired by XRF imaging of *Alessandro Vittoria* (fig. 1). Iron is the primary component of earth pigments, such as ochers, sienna, and various brown and red earths, which are used in paint mixtures to deepen tones and model form.

his Roman cuirass, the molded torso of which is foreshortened, its empty neck aligned similarly toward the viewer. There Veronese juxtaposes the Christian saint and his Roman armor; here the modern and ancient worlds coexist in the sculptor's realm.[15] Finally, as our analysis has confirmed, Veronese blocked out another sculpture in a niche in the background. Comparable examples appear in numerous works by the artist, including other portraits (fig. 11), but only here in an abbreviated fashion that gives no sign of the sculpture's purported material, implying an architectural setting without competing with the physicality of the other pieces. The collegial relationship between painter and

sitter could account for Veronese's careful consideration of the sculptural elements of the portrait.

Although Vittoria's age in the portrait is difficult to pinpoint, his dark, clipped beard, graying hair, and the prominent veins on his temple suggest he is about fifty and the painting may date to about 1575 or a few years later. The subtle twist of the body, the glance away from the viewer, and the sober expression are reminiscent of portraits by Jacopo Bassano (ca. 1510–1592) of the 1570s with which this painting has been compared, and coincide with Veronese's more general interest in that artist at that time.[16] Only a handful of portraits date to the last decade or so of Veronese's career. The latest ones, such

fig. 9 Lead distribution map acquired by XRF imaging of *Alessandro Vittoria* (fig. 1). This XRF map provides an enhanced image of the lead white paint used to construct the statue, depicted from the waist down, standing on a pedestal base in the background upper left, which is largely illegible when the surface of the painting is viewed with the unaided eye. The small black spots distributed throughout the image are locations where the paint layer and ground preparation are lost.

as a portrait of the jeweler and merchant Hans Jakob König (Castle Picture Gallery, Prague Castle, Prague), with a likely date of 1583, are even more somber than that of Vittoria, especially as we now know that his doublet began as a more colorful blue.[17] However, they share the rather reserved facial expressions that add to their powerful impact.

Veronese's portrait of his colleague Vittoria is one of the finest examples of a group of paintings for which Venice was noted: artists capturing the appearance of other artists.[18] Despite the physical changes over time that we have observed, it remains one of the artist's most perceptive portraits, and one that speaks eloquently about relations between two of the most significant artists active in the city in the later decades of the sixteenth century.

ANDREA BAYER
Jayne Wrightsman Curator, Department of European Paintings, The Metropolitan Museum of Art

DOROTHY MAHON
Conservator, Department of Paintings Conservation, The Metropolitan Museum of Art

SILVIA A. CENTENO
Research Scientist, Department of Scientific Research, The Metropolitan Museum of Art

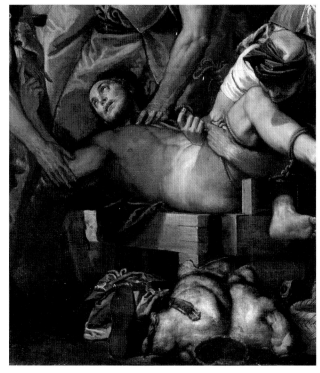

fig. 10 Paolo Veronese. Detail of *The Martyrdom of Saint Sebastian*, ca. 1565. Oil on canvas, 140 × 212½ in. (355 × 540 cm). San Sebastiano, Venice

fig. 11 Paolo Veronese. *Portrait of a Man*, ca. 1560, or 1576–78. Oil on canvas, 75⅝ × 52¾ in. (192.1 × 134 cm). The J. Paul Getty Museum, Los Angeles, Gift of J. Paul Getty (71.PA.17)

NOTES

1 Andrea Bayer thanks Thomas Martin for his insightful comments. See Venturi 1937; Valentiner 1942; and Salinger 1946 (Salinger's observations were built on earlier insights by Alfred M. Frankfurter; Memorandum, February 1937, Archives, Department of European Paintings). These authors based the identification of Vittoria on the similarity of the painted portrait with Vittoria's memorial bust made for his tomb in San Zaccaria, Venice, designed between about 1584 and 1595, as well as the statuette.

2 Alfeld et al. 2011.

3 Alfeld et al. 2013; Noble et al. 2012; Mahon et al. n.d. (forthcoming).

4 The XRF instrument used here consists of a measuring head that is moved across the painting surface by means of a motorized X-Y stage with a maximum travel range of 80 × 60 cm. The measuring head includes a 30 W Rh-target micro-focus X-ray tube and a Silicon Drift Detector (SDD) to collect the fluorescence signal. The X-ray source was operated at 50kV and 500 mA, and the resulting beam was focused by means of a polycapillary optic. The overall painting was scanned at 140 msec/pixel with a 600 micron step-size. The spectra were processed employing a combination of Pymca and Datamuncher software as described by Matthias Alfeld and Koen Janssens (2015, p. 777) and by the software provided by Bruker® for the M6 Jetstream instrument. We thank Giulia Olmeda, who at the time the painting was analyzed was a visiting graduate student from the Università degli Studi di Padova, for her assistance with the XRF mapping. We are also thankful to Joris Dik, Delft University of Technology, and Koen Janssens, University of Antwerp, for the loan of an XRF scanner prototype to the Metropolitan Museum, and to Geert Van der Snickt, University of Antwerp, for the initial processing of the data.

5 See Gettens and Fitzhugh 1993.

6 Mühlethaler and Thissen 1993.

7 Another feature visible in the XRF map of cobalt, abandoned at an early stage, is an object that cannot be identified with certainty, extending vertically from the waistline of the doublet. Mahon et al. 2010.

8 The authors thank Walter B. Denny, University Distinguished Professor of Islamic Art, University of Massachusetts, Amherst, and Melinda Watt, curator, Department of European Sculpture and Decorative Arts, and supervising curator, Antonio Ratti Textile Center, The Metropolitan Museum of Art, for their pertinent observations about the fabric. Examples of velvets can be found in Monnas 2012, especially nos. 40 (pp. 130–31), and 46 (pp. 142–43); on Venetian velvets in general, see Hills 1999, pp. 182–85. Examples of comparable textiles with embroidery and appliqué can be found in the Metropolitan Museum's collection and include a French band (16.32.333), an Italian runner (41.190.78), and a (possibly) Italian panel (41.190.175). All may be seen at www.metmuseum.org/collections.

9 The depiction of a statue was suggested orally by Xavier Salomon; and by Linda Borean in Marini and Aikema 2014, p. 140, no. 2.9.

10 The complicated issue of possible portraits of Campagna is outside the scope of this article. See Timofiewitsch 1972, pp. 32–34, for the full argument (fig. 124).

11 While preparing the Museum's catalogue of Venetian paintings, volume 2 of *Italian Paintings: A Catalogue of the Collection of The Metropolitan Museum of Art* (1973), the authors Federico Zeri and Elizabeth E. Gardner exchanged letters about the debate over the identification of the sitter as Alessandro Vittoria or Girolamo Campagna (Archives, Department of European Paintings, MMA). The following were inclined to accept Timofiewitsch's identification of Girolamo Campagna: Pignatti 1976, pp. 95, 154, no. 277; Pallucchini 1984, pp. 155, 188, no. 255; Rearick 1988, p. 192; and Pignatti and Pedrocco 1995, vol. 1, pp. 432–33, no. 325. For the re-identification as Alessandro Vittoria, see especially Kryza-Gersch 1999, pp. 153–56, 162, no. 3.

12 Kryza-Gersch 1999, pp. 153–56, 162, no. 3; Bayer 2005, pp. 20–25; Garton 2008, pp. 126–32; Koering 2009, pp. 180–86; Borean in Marini and Aikema 2014, p. 140.

13 Martin 1998, p. 119; Salomon 2014, p. 98.

14 Fiorentini 2007, pp. 227–28.

15 For further interpretation of the sculpture in the painting, see Garton 2008, pp. 129–32.

16 Pignatti 1976, vol. 1, p. 154. Zeri and Gardner 1973, p. 87, dated the painting about 1566, connecting it more closely with the first mention of a bronze of that subject by Vittoria.

17 For the portrait of Hans Jakob König, see Andrew John Martin in Marini and Aikema 2014, pp. 178–79, no. 3.3.

18 On this subject, see Fiorentini 2007; Koering 2009; and Borean 2014, for developments in the following century.

REFERENCES

Alfeld, Matthias, et al.
2011 Alfeld, Matthias, Koen Janssens, Joris Dik, Wout de Nolf, and Geert van der Snickt. "Optimization of Mobile Scanning Macro-XRF Systems for the *in situ* Investigation of Historical Paintings." *Journal of Analytical Atomic Spectrometry* 26, no. 5, pp. 899–909. First published online March 21, 2011, http://pubs.rsc.org/en/content/articlelanding/2011/ja/c0ja00257g#!divAbstract.
2013 Alfeld, Matthias, Wout De Nolf, Simone Cagno, Karen Appel, D. Peter Siddons, Anthony Kuczewski, Koen Janssens, Joris Dik, Karen Trentelman, Marc Walton, and Andrea Sartorius. "Revealing Hidden Paint Layers in Oil Paintings by Means of Scanning Macro-XRF: A Mock-up Study Based on Rembrandt's 'An Old Man in Military Costume.'" *Journal of Analytical Atomic Spectrometry* 28, no. 1, pp. 40–51. First published online November 22, 2012, http://pubs.rsc.org/en/content/articlelanding/2013/ja/c2ja30119a#!divAbstract.

Alfeld, Matthias, and Koen Janssens
2015 "Strategies for Processing Mega-Pixel X-ray Fluorescence Hyperspectral Data: A Case Study on a Version of Caravaggio's Painting *Supper at Emmaus.*" *Journal of Analytical Atomic Spectrometry* 30, no. 3, pp. 777–89. First published online February 12, 2015, http://pubs.rsc.org/en/content/articlelanding/2015/ja/c4ja00387j#!divAbstract.

Bayer, Andrea
2005 "North of the Apennines: Sixteenth-Century Italian Painting in Venice and the Veneto." *MMAB* 63 (Summer).

Borean, Linda
2014 "L'artista e il suo doppio: Ritratti di pittori del Seicento veneziano." *Artibus et historiae* 35, no. 70, pp. 61–82.

Fiorentini, Erna
2007 "Identità artistica nella retorica del mezzo espressivo: Vittoria, Campagna e altri scultori ritratti da pittori e il ruolo del bozzetto nel Veneto." In *Il ritratto nell'Europa del Cinquecento: Atti del convegno, Firenze, 7–8 novembre 2002*, edited by Aldo Galli, Chiara Piccinini, and Massimiliano Rossi, pp. 217–41. Florence: Leo S. Olschki.

Garton, John
2008 *Grace and Grandeur: The Portraiture of Paolo Veronese.* London: Harvey Miller.

Gettens, Rutherford J., and Elizabeth West Fitzhugh
1993 "Azurite and Blue Verditer." In *Artists' Pigments: A Handbook of Their History and Characteristics*, vol. 2, edited by Ashok Roy, pp. 23–35. Washington, D.C.: National Gallery of Art.

Hills, Paul
1999 *Venetian Colour: Marble, Mosaic, Paintings, and Glass, 1250–1550.* New Haven and London: Yale University Press.

Koering, Jérémie
2009 "L'art en personne(s)." In *Titien, Tintoret, Véronèse: Rivalités à Venise, 1540–1600*, edited by Vincent Delieuvin and Jean Habert, pp. 178–99. Exh. cat., Musée du Louvre, Paris. Paris: Hazan; Musée du Louvre Editions.

Kryza-Gersch, Claudia
1999 "Ritratti di scultori—ritratti di sculture: Osservazioni sulla rappresentazione di una professione." In *"La bellissima maniera": Alessandro Vittoria e la scultura veneta del Cinquecento*, edited by Andrea Bacchi, Lia Camerlengo, and Manfred Leithe-Jasper, pp. 153–65. Exh. cat., Castello del Buonconsiglio, Trent. Trent: TEMI.

Mahon, Dorothy, et al.
2010 Mahon, Dorothy, Silvia A. Centeno, Mark T. Wypyski, Xavier F. Salomon, and Andrea Bayer. "Technical Study of Three Allegorical Paintings by Paolo Veronese: *The Choice between Virtue and Vice, Wisdom and Strength,* and *Mars and Venus United by Love.*" *Metropolitan Museum Studies in Art, Science, and Technology* 1, pp. 83–108.
n.d. Mahon, Dorothy, Silvia A. Centeno, Mark T. Wypyski, Geert van der Snickt, Joris Dik, and Koen Janssens. "Rembrandt's *Aristotle with a Bust of Homer* Revisited: Technical Examination and New Insights" (paper presented at the National Gallery, London, November 13, 2014). In *Rembrandt Now: Technical Practice, Conservation, and Research.* London: Archetype Press and National Gallery Publications. Forthcoming.

Marini, Paola, and Bernard Aikema, eds.
2014 *Paolo Veronese: L'illusione della realtà.* Exh. cat., Palazzo della Gran Guardia, Verona. Milan: Mondadori Electa.

Martin, Thomas
1998 *Alessandro Vittoria and the Portrait Bust in Renaissance Venice: Remodelling Antiquity.* Oxford and New York: Clarendon Press.

Monnas, Lisa
2012 *Renaissance Velvets.* London: V&A Publishing.

Mühlethaler, Bruno, and Jean Thissen
1993 "Smalt." In *Artists' Pigments: A Handbook of Their History and Characteristics*, vol. 2, edited by Ashok Roy, pp. 113–30. Washington, D.C.: National Gallery of Art.

Noble, Petria, Annelies van Loon, Matthias Alfeld, and Joris Dik
2012 "Rembrandt and/or Studio, *Saul and David,* c.1655: Visualising the Curtain Using Cross-Section Analyses and X-ray Fluorescence Imaging." *Technè*, no. 35, pp. 36–45.

Pallucchini, Rodolfo
1984 *Veronese.* Milan: Mondadori.

Pignatti, Terisio
1976 *Veronese.* 2 vols. Venice: Alfieri Edizioni d'Arte.

Pignatti, Terisio, and Filippo Pedrocco
1995 *Veronese.* 2 vols. Milan: Electa.

Rearick, W. R.
1988 *The Art of Paolo Veronese, 1528–1588.* Exh. cat. Washington, D.C.: National Gallery of Art.

Salinger, Margaretta
1946 "Veronese's Portrait of the Sculptor Vittoria." *MMAB* 5 (Summer), pp. 7–14.

Salomon, Xavier F.
2014 *Veronese.* Exh. cat., National Gallery, London. London: National Gallery Company.

Timofiewitsch, Wladimir
1972 *Girolamo Campagna: Studien zur venezianischen Plastik um das Jahr 1600.* Munich: Fink.

Valentiner, Wilhelm R.
1942 "Alessandro Vittoria and Michelangelo." *Art Quarterly* 5, no. 2 (Spring), pp. 149–57.

Venturi, Adolfo
1937 "Per Paolo Veronese." *L'arte* 40, n.s., 8, no. 3 (July), pp. 210–15.

Zeri, Federico, and Elizabeth E. Gardner
1973 *Italian Paintings: A Catalogue of the Collection of The Metropolitan Museum of Art.* Vol. 2, *Venetian School.* New York: MMA.

FURIO RINALDI

The Roman *Maniera*: Newly Identified Drawings

Notoriously labeled by Federico Zeri as "arte senza tempo" (art without time), the Roman artistic community of the late sixteenth century was later revealed by John A. Gere and Philip Pouncey to be a vital and experimental hub of activity for drawing in particular.[1] Transitional and contradictory, but nonetheless somewhat nostalgic, during the passage from Late Mannerism to Baroque, Rome flourished as an exciting center of development for drawing, mostly due to the varied backgrounds of the artists involved. A higher demand for rapidly executed large frescoes and the progressive failure of traditionally organized Renaissance workshops—based on Raphael's method in the Vatican *Stanze*—forced personalities with diverse styles to join forces, resulting in a network of shared influences. In contrast to the somewhat superficial stylistic uniformity that the collaborations produced in painting, this dynamic melting pot produced an extraordinary variety of styles and techniques in drawing, especially in comparison to Florence, where the local school of drawing was regulated by the rules of the Accademia delle Arti del Disegno, founded in 1563. Highlighting the mutual relationships and influences among artists working in Rome from the 1550s to the early decades of the seventeenth century, this article presents seven newly identified and attributed Roman drawings in The Metropolitan Museum of Art. Astonishing in their experimentation and diversity, several were created for prestigious commissions.

THE LEGACY OF DANIELE DA VOLTERRA:
PELLEGRINO TIBALDI AND GIROLAMO MUZIANO

Two impressive, large sheets in the Metropolitan Museum (figs. 1, 3) provide critical visual evidence for the beginnings of two main protagonists in the Roman art world of the mid-1550s. Trained in the workshop of Daniele da Volterra (1509–1566), Michelangelo's protégé and last pupil in Rome, Pellegrino Tibaldi (1527–1596) and Girolamo Muziano (1528–1592) played instrumental roles both in keeping Michelangelo's legacy alive—especially at a time when it was severely challenged following the infamous unveiling of the

fig. 2 Pellegrino Tibaldi. *Saint Elizabeth,* ca. 1554. Red chalk, 16⅛ × 11⅛ in. (41.1 × 28.2 cm). Watermark: "five stars in a circle"; close to Briquet 6098; annotated at upper right in pen and brown ink: "Pord[eno]ne." Private collection (courtesy Pandolfini Casa d'Aste, Florence)

Last Judgment with its outrageously explicit nudes—and in spreading Daniele's stylized artistic language beyond the confines of Rome. The monumental study for a standing Saint Peter (fig. 1) entered the Museum with an attribution to Daniele himself but is instead to be assigned with confidence to the young Pellegrino Tibaldi and dated right after his collaboration with Daniele in the chapel of Lucrezia della Rovere at Trinità dei Monti (1548–49).[2] Tibaldi finely chiseled the figure on paper with highly polished black chalk, using a characteristic technique that he derived directly from Daniele and adopted shortly afterward in his monumental study for the standing Saint Elizabeth, frescoed by the artist in the Poggi Chapel, Bologna, about 1554 (fig. 2).[3] Comparable in size, both figures are rendered with the same tight crosshatching and share similar disproportions between the massive bodily presences and the small, pointy hands. The newly attributed sheet at the Metropolitan Museum can possibly be associated with Tibaldi's lost frescoes of Saints Peter and Paul executed by November 1553 (the date of the payments) in the Roman church of Sant'Andrea in Via Flaminia, and highly praised by Giorgio Vasari in 1568, who claimed to own a drawing for the figure of Saint Peter.[4]

The flowing pen-and-ink line of Perino del Vaga combined with Michelangelo's greatness and figural monumentality are the two main stylistic qualities of a large sheet depicting the Last Supper, in the Museum since 1880 with a traditional attribution to Girolamo Romanino (fig. 3).[5] The drawing can be identified instead as an important early work by the much younger Girolamo from Brescia, Muziano, who moved from his native Veneto to Rome during the early 1550s and soon became a key personality of late Roman Mannerism. The Metropolitan Museum's sheet is connected to a more typical, highly finished drawing by the artist on the same subject in the Louvre (fig. 4):[6] almost the same size, it was realized in Muziano's distinctive, polished red-chalk technique, derived from his admiration for the work of Daniele da Volterra. The drawing in the Metropolitan Museum clearly constitutes a preparatory step for the Louvre's *Last Supper*, as seen in its sketchier nature, the number of *pentimenti* and tentative outlines visible in its black-chalk underdrawing, and the presence in the center of the composition of the plate with viands, ultimately excluded in the design in red chalk. Possibly executed in preparation for a series of lost canvases depicting the Passion commissioned about 1561 from the artist by his major patron, Ippolito II d'Este, the sheet may also have been related, in view of its size and finish, to an unexecuted (or lost) composition

fig. 3 Here attributed to Girolamo Muziano (Italian, 1528–1592). *The Last Supper*, ca. 1555. Pen and brown ink, brush and brown wash, over black chalk, 14⅝ × 16⅛ in. (37.1 × 41 cm). Annotated at lower right in pen and ink: "1480–1560 Romanino da Brescia"; on the verso in graphite: "Romanino." The Metropolitan Museum of Art, Gift of Cornelius Vanderbilt, 1880 (80.3.141)

fig. 4 Girolamo Muziano. *The Last Supper*, ca. 1555. Red chalk, 13⅝ × 14⅝ in. (34.5 × 37 cm). Annotated in pen and brown ink at lower left: "Hieronemo Muciano." Musée du Louvre, Département des Arts Graphiques, Paris (5097)

meant to be engraved by the artist's longtime partner Cornelis Cort. In 1568, Cort produced a similar print of a Last Supper on the basis of a drawing by Muziano.[7]

The unusual technique adopted in the Metropolitan Museum's sheet suggests an earlier dating, which seems further confirmed by the sketches on its laid-down verso, visible only in transmitted light. The main figure on the verso, a seated figure with right arm raised, closely resembles an early idea for the allegory of Spring, frescoed by the young Muziano on the ceiling of the Salone della Caminata in the palazzo of Girolamo Simoncelli in Torre San Severo, Orvieto. This decoration was taken on by the artist in 1558–59 and ultimately completed by his pupil Cesare Nebbia in 1570–73.[8]

The Metropolitan Museum's sheet opens a new chapter on Muziano's stylistic spectrum and early Roman influences. At his arrival in Rome in the early

1550s, he was attracted to the refined draftsmanship of Daniele da Volterra, and it was within Daniele's Roman workshop that the artist probably found his initial training, as argued by Patrizia Tosini, who detected Muziano's presence in the frescoes of the Stanza di Cleopatra at the Vatican.[9] The sculptural quality of Muziano's numerous highly finished chalk drawings has somewhat hampered a full understanding of the artist's wider graphic abilities. During his career, Muziano would progressively enhance his *michelangiolismo* by reinforcing the plastic quality of his drawing (ultimately becoming a favorite of Tommaso de' Cavalieri, Michelangelo's beloved Roman nobleman), but the Metropolitan Museum's sheet still attests his early Roman influences. It shows Muziano's proximity to the sketchier, more dynamic draftsmanship of his peer Taddeo Zuccaro, a rising star in Rome during the early 1550s and the principal exponent of vibrant, almost "electric," techniques in pen and ink. The friendship and mutual influences between the two artists was recorded as early as 1648 by author, painter, and collector Carlo Ridolfi (1594–1658) and reiterated in modern scholarship with particular emphasis on their graphic

work, by John A. Gere and John Marciari, who both suggested a joint collaboration between Zuccaro and Muziano on the frescoes of Santa Caterina della Rota (ca. 1552–53).[10] Muziano's early double-sided sheet in the Rijksmuseum, made for one of the prophets frescoed on the lunette at Santa Caterina, provides the closest stylistic comparison for the Metropolitan Museum's drawing, similarly rendered in bold, flowing pen and brown ink, and brown wash over black chalk.[11]

MARCO PINO

Much like Muziano and Tibaldi, Marco Pino (1521–1583) was reared in the Roman workshop of Daniele da Volterra, but due to his early training with Perino del Vaga, Pino developed in Rome a far more layered and eclectic drawing style that reflects his restless travels between Siena, Rome, and Naples. Daniele's *Assumption of the Virgin*, frescoed with the help of Pino and Pellegrino Tibaldi in the Della Rovere chapel at Trinità dei Monti (1547–51), appears to be the main figural reference point for a hitherto unattributed drawing of a seated Virgin for an *Assumption* (fig. 5). The sheet's style, technique, and figure closely resemble a

fig. 5 Here attributed to Marco Pino (Italian, 1521–1583). Study for a Virgin in the *Assumption*, 1570–71. Pen and brown ink, brush and brown wash, squared in black chalk, 8½ × 6¾ in. (21.6 × 17 cm). The Metropolitan Museum of Art, Gift of Cornelius Vanderbilt, 1880 (80.3.142)

fig. 6 Marco Pino. *Christ in Pietà with the Virgin and Two Angels*, 1568–71. Pen and brown ink, brush and brown wash over black chalk, 9¼ × 5½ in. (23.4 × 14 cm). Musée du Louvre, Département des Arts Graphiques, Paris (22)

pen-and-ink study for the *Pietà* in the Louvre (fig. 6), executed by Pino about 1568–71 for a canvas in Santa Maria in Aracoeli.[12] Datable about the same years, 1570–71, the Metropolitan Museum's study for the *Assumption* records Pino's mature drawing style at the time of his involvement in the decoration of the Oratorio del Gonfalone, in harmony with the dynamic and luminous techniques developed there by Federico Zuccaro and Raffaellino da Reggio. Although the design cannot be linked precisely to any of Pino's finished productions, the drawing possibly records an early idea for his *Assumption of the Virgin*, a late work executed in Naples for the church of Santi Severino e Sossio directly after his departure from Rome in 1571.[13]

RAFFAELLINO DA REGGIO

During his almost meteoric presence in the city, limited to less than ten years, Raffaellino Motta da Reggio (1550–1578) occupied a primary position on the Roman scene. He was active with Marco Pino on the frescoes of the Oratorio del Gonfalone (ca. 1570–73), the iridescent temple of late Roman Mannerism, and equally influenced by the draftsmanship of Taddeo Zuccaro, for which Gere has rightly considered him that artist's true heir, even more than Zuccaro's brother Federico. During the papacy of Gregory XIII Boncompagni (r. 1572–85), who promoted and attracted artists from his native region of Emilia and Romagna, Raffaellino's highly individual, luminous draftsmanship was equally motivated by the quirky manner of his first local master, Lelio Orsi, and the elegance of Taddeo, relying mostly on a strongly pictorial use of brush and washes, over freely executed black- or red-chalk underdrawings.

A sheet in the Metropolitan Museum is an important addition to Raffaellino's limited catalogue of preparatory drawings (fig. 7).[14] The drawing entered the Museum in 1880 as "school of Tintoretto," and was subsequently filed as "anonymous seventeenth century." It is in fact a gleaming brush *modello* for the scene of Christ at the home of Simon the Pharisee (Luke 7:36–50) frescoed by Raffaellino on the vault of the tenth bay in the second-floor Loggia of Gregory XIII between

fig. 8 Raffaellino Motta da Reggio. *Christ and the Magdalen at the Home of Simon the Pharisee*, 1575–77. Fresco. Vatican City, Vatican Palace, Gregorian Logge

October 1575 and September 1577 (fig. 8).[15] The style and function of the sheet match other highly finished drawings produced by Raffaellino for the same endeavor at the Vatican, including studies for *Christ's Entry into Jerusalem* and the *Washing of the Apostles' Feet*, frescoed on the same vault of the Loggia.[16] Despite some stiffness in execution and an apparent uniformity with the composition of the final fresco, the drawing exhibits several *pentimenti* in the black chalk outlines and differences in scale and positions from the figures in the background of the scene. Overall, the composition reflects the state of the fresco, but should not be considered a copy. As the frescoes in the Gregorian Loggia were the result of a joint effort of several artists employed in the workshop of Lorenzo Sabatini (ca. 1530–1576), Raffaellino was obliged to define his compositions on paper with a painstaking degree of finish (he often produced several copies of the same scenes), in case the painting was ultimately assigned to another artist in Sabatini's entourage.[17] Raffaellino's distinctive pictorial style, praised by artist-authors Giovanni Baglione (1566–1643) and Karel van Mander (1548–1606), who visited Rome at the height of the artist's activity and fame, is fully expressed in this drawing. He conveys lighting through a masterly *chiaroscuro* brush technique that infuses a liquid quality into the composition.[18]

TWO DRAWINGS BY GIOVANNI GUERRA

Similarly related to an early decorative stage of the Gregorian Logge, a monumental design (fig. 9) for an ornamental architectural ceiling compartment was

acquired by the Metropolitan Museum's curator Jacob Bean in 1971 with an attribution to Giovanni Alberti. The reattribution here suggests that the drawing is instead an important missing link to the first Roman activity of the Modenese artist Giovanni Guerra (1544–1618).[19] Finely drawn in pen, ink, and wash on the recto, and quickly sketched on the verso with a crude architectural rendering of a floor plan, this hitherto unpublished sheet relates in style to Guerra's fragmentary designs pasted about 1690 on two leafs of Sebastiano Resta's (1635–1714) book of ornamental drawings, the *Libro d'Arabeschi*. Still preserved in its original seventeenth-century binding at the Biblioteca Comunale of Palermo, these fragments were attributed by Resta to Federico Zuccaro but astutely recognized by Simonetta Prosperi Valenti Rodinò as Guerra's proposals for the architectural compartments of the Gregorian Logge.[20] The fragments in Palermo feature ornamental projects with allegories of the Church, Religion, and— most importantly—the Boncompagni papal arms of Gregory XIII (a dragon). Comparable techniques, facial types, and recurring decorative motifs appear on the sheets in Palermo and New York. The putti playfully clutch the volutes under the pendentives, while the female figure with a globe (an allegory of Faith?) in a niche at the bottom left of the Metropolitan Museum's sheet finds her sisters in the female allegories in Palermo.

Although undocumented and unrecorded by early sources, Guerra's involvement in the Logge was very likely promoted once again by Lorenzo Sabatini, his father-in-law and headmaster of the Vatican decorative tasks under Pope Gregory XIII. Guerra's effervescent decorative idea for the Logge was, however, ultimately not translated into paint: when Sabatini died in 1576, Guerra lost his powerful mentor and the commission was ultimately assigned to Marco Marchetti da Faenza, who completed the ornaments in 1577.[21] Nevertheless, the sheet in the Metropolitan Museum clearly records Guerra's ambition as a designer and his strong ability in elaborating trompe l'oeil. He invented quite early a taste for architectural illusionistic complexity that would flourish in the Vatican only decades later, especially in the work of the brothers Giovanni and Cherubino Alberti in the Sala Clementina. Especially innovative—and repeatedly inserted by Guerra on the sheets in Palermo and the Metropolitan Museum—is the motif of foreshortened blustered *oculi* with flying putti that will appear in the artist's later decoration of the dome of San Girolamo degli Schiavoni (1589–90). His architectural insets would soon be copied by

fig. 9 Here attributed to Giovanni Guerra (Italian, 1544–1618). *Design for Ceiling Compartment with Allegory of Faith(?)*, ca. 1575. Pen and brown ink, brush with brown and gray wash, ruling and compass work, over traces of black chalk, 21 × 15¼ in. (53.2 × 38.9 cm). Watermark: "crescent." The Metropolitan Museum of Art, Purchase, Harris Brisbane Dick Fund and Joseph Pulitzer Bequest, 1971 (1971.513.44)

Giovanni and Cherubino Alberti, becoming one of their most quoted decorative trademarks, appearing, for example, in the frescoes in the Old Sacristy of San Giovanni in Laterano (about 1600).[22]

Unlike the fragments pasted on Resta's codex in Palermo, the Metropolitan Museum's drawing is fully preserved in its original size (possibly a *mezzano* format). In this respect, it is worth noting that Sebastiano Resta himself specified at the bottom of folio 74 of the Palermo codex that "The best preserved portions of

these ornaments are placed in the third volume of the *Pittori per serie*" (*Le portioni più sane di questi ornamenti stanno collocate nel terzo tomo delli Pittori per serie*), a reference to fully preserved designs that he kept in his book of drawings titled *Serie dei pittori*. Sold by Resta to Matteo Marchetti, bishop of Arezzo, the book was eventually dismembered and sold in England with Lord Somers's collection in 1717.[23]

After these bumpy beginnings, Guerra's Roman career flourished under the brief tenure of

fig. 10 Attributed to Giovanni Guerra. *Vestal Virgin*, ca. 1585–90. Pen and brown ink, brush and brown wash, 7 × 4½ in. (17.8 × 11.3 cm). The Metropolitan Museum of Art, Gift of Cornelius Vanderbilt, 1880 (80.3.122)

Felice Peretti Montalto, Pope Sixtus V, between 1585 and 1590, when he was charged with countless decorative and architectural renovations in the city. Datable to this period is a far more recognizable sheet easily attributable to Guerra (fig. 10), drawn with his later and typically vibrant pen-and-ink technique, and a highlight in his relationship with his major patron.[24] The sheet reproduces rather faithfully a celebrated Roman sculpture after a Greek prototype of the third century B.C. known as the *Old Drunkard* or *Drunken Crone*, depicting a seated, draped aged woman, possibly making a votive offering of a wine jar to the god Dionysus. Only two copies of this extraordinary sculpture survive: one in the Glyptothek in Munich, and the other in the Capitoline Museums in Rome.[25] Although the Capitoline version was unearthed during the renovation of the Basilica of Sant'Agnese in Via Nomentana in 1620, thus only after Guerra's death in 1618, the version in Munich was preserved in the second floor of Villa Peretti Montalto, the Roman residence of the future pope Sixtus V, where Guerra would have seen it.[26]

It was possibly conceived as an allegorical emblem, or an iconographic idea for a decorative element, but

Guerra transformed the original antique source, adding the statue's missing right arm and shaping the wine jar into a flaming urn. Following a recurring practice in his graphic work, Guerra annotated in pen and ink an inscription in capital letters that reads "Amate virg. [ines] vestal inveterate in sacris obsequis . . ." (beloved aged vestal virgins in the sacred service [. . .]), thus clarifying the subject as an aged Vestal Virgin. Unfortunately, the figure does not seem to appear in Guerra's collection of emblems dedicated to Sixtus V (*Varii emblemi hieroglifici*, published in Rome in 1589), nor in other figural inventions that he developed in his frescoes at the Palazzetto Cenci or at Villa Peretti Montalto, Rome, where similarly seated allegorical female figures are also featured.[27]

FAMILY THREADS

An ornamental design (fig. 11) formerly catalogued as a work by Andrea Lilio provides solid groundwork for reestablishing the personality of Elisabetta Catanea Parasole (ca. 1580–1617), the celebrated designer of textile pattern books and needlework manuals, and her connections with artists from the workshop of Giuseppe Cesari, called Cavaliere d'Arpino (ca. 1568–1640), namely her husband, the painter Rosato Parasole (doc. 1592–1622), and her nephew Bernardino Parasole (1594–?before 1642).[28]

Vividly drawn with pen and brown ink, with washes and white gouache over black and red chalks, the sheet is incised for transfer with a stylus over the contours of its right half. It is the preparatory drawing for the engraved frontispiece of Elisabetta Parasole's most accomplished and celebrated work, the textile pattern book *Teatro delle nobili et virtuose donne (Theater of the Noble and Virtuous Women)*, published by Mauritio Bona in Rome in 1616 (fig. 12).[29] Marking a crucial turning point in the affirmation of women in the histories of design and printmaking, Elisabetta Parasole's *Teatro* is the reedition of her overwhelmingly successful textile book of 1610, *Fiore d'ogni virtù per le nobili et honeste matrone (Flower of Virtues for Noble and Honest Women*, published in Rome by Antonio Facchetti) and includes twelve additional plates of textile and lace patterns for needlework and a new frontispiece. The *Teatro*'s fame was recorded by the biographer Giovanni Baglione, who mentioned its newly added frontispiece in his *Le vite de'pittori, scultori et architetti* (1642) with an attribution to the engraver Francesco Villamena.[30]

Measuring almost the same size as the engraving, the Metropolitan Museum's sheet is evidently an early idea for the title page, apart from some differences in

fig. 11 Here attributed to Rosato Parasole (Italian, doc. 1592–1622) or Bernardino Parasole (Italian, 1594–?before 1642). *Design for a Frontispiece with Allegories of Intelletto and Operatione Perfetta*, ca. 1616. Pen and brown ink, brush and brown wash, white gouache over black and red chalk, contours incised with a stylus over the right half of the sheet, sheet 7⅛ × 9¼ in. (18.1 × 23.6 cm), drawing 6⅞ × 9 in. (17.5 × 23 cm). Annotated in pen and brown ink in the upper medallion: "Andrea d'/Ancona," and illegible note at lower right: [Cherubino Alberti]. The Metropolitan Museum of Art, Rogers Fund, 1970 (1970.113.4)

fig. 12 Francesco Villamena (Italian, 1564–1624). Engraved title page for Elisabetta Catanea Parasole (Italian, ca. 1580–1617), *Teatro delle nobili et virtuose donne*. Published by Mauritio Bona, Rome, 1616. Engraving, 7½ × 9⅞ in. (19 × 25 cm). The Metropolitan Museum of Art, Rogers Fund, 1919 (19.51[1])

the final print. Following a common practice in frontispiece designs, the drawing leaves the two medallions blank, thus without the portrait of the Princess of France and Spain, Elisabetta of Bourbon (1602–1644) (to whom the book is dedicated), and her coat of arms. Furthermore, the sheet presents two allegorical figures at the lower corners that will be later discarded from the final design and replaced by emblems of two crossed flaming trunks. The allegorical figures find matches in Cesare Ripa's allegories illustrated in his *Iconologia*: at left is the emblem of *Intelletto* (Intellect), a crowned young man holding a scepter and accompanied by an eagle, while *Operatione Perfetta* (Perfect Operation, or Better Realization) is embodied at right by a reclining young woman holding a mirror and a square.[31] Although virtuosity, precision, and patience are required in needlework, the two allegories were ultimately eliminated from the final engraving in order to give due prominence to the portrait of Elisabetta of Bourbon.

With regard to the drawing's attribution, its style and technique embody the qualities of a draftsman belonging to the workshop of Giuseppe Cesari, Cavaliere d'Arpino, as demonstrated by the recognizable and expressive facial features, the compressed anatomies, and the dynamic flow of pen and ink. As the husband of Elisabetta (to whom he was engaged in 1593) and a prominent assistant in Arpino's Roman workshop, Rosato Parasole could be the author responsible for it. Virtually unknown as a draftsman, Rosato Parasole is well documented in Saint Peter's between 1601 and 1611 as an artist from Arpino's entourage who was active on the basilica's celebrated mosaics in its dome and drum.[32]

As a possible alternative, the name of Bernardino Parasole (1594–?before 1642) may be offered. The nephew of Elisabetta and Rosato and—most importantly—the son of the Roman printmakers Girolama (Geronima) Cagnaccia and Leonardo Norcino Parasole, Bernardino was also well acquainted with printmaking and design processes, and like his uncle joined the workshop of the Cavaliere d'Arpino at a young age, as later recorded by Baglione.[33] Stylistically devoted to the pictorial manner of his master, Bernardino Parasole's securely attributed works, such as two painted ovals with Angels in Glory now in the Capodimonte, Naples—paid for in May 1623 by the abbot of Montecassino, Don Pietro da Verona—show a series of flying putti that are strikingly close to those drawn on the cartouche of the sheet.[34] As a talented son of two celebrated printmakers, Bernardino Parasole could well have been involved in the design process of the frontispiece of his aunt's *Teatro.*

If indeed the drawing is by either Rosato or Bernardino Parasole, many other drawings may now be attributed to the hands of the recognizable draftsmen. A dynamic bacchanal with a reclining Silenus in Columbus, Ohio,[35] certainly belongs to the same hand, while other drawings by the Parasoles may appear among a corpus recently attributed to another member of Arpino's circle, Cesare Rossetti (ca. 1560–1644).[36]

Throughout his career, the Cavaliere d'Arpino was significantly involved in printmaking and produced designs for title pages, celebratory prints, and reproductive engravings after his paintings and drawings. He used the help of engravers based in Rome such as Raffaele Guidi, Philippe Thomassin, Johann Fredrich Greuter, and Francesco Villamena.[37] Villamena, according to Baglione, was the engraver of the *Teatro* frontispiece. Based on the Metropolitan Museum's newly attributed sheet, this activity can now be extended to other members of the Cavaliere's workshop. The Cavaliere, the last proponent of the stylistic language that derived from Raphael and Michelangelo and was echoed by Perino del Vaga, Daniele da Volterra, and Girolamo Muziano, embodied in his drawings the contradictions of a transitional period that we have outlined here through some of its key personalities. With a career spanning more than six decades, Arpino played a critical role in keeping the legacy of Renaissance drawing alive in Rome. He outlived by many years Annibale Carracci, whose radical naturalism set new standards. His own draftsmanship, stylish and nostalgic, sounded a swan song that could not survive the clarion call with which Caravaggism would challenge traditional design practices.

ACKNOWLEDGMENTS

I thank Carmen Bambach, James David Draper, Marco Simone Bolzoni, George Goldner, John Marciari, Nadine M. Orenstein, Simonetta Prosperi Valenti Rodinò, Femke Speelberg, Patrizia Tosini, and Mark P. McDonald.

FURIO RINALDI
Associate Specialist, Old Master Drawings, Christie's, New York

NOTES

1 Zeri 1957; Gere 1971; Gere and Pouncey 1983.

2 See the entry by Carmen C. Bambach (2007) on metmuseum.org /collection (as Daniele da Volterra).

3 See Roli 1987, pp. 34–36, ill., and Pandolfini Casa d'Aste 2014, pp. 154–58, lot 26. I thank Antonio Berni for providing me with a photograph of the drawing.

4 Tibaldi was paid for the frescoes at Sant'Andrea on November 25, 1553 ("Reg. Edifici Pubblici 1552–55," year 1553, fol. 25, Archivio di Stato, Rome). See Briganti 1945, pp. 70, 74, 107. Vasari's claim for owning a study by Tibaldi for the Saint Peter is recorded in his 1568 edition of the *Vite*: "fece un San Pietro e un Santo Paolo, che furono due molto lodate figure; il disegno di quel San Pietro è nel nostro libro" ("he painted Saint Peter and Saint Paul, which were two figures much praised; the drawing for the Saint Peter is in our book [Vasari's *Libro de' Disegni*]"); see Vasari [1568] 1966–87, vol. 6, p. 148. Two studies for Saints Peter and Paul—the latter, possibly the same one owned by Vasari—were in possession of Sebastiano Resta in 1684 (Agosti, Grisolia, and Pizzoni 2016, p. 87).

5 An undated attribution to "copy after Taddeo Zuccaro" was annotated by curator Jacob Bean on the mount.

6 See Tosini 2008, pp. 156, 159, fig. 142.

7 On Muziano's commissions for Ippolito II d'Este and his *Last Supper* engraved by Cornelis Cort, see ibid., pp. 156–57, 166, fig. 150.

8 On the Palazzo Simoncelli, see ibid., pp. 340–43, no. A9.

9 On Daniele da Volterra and Muziano, see ibid., pp. 48, 321, 481, and Rinaldi 2016, pp. 71–74.

10 Ridolfi 1648, part 1, p. 265; Gere 1966, pp. 417–18; Marciari 2002, pp. 113–17.

11 Rijksprentenkabinett, Amsterdam, RP-T-1949-445 verso; see Marciari 2002, pp. 117–19, fig. 7, and Tosini 2008, pp. 324–25, fig. 3a. John Marciari pointed out this drawing and verified my attribution to Muziano of the Metropolitan Museum's sheet on a visit to the Museum in March 2016.

12 See Monbeig-Goguel 1972, p. 102, no. 120, ill., and Zezza 2003, p. 319, no. C.32, ill. On the panel in Santa Maria in Aracoeli, see ibid., p. 279, no. A.71, ill.

13 On the painting, see Zezza 2003, p. 272, no. A.52, ill.

14 The artist's catalogue of drawings was recently discussed by Marco Simone Bolzoni (2016).

15 The attribution to Raffaellino of this scene in the Loggia dates back to Giovanni Baglione's *Vita* of the artist (1642, p. 26).

16 For an overview of the artist's drawings for the Logge, see Marciari 2006 and Bolzoni 2016, pp. 156–60, 187–88, 192, 194–95, figs. 14–16, 19–21, nos. A14, A19, A39, A40, A50, and A51 (the latter in my view is not autograph).

17 In conversation (July 2016), George R. Goldner agreed to an attribution to the artist, whereas both Marco Simone Bolzoni and Carmen C. Bambach consider the drawing to be a copy from the workshop of Raffaellino. He may have been assisted by his own collaborators during the decoration of the Logge. Raffaellino's common practice of replicating his own drawn *modelli* is discussed by Bolzoni (2016, pp. 158, 161). At least another sheet connected to the same scene in the loggia is known: Teylers Museum, Haarlem (D 43; Pen and brown ink, brush and gray-brown wash, white gouache, 9⅞ × 11⅞ in. [25 × 30.3 cm]); see Van Tuyll van Serooskeren 2000, p. 291, no. 276, ill., and Bolzoni 2016, p. 158. A second version is said to be in the J. F. Willumsens Museum, Frederikssund, as indicated by Chris Fischer on an undated note in the department's files.

18 Baglione 1642, p. 26; Van Mander 1604, fol. 193v; and Bolzoni 2016, pp. 147, 201.

19 Simonetta Prosperi Valenti Rodinò confirmed the attribution of the sheet to Guerra in 2014.

20 Giovanni Guerra. *Fragmentary Designs with Ornamental Architectural Ceiling Compartment with Allegory Church, Religion and Boncompagni Papal Arms*, ca. 1575, assembled by Sebastiano Resta (1635–1714), ca. 1690. Pen and brown ink, washes, over black chalk, 13¾ × 16⅛ in. (35 × 41 cm). Biblioteca Comunale di Palermo, *Libro d'Arabeschi* (fol. 74). Folio 74 is annotated by Resta: "frammenti dell'Ornato in più modi disegnato / da federigo Zuccaro per la Cappella Paolina sotto GreG[ori]o XI[II] / Il Baglione li attribuisce à federigo Zuccaro, ma à me paiono di Lorenzo Sabbatini da Bologna / In ogni modo bisogna credere più al Baglione per essere / stato quello che fù, e per essere stato quasi di quel tempo / Le portioni più sane di questi ornamenti stanno collocate nel terzo Tomo delli Pittori per serie" ("fragments of Ornaments drawn in different ways / by Federico Zuccaro for the Pauline Chapel under Gregory XI[II] / Baglione attributed them to Federico Zuccaro, but it seems to me that they are by Lorenzo Sabatini from Bologna / In any case we should trust Baglione because / he was who he was, and he was there at the time / The best preserved [most intact] portions of these ornaments are placed [pasted] in the third volume of the *Pittori per serie*"). See Prosperi Valenti Rodinò 2007, pp. 146–49, nos. 74, 76.

21 On Guerra, Sabatini, and the development of the decoration in the Gregorian logge, see Parma Armani 1978, p. 22; Prosperi Valenti Rodinò 2000; Pierguidi 2002, p. 446n52; and Prosperi Valenti Rodinò 2007, pp. 146–47.

22 On Giovanni and Cherubino Alberti, see Pierguidi 2002, p. 439, figs. 9, 10.

23 On the fate of Sebastiano Resta's books of drawings, see Warwick 2000. That the Metropolitan Museum's sheet was likely part of this book is further attested by the fact that similar designs ascribed to Federico Zuccaro are described by Resta in the annotated description of *Serie dei pittori* under the numbers 55, 58–63, in Lansdowne MS 802, Book L, British Library, London.

24 A tentative attribution to Giovanni Guerra was suggested by Mary Vaccaro on July 22, 2008, in a note on the mount.

25 On the two versions of the *Old Drunkard* in Rome (Musei Capitolini, 299) and Munich (Glyptothek, 473) see Dimartino 2008.

26 The Munich version is recorded on the second floor of Villa Peretti Montalto in 1655 but may have been acquired by Felice Peretti much earlier, by the late 1580s (the villa was built from 1586). On the sculpture's early provenance, see Rausa 2005, pp. 107–8, and Dimartino 2008, pp. 67, 77nn7–8.

27 On the frescoes in Palazzetto Cenci, Rome (1583), see Bevilacqua 1985; on those at Villa Peretti Montalto, see Tosini 2015, pp. 41–45.

28 The sheet was published by Jacob Bean and Lawrence Turčić (1982, p. 125, no. 116) as by Andrea Lilio, and by Luciano Arcangeli (1985, p. 91) as not by Andrea Lilio.

29 Parasole 1616. See Speelberg 2015, pp. 44–46, figs. 54–56. A full version with forty-five woodcut designs is in the Biblioteca Casanatense, Rome (Rari 700); see Cavarra 1998, pp. 177–78, no. 14, ill.

REFERENCES

30 Baglione 1642, pp. 394–95: "Isabella Parasoli Romana fu moglie di Lionardo, e fece di sua inventione un Libro intagliato con diverse forme di merletti, & altri lavori per le Dame, con il Fronstispitio da Francesco Villamena operato" ("Isabella Parasole from Rome was the wife of Leonardo, and designed from her own invention a Book engraved with various shapes of laces, and other works for Women, with a frontispiece produced by Francesco Villamena"). Most of the literature on Elisabetta Parasole and her work (see note 29 above) is tainted by Baglione's information that she was married to Leonardo Parasole, not Rosato. Baglione's misleading information derives from the identification of Elisabetta with the female engraver Girolama (Geronima) Parasole Cagnacci (ca. 1567–1622), wife of Rosato's brother Leonardo Norcino Parasole (1542 or 1552–1612) and mother of the painter Bernardino Parasole, who like his uncle was active in the Roman workshop of Cristoforo Roncalli and Cavaliere d'Arpino. See Pupillo 2009, pp. 845–49; Vodret 2011, p. 494, no. 1984; Mancino 2015b; and Fara 2016, pp. 71–73.

31 Ripa 1603, p. 238: "Intelletto. Giovanetto ardito, vestito d'oro, in capo terrà una corona medesimamente di oro [. . .] nella destra mano terrà uno scettro, e con la sinistra mostrerà un'aquila, che gli sia vicina"; and p. 369: "Operatione perfetta. DONNA che tiene con la destra mano uno specchio, & con la sinistra uno squdro, & un compasso." ("Intellect. Young bold man, dressed in gold, crowned with golden laurel [. . .] in his right hand holds a scepter, with his left [hand] is showing an eagle, very close to him; Perfect operation: WOMAN holding a mirror with her right hand, and with the left [hand] a square and a compass.")

32 Born in Visso (Marcerata), Rosato Parasole was active in the workshop of Cesari at Saint Peter's where, on the basis of the master's cartoons, he painted the lunette with the Virgin Mary in the Clementine chapel (1601) and the dome of the crossing (1608–11). For documents, see DiFederico 1983, pp. 65–66, 68. Further biographical information on Rosato can be found in Vodret 2011, pp. 38, 116, 130, 137, 149, 155, 494, no. 1984: Elisabetta and Rosato's son Cristoforo was born in 1600 and named after his godfather, the painter Cristoforo Roncalli, known as Pomarancio. After Elisabetta's death on May 12, 1617, Rosato married the widow Clarice Cortellacci in Rome on July 29, 1618.

33 Baglione 1642, p. 395. See Pupillo 2009 and Mancino 2015a.

34 Museo di Capodimonte, Naples (788 and 790). Oil on panel, each 10⅞ × 15⅞ in. (27.5 × 40.3 cm). On the paintings and related documents, see Röttgen 1973, p. 135, no. 55, ill.

35 *Bacchanal* (recto); *Saint John the Baptist* (verso). Pen and brown ink, brush and brown wash, white gouache, over black chalk, on rose tinted paper (recto); red and black chalk (verso), 7 × 5¾ in. (17.8 × 14.6 cm). Columbus Museum of Art, Gift of Frederick W. Schumacher (34.051). See Olszewski 2008, vol. 2, p. 380, no. 305 (as attributed to Giulio Romano).

36 The group of drawings attributed to Cesare Rossetti recently published in Bolzoni 2013 seems stylistically inconsistent. In my opinion at least two different personalities can be isolated from this group, one being Bernardino or Leonardo Parasole.

37 For prints after designs by Giuseppe Cesari, see Röttgen 2002, pp. 510–21, nos. I–XIV.

Agosti, Barbara, Francesco Grisolia, and Maria Rosa Pizzoni, eds.
2016 *Le postille di Padre Resta alle vite del Baglione*. Milan: Officina Libraria.

Arcangeli, Luciano, ed.
1985 *Andrea Lilli nella pittura delle Marche tra Cinquecento e Seicento*. Exh. cat., Pinacoteca Civica Francesco Podesti, Ancona. Rome: Multigrafica.

Baglione, Giovanni
1642 *Le vite de' pittori, scultori et architetti; dal pontificato di Gregorio XIII del 1572, in fino a' tempi di Papa Urbano Ottavo nel 1642*. Rome: Nella Stamperia d'Andrea Fei.

Bean, Jacob, and Lawrence Turčić
1982 *15th and 16th Century Italian Drawings in The Metropolitan Museum of Art*. New York: MMA.

Bevilacqua, Mario
1985 "Palazzetto Cenci a Roma: Un'aggiunta per Martino Longhi il Vecchio e un contributo per Giovanni Guerra pittore." *Bollettino d'arte*, ser. 6, 70, no. 31–32, pp. 157–87.

Bolzoni, Marco Simone
2013 "Cesare Rossetti, 'amico' del Cavalier d'Arpino: Un nuovo dipinto e alcune note sull'opera grafica." *Storia dell'arte* 136, no. 36, pp. 46–64.
2016 "The Drawings of Raffaellino Motta da Reggio." *Master Drawings* 54, no. 2, pp. 147–204.

Bolzoni, Marco Simone, Furio Rinaldi, and Patrizia Tosini, eds.
2016 *Dopo il 1564: L'eredità di Michelangelo a Roma nel tardo Cinquecento/After 1564: Michelangelo's Legacy in Late Cinquecento Rome*. Rome: De Luca Editori d'Arte.

Briganti, Giuliano
1945 *Il Manierismo e Pellegrino Tibaldi*. Rome: Cosmopolita.

Cavarra, Angela Adriana
1998 *Donna è . . . : L'universo femminile nelle raccolte casanatensi*. Exh. cat., Biblioteca Casanatense, Rome. Milan: Aisthesis.

DiFederico, Frank
1983 *The Mosaics of Saint Peter's: Decorating the New Basilica*. University Park: Pennsylvania State University Press.

Dimartino, Alessia
2008 "*Anus Ebria*: Immagini di una donna tra vecchiaia e ubriachezza." *Prospettiva*, no. 129 (January), pp. 67–80.

Fara, Giovanni Maria, ed. and ann.
2016 *Giovanni Baglione: Intagliatori*. Pisa: Edizioni della Normale (Scuola Normale Superiore).

Gere, John A.
1966 "Girolamo Muziano and Taddeo Zuccaro: A Note on an Early Work by Muziano." *Burlington Magazine* 108, no. 761, pp. 417–18, 419.
1971 *Il manierismo a Roma*. Milan: Fabbri.

Gere, John A., and Philip Pouncey
1983 *Italian Drawings in the Department of Prints and Drawings in the British Museum*. Vol. 5, *Artists Working in Rome, c. 1550 to c. 1640*. 2 vols. London: British Museum Publications.

Guerra, Giovanni
1589 *Varii emblemi hieroglifici usati nelli abigliamenti delle pitture fatte in diversi luochi nelle fabriche del S.ᵐᵒ S.ʳ Nostro papa Sixto V P.O.M all'ill.ᵐᵃ et eccel.ᵐᵃ s.ʳᵃ la S.ʳᵃ D. Camilla Perretti; Giovanni Guerra pittore et invent*. Rome: N.p.

Mancino, Maria Rosa
2015a "Parasole Cagnaccia, Geronima." In *Dizionario biografico degli Italiani*, vol. 81. Rome: Treccani. Available online: www.treccani.it/enciclopedia/geronima-parasole-cagnaccia _(Dizionario-Biografico)/.

2015b "Parasole Catanea, Elisabetta." In *Dizionario biografico degli Italiani*, vol. 81. Rome: Treccani. Available online: www.treccani.it/enciclopedia/elisabetta-parasole-catanea _(Dizionario-Biografico)/.

van Mander, Karel

1604 *Het Schilder-Boeck*. . . . Haarlem: Paschier van Wesbusch.

Marciari, John

2002 "Girolamo Muziano and the Dialogue of Drawings in Cinquecento Rome." *Master Drawings* 40, no. 2 (Summer), pp. 113–34.

2006 "Raffaellino da Reggio in the Vatican." *Burlington Magazine* 148, no. 1236 (March), pp. 187–91.

Monbeig-Goguel, Catherine

1972 *Vasari et son temps: Maîtres toscans nés après 1500, morts avant 1600*. Paris: Editions des Musées Nationaux.

Olszewski, Edward J.

2008 *A Corpus of Drawings in Midwestern Collections. Sixteenth-Century Italian Drawings*. 2 vols. London: Harvey Miller.

Pandolfini Casa d'Aste, Florence

2014 *Capolavori da collezioni italiane*. Sale cat., Palazzo Ramirez-Montalvo, October 28.

Parasole, Elisabetta Catanea

1610 *Fiore d'ogni virtù per le nobili et honeste matrone; dove si vedono bellissimi lavori di ponto in aria, reticella, di maglia & a piombini. Dissegnati da Isabetta Catanea Parasole*. Rome: Antonio Facchetti.

1616 *Teatro delle nobili et virtuose donne dove si rappresentano varij Disegni di Lavori nuovamente. Inventati, et disegnati da Elisabetta Catanea Parasole Romana*. [2nd ed.] Rome: Mauritio Bona.

Parma Armani, Elena

1978 *Libri di immagini, disegni e incisioni di Giovanni Guerra (Modena 1544–Roma 1618)*. Edited by Enrichetta Cecchi Gattolin. Exh. cat., Palazzo dei Musei, Modena. Modena: Tipolito Cooptip.

Pierguidi, Stefano

2002 "Alle radici dell'*Iconologia*: I rapporti di Cesare Ripa con Ignazio Danti, Giovanni Alberti e Giovanni Guerra." *Arte cristiana* 90, no. 813, pp. 433–48.

Prosperi Valenti Rodinò, Simonetta

2000 "Disegni giovanili di Giovanni Guerra." In *L'arte nella storia: Contributi di critica e storia dell'arte per Gianni Carlo Sciolla*, edited by Valerio Terraroli, Franca Varallo, and Laura De Fanti, pp. 413–22. Milan: Skira.

2007 *I disegni del Codice Resta di Palermo*. Exh. cat., Civica Galleria d'Arte Moderna, Palermo. Cinisello Balsamo: Silvana.

Pupillo, Marco

2009 "Gli incisori di Baronio: Il maestro 'MGP,' Philippe Thomassin, Leonardo e Girolama Parasole (con una nota su Isabella/Isabetta/Elisabetta Parasole)." In *Baronio e le sue fonti: Atti del Convegno Internazionale di Studi, Sora, 10–13 ottobre 2007*, edited by Luigi Gulia, pp. 831–66. Sora: Centro di Studi Sorani Vincenzo Patriarca.

Rausa, Federico

2005 "L'Album Montalto e la collezione di sculture antiche di Villa Peretti Montalto." *Pegasus: Berliner Beiträge zum Nachleben der Antike* 7, pp. 97–132.

Ridolfi, Carlo

1648 *Le maraviglie dell'arte; ouero, Le vite de gl'illustri pittori veneti, e dello stato*. Venice: Presso Gio. Battista Sgaua.

Rinaldi, Furio

2016 "Michelangelo e il disegno a Roma: Continuità e sopravvivenza di uno stile dopo il 1564." In Bolzoni, Rinaldi, and Tosini 2016, pp. 56–81.

Ripa, Cesare

1603 *Iconologia; overo, Descrittione di diverse Imagini cavate dall'antichità, & di propria inventione*. Rome: Lepido Facij.

Roli, Renato

1987 "Due disegni di Pellegrino Tibaldi." *Paragone*, n.s., 38, no. 443, pp. 34–36.

Röttgen, Herwarth

1973 as ed. *Il Cavalier d'Arpino*. Exh. cat., Palazzo Venezia, Rome. Rome: De Luca.

2002 *Il Cavalier Giuseppe Cesari D'Arpino: Un grande pittore nello splendore della fama e nell'incostanza della fortuna*. Rome: Bozzi.

Speelberg, Femke

2015 "Fashion & Virtue: Textile Patterns and the Print Revolution, 1520–1620," *MMAB* 53, no. 2 (Fall).

Tosini, Patrizia

2008 *Girolamo Muziano, 1532–1592: Dalla Maniera alla Natura*. Rome: Ugo Bozzi.

2015 *Immagini ritrovate: Decorazione a Villa Peretti Montalto tra Cinque e Seicento*. Rome: De Luca.

van Tuyll van Serooskeren, Carel

2000 *The Italian Drawings of the Fifteenth and Sixteenth Centuries in the Teyler Museum*. Haarlem: Teylers Museum.

Vasari, Giorgio

1966–87 *Le vite de' più eccellenti pittori, scultori e architettori, nelle redazioni del 1550 e 1568*. 8 vols. Edited by Rosanna Bettarini and Paola Barocchi. Florence: Sansoni; Studio per Edizioni Scelte.

Vodret, Rossella, ed.

2011 *Alla ricerca di "Ghiongrat": Studi sui libri parrocchiali romani (1600–1630)*. Rome: L'Erma di Bretschneider.

Warwick, Genevieve

2000 *The Arts of Collecting: Padre Sebastiano Resta and the Market for Drawings in Early Modern Europe*. Cambridge: Cambridge University Press.

Zeri, Federico

1957 *Pittura e Controriforma: L'arte senza tempo di Scipione da Gaeta*. Turin: Einaudi.

Zezza, Andrea

2003 *Marco Pino: L'opera completa*. Milan and Naples: Electa Napoli.

MARTINA COLOMBI

The Madonna and Child with Saints Francis and Dominic and Angels by Giulio Cesare Procaccini: A Masterpiece from the Archinto Collection

In 1979, The Metropolitan Museum of Art acquired the *Madonna and Child with Saints Francis and Dominic and Angels,* a major altarpiece by the painter Giulio Cesare Procaccini (1574–1625) (fig. 1). The same year, in an article in this journal, Keith Christiansen published the painting together with documents relating to its commission in 1612, its presumed installation in the church of the Madonna dei Miracoli in the town of Corbetta, just west of Milan, and its eventual replacement by a copy.[1] Christiansen conjectured that the work was installed in the church—in a frame designed by Procaccini—after its completion in 1613, and that it was later removed from its frame and replaced. As it turns out, this account of the picture's history is partly inaccurate, for Procaccini's painting never made it to its intended destination.

Let us begin at the end of the story as it can now be reconstructed. On May 18, 1863, at Hôtel Drouot in Paris, the Metropolitan Museum's picture appeared in a sale of paintings from the famous collection of Giuseppe Archinto (1783–1861).[2] A Milanese count known for his eccentric and dissolute ways, Archinto had squandered his estate, forcing his son Luigi (1821–1899) to sell off the family's property after his father's death. On this occasion, ninety-five pieces were sold—probably the most significant works of the collection. Among those mentioned in the sale catalogue is a painting by Giulio Cesare Procaccini that, judging from its description, must be the one now in the Metropolitan Museum: "The Holy Virgin and Child Jesus, surrounded by angels, between two saints. Canvas. H. 255 cm, L. 143 cm."[3]

The painting was made for the chapel dedicated to Saints Francis and Dominic in the church of the Madonna dei Miracoli in Corbetta. In November 1612, the deputies of the church gave Filippo Spanzotta and his brother Gaspare the responsibility of providing the chapel's decoration, including an altarpiece by an esteemed painter that was to be completed within one year.[4] Whether the picture was finished in time is uncertain, but it was not installed in the chapel. This is made clear by two successive wills (dated 1625 and 1637) in which Filippo Spanzotta charged his heirs with placing an appropriate painting on the altar, which was apparently still bare.[5] As this request does not appear in Spanzotta's final will, drafted in 1640, his obligation must have been fulfilled by then—but not by the work he had commissioned from Procaccini.[6] Instead, the nobleman had a copy made for the chapel and, as we will explain, most probably retained Procaccini's altarpiece for himself.[7] The painting registered in the 1642 inventory of the church's possessions must be the copy, which in the mid-twentieth century was transferred to the rector's office, where it was housed until 2011.[8] It was then restored and placed in the museum of the church, located nearby. That Spanzotta kept Procaccini's original is supported by the posthumous inventory of Spanzotta's assets. Drafted in 1641, the inventory mentions a painting depicting "Our Lady with the image of the Saints Francis and Dominic."[9]

Although the precise moment when the picture entered the Archinto collection is not known, it was possibly a short time after Spanzotta's death. What can be said with certainty is that there was a close bond between the Archinto family and the church of the Madonna dei Miracoli that can be traced back to Carlo Archinto (1670–1732). A document in the Archinto archives dated May 4, 1717, states that the sanctuary received two hundred lire from Count Carlo acting as the executor of his wife, Giulia Barbiano di Belgiojoso, who had died two years earlier.[10] In his own last will, dated December 12, 1732, the count bequeathed to the church his Golden Fleece collar encrusted with diamonds.[11]

Just over a decade earlier, in 1721, the British traveler Edward Wright had visited Count Carlo's home and noted "two large and fine pieces of Jul. Ces. Procaccini."[12] One of the two—unfinished—depicted the Massacre of the Innocents; the other, not described, was possibly the painting commissioned for the church in Corbetta. Procaccini's painting was certainly displayed in Palazzo Archinto by 1772, when it is specifically mentioned by the Bolognese painter and collector Marcello Oretti: "Archinto residence. . . . An altarpiece with the Virgin, Child, S. Dominic and S. Francis by Giulio Cesare Procaccini . . . ."[13]

Documents from the nineteenth century are of great interest as well. In 1844, the historian Cesare Cantù mentioned in a brief description of his tour of the Archinto collection a Virgin Mary in Glory by Giulio Cesare Procaccini[14]—probably the same painting that was to attract the attention of Otto Mündler, who visited Palazzo Archinto in the company of Giovanni Morelli and Clementina Reichmann (Mme Frizzoni) on January 13, 1856.[15] Mündler's *Travel Diaries* are the last record of the famous Milanese collection before its dispersal, the most tragic and significant episode of which was the 1863 auction in Paris, referred to above. A copy of the auction catalogue in the Museo Poldi Pezzoli, Milan, contains manuscript annotations indicating that an Italian named Scotti purchased the painting by Giulio Cesare Procaccini, while Otto Mündler scored lot number one: a Head of a Child by Correggio—a study for his *Madonna with Saint George* now in the Gemäldegalerie Alte Meister, Dresden.[16]

We then lose track of the Metropolitan Museum's picture until 1978, when it was offered for sale in London, first by Colnaghi's[17] and then by Matthiesen Gallery, London.[18] By purchasing this splendid altarpiece in 1979, the Museum fulfilled the expectations of the experts at the 1863 sale in Paris: in the catalogue, they described the work as a "really museum-worthy painting."[19]

ACKNOWLEDGMENTS

The research for this article would not have been possible without the support of Giovanni Agosti and Jacopo Stoppa and the generous help of Manfredo and Rosellina Archinto, Keith Christiansen, Giulia Kimberly Colombo, and Mariasilvia Cortelazzi.

MARTINA COLOMBI
Postgraduate candidate in the Department of Cultural Heritage and Environment, University of Milan

fig. 1 Giulio Cesare Procaccini (Italian, 1574–1625). *Madonna and Child with Saints Francis and Dominic and Angels.* Oil on canvas, 101⅛ × 56⅜ in. (256.9 × 143.2 cm). The Metropolitan Museum of Art, Purchase, Enid A. Haupt Gift, 1979 (1979.209)

NOTES

1 See Christiansen 1979, in which the author logically assumed that an inventory of church property drawn up in 1642 referred to the museum's altarpiece; however, as will be shown, it describes the copy, today in the museum of the church. See also Brigstocke 1980, p. 39; Rosci 1993, pp. 84–85; and Brigstocke 2002, pp. 84–85.

2 The original core of the Archinto collection was made up mainly of sixteenth-century Venetian and Lombard works and was assembled by Filippo Archinto (1495–1558). In the following centuries, the collection was augmented by other notable family members, including Ottavio (1584–1656), Carlo (1670–1732), and Filippo (1697–1751). Their acquisitions included not only paintings but also ancient sculpture, drawings, tapestries, books, precious objects, and musical and scientific instruments. An inventory of the paintings in the collection, dated April 10, 1741 (Archivio Archinto, Milan, fascicolo 148), included some five hundred and fifty works (unfortunately without attribution). For further information on the family, see Litta 1843 and Forte 1932.

3 "La sainte Vierge et l'Enfant Jésus, entourés d'une gloire d'anges, apparaissent à deux saints. Toile. H. 2 m. 55 c. L. 1 m. 43 c." Archinto sale 1863, lot 50, p. 13. The subject, material, and dimensions of the Museum's painting are a perfect match.

4 The brothers were descendants of Giovanni Ambrogio Spanzotta, who in the second half of the sixteenth century had financed the restoration and enlargement of the church.

5 Archivio di Stato di Milano, Notarile, fascicoli 28174 (March 17, 1625) and 28177 (April 11, 1637).

6 Ibid., fascicolo 29446 (October 11, 1640).

7 The copy was first mentioned in Bona Castellotti 1978, especially pp. 89–90. The painting, which measures 105½ × 58¼ in. (268 × 148 cm), was initially attributed to Procaccini but was recognized as a later copy after the original version was discovered.

8 "Inventario," 1642, Archivio della Chiesa della Madonna dei Miracoli, Proprietà del Santuario, Cartella VI, fascicolo 2.

9 "Nostra Signora con l'immagine dei Santi Francesco e Domenico." Archivio di Stato di Milano, Notarile, fascicolo 29446 (January 11, 1641). For further information on the history of the two paintings, see Comincini 1999, pp. 150–51, 188. Additional hypotheses about the relationship of these works are provided in the same volume by Cavalieri 1999, pp. 38–39, 184.

10 "Legato disposto da Giulia Archinto, nata Barbiano di Belgiojoso, moglie di Carlo," Milan, May 4, 1717, Archivio Archinto, Milan, fascicolo 138.

11 "Testamento di Carlo Archinto, figlio di Filippo e di Camilla Stampa," Milan, December 12, 1732, Archivio Archinto, Milan, fascicolo 114.

12 Wright 1730, vol. 2, p. 470.

13 "Casa Archinti . . . . Una Tavola d'altare con la Mad.a Bamb.o | S. Dom.o e S. Francesco di Giul. Ces. Procaccino . . . ." Marcello Oretti, "Libro Quarto | Miscellanee | Pitture nella città | di Milano || Raccolte e scritte in d.a Città | da Marcello Oretti | nell'Anno 1772," Biblioteca dell'Archiginnasio, Bologna, ms. 96*bis*. The first printed edition of the manuscript is forthcoming. For further information on the author and the manuscript, see Stoppa 2015, especially p. 199.

14 Cantù 1844, vol. 2, p. 280.

15 Mündler [1855–58] 1985, p. 93: "13 January. Sunday. Milan. With Morelli & Mme Frizzoni to Palazzo Archinti, where visitors are very seldom admitted. Besides a large and excellent Procaccini, a Titian, Portrait of a Cardinal seated with a transparent white curtain covering half of his face; and a fine portrait of a man, of Leonardo's school. There is a precious portrait of a young man, of 20, of the Archinti family, painted in '1494,' and most likely by Leonardo da Vinci, whose beautiful modelling & execution it certainly has." The four paintings mentioned by Otto Mündler are the one by Procaccini, which is probably the altarpiece in the Metropolitan Museum's collection; Titian's *Portrait of Archbishop Filippo Archinto*, today in the Philadelphia Museum of Art, 204); an unknown male portrait of the "Leonardeschi" school; and *Portrait of a Man Aged Twenty* (*The Archinto Portrait*), attributed to Marco d'Oggiono and today in the National Gallery, London (NG1665). Both Titian's and d'Oggiono's paintings were auctioned at the Archinto sale in Paris in 1863. The present author's research into the catalogue of that sale has revealed the provenance of paintings, the history of which was previously unknown. The most important among these are Scipione Pulzone's *Cardinal Ferdinando de' Medici* (Art Gallery of South Australia [985P39]), and, most likely, Giovanni Antonio Boltraffio's *Portrait of a Youth Crowned with Flowers* (North Carolina Museum of Art [GL.60.17.40]). *The Temptations of Saint Anthony*, by Camillo Procaccini, Giulio Cesare's older brother, is not mentioned in the sale catalogue but was seen in the Archinto mansion by Carlo Cesare Malvasia (1678, vol. 1, p. 285) and Marcello Oretti (1772; see note 13 above). The painting was exhibited by the Milanese Galleria Nobili in 2015.

16 Archinto sale 1863, lot 1, p. 5, and lot 50, p. 13. The names "Mündler" and "Scotti" are handwritten next to the descriptions of the paintings.

17 Brigstocke 1980, p. 39; Hall 1992, p. 31.

18 Colnaghi's built an international reputation in the field of Italian Baroque painting in the 1970s. Michael Simpson, director of the paintings department, was joined by Patrick Matthiesen at the beginning of the decade. Matthiesen established his own gallery in 1978. See Howard 2010, especially pp. 48–49.

19 "page vraiment digne d'un musée." Archinto sale 1863, introduction, p. 4.

REFERENCES

Archinto sale
1863 *Catalogue des tableaux anciens de feu M. le comte Archinto de Milan*. Sale, Hôtel Drouot, Paris, May 18.

Bona Castellotti, Marco
1978 "Aggiunte al catalogo di Melchiorre Gherardini." *Paragone: Arte* 29, no. 345, pp. 87–94.

Brigstocke, Hugh
1980 "G. C. Procaccini et D. Crespi: Nouvelles découvertes." *Revue de l'art* 48, pp. 30–39.
2002 *Procaccini in America*. Edited by Nicholas H. J. Hall. Exh. cat. New York: Hall & Knight.

Cantù, Cesare, ed.
1844 *Milano e il suo territorio*. Engravings by L. Cherbuin. 2 vols. Milan: Luigi di Giacomo Pirola.

Cavalieri, Federico
1999 "Spigolature di pittura milanese, con qualche eccezione: Da Bergognone ad Arduino." In *Pittura nell'Abbiatense e nel Magentino: Opere su tavola e tela, secoli XV–XVIII*, by Federico Cavalieri and Mario Comincini, pp. 9–56, 182–85. Abbiategrasso: Società Storica Abbiatense.

Christiansen, Keith
1979 "An Altarpiece by Giulio Cesare Procaccini." *MMJ* 14 (pub. 1980), pp. 159–66.

Comincini, Mario
1999 "Spigolature d'archivio." In *Pittura nell'Abbiatense e nel Magentino: Opere su tavola e tela, secoli XV–XVIII*, by Federico Cavalieri and Mario Comincini, pp. 141–66, 188–91. Abbiategrasso: Società Storica Abbiatense.

Forte, Francesco
1932 *"Archintea Laus": Giunte e note alla genealogia degli Archinto, patrizi milanesi, pubblicata da Pompeo Litta*. Milan: Arti Grafiche Rovida e Gadda.

Hall, Nicholas H. J., ed.
1992 *Colnaghi in America: A Survey to Commemorate the First Decade of Colnaghi New York*. New York: Colnaghi.

Howard, Jeremy
2010 "Colnaghi 1940–2001." In *Colnaghi, Established 1760: The History*, edited by Jeremy Howard, pp. 47–53. London: Colnaghi.

Litta, Pompeo
1843 *Famiglie celebri d'Italia*. Vol. 1, fasc. 11, *Archinto di Milano*. Milan: Paolo Emilio Giusti Stampatore.

Malvasia, Carlo Cesare
1678 *Felsina pittrice: Vite de' pittori bolognesi*. 2 vols. Bologna: Erede di Domenico Barbieri.

Mündler, Otto
1985 *The Travel Diaries of Otto Mündler, 1855–1858*. Edited by Carol Togneri Dowd. Walpole Society 51. [London]: Walpole Society.

Rosci, Marco
1993 *Giulio Cesare Procaccini*. Soncino: Edizioni dei Soncino.

Stoppa, Jacopo
2015 "Il *curriculum* di Ferdinando Porta nelle carte di Marcello Oretti." *Prospettiva*, no. 157–58 (January–April), pp. 192–204.

Wright, Edward
1730 *Some Observations Made in Travelling through France, Italy &c. in the Years 1720, 1721, and 1722*. 2 vols. London: Tho. Ward & E. Wicksteed.